The Ethics of Deconstruction

D1489712

B

For Anthea

The Ethics of Deconstruction:

Derrida and Levinas

Simon Critchley

BLACKWELL
Oxford UK & Cambridge USA

First published 1992

Blackwell Publishers
108 Cowley Road
Oxford OX4 1JF
UK

Three Cambridge Center
Cambridge, Massachusetts 02142
USA

British Library Cataloguing in Publication Data

A CIP catalogue record for this book is available from the British Library.

Library of Congress Cataloging-in-Publication Data

Critchley, Simon, 1960–
The ethics of deconstruction: Derrida and Levinas/Simon
Critchley.
p. cm.
Includes bibliographical references and index.
ISBN 0–631–17785–X (hardback)–ISBN 0–631–17786–8 (pbk.)
1. Derrida, Jacques. 2. Levinas, Emmanuel. 3. Deconstruction—
History. 4. Ethics, Modern—20th century. I. Title.
B2430.D484C75 1992
170—dc20 91–46361
CIP

Typeset in 11 on 13pt Garamond by Graphicraft Typesetters Ltd, Hong Kong
Printed in Great Britain

This book is printed on acid-free paper

Contents

Abbreviations

WORKS BY DERRIDA

A   *Altérités* (Osiris, Paris, 1986).

AF   *L'Archéologie du frivole. Lire Condillac* (Denoël/Gonthier, Paris, 1976).

AT   'Of an Apocalyptic Tone Recently Adopted in Philosophy', tr. J. P. Leavey, *Oxford Literary Review*, 6, no. 2 (1984), pp. 3–37.

CP   *La carte postale de Socrate à Freud et au-delà* (Flammarion, Paris, 1980).

D   *La dissémination* (Seuil, Paris, 1972).

E   *De l'esprit. Heidegger et la question* (Galilée, Paris, 1987).

ECM 'En ce moment même dans cet ouvrage me voici', *in Textes pour Emmanuel Levinas*, ed. F. Laruelle (Jean-Michel Place, Paris, 1980), pp. 21–60.

ED   *L'écriture et la différence* (Seuil, Paris, 1967).

EN   'Envoi', Actes du XVIIIe Congrès des Sociétés de Philosophie de Langue Française (Vrin, Paris, 1980).

EP   *Epérons. Les styles de Nietzsche* (Flammarion, Paris, 1978).

FC   *Feu la cendre* (Editions des Femmes, Paris, 1987).

FH   *Les fins de l'homme. A partir du travail de Jacques Derrida* (Galilée, Paris, 1981).

G   *De la grammatologie* (Minuit, Paris, 1967).

GL   *Glas* (Denoël/Gonthier, Paris, 1981).

GLtr *Glas*, tr. J. P. Leavey and R. Rand (University of Nebraska Press, Lincoln, 1986).

LI   *Limited Inc.* (Galilée, Paris, 1990).

LItr   *Limited Inc.* (Northwestern University Press, Evanston, 1988).

LSS 'Like the Sound of the Sea Deep within a Shell: Paul de Man's War', tr. Peggy Kamuf, *Critical Inquiry*, 14, no. 3 (1988), pp. 590–652.

LVP *La vérité en peinture* (Flammarion, Paris, 1978).

M *Marges de la philosophie* (Minuit, Paris, 1972).

MP *Margins of Philosophy*, tr. A. Bass (University of Chicago Press, Chicago, 1982).

MPM *Mémoires pour Paul de Man* (Galilée, Paris, 1988).

MPMtr *Memoires for Paul de Man* (Columbia University Press, New York, 1986).

OG *Of Grammatology*, tr. Gayatri Spivak (Johns Hopkins University Press, Baltimore, 1976).

ORG *L'origine de la géométrie* (Presses Universitaires de France, Paris, 1962).

OS *Of Spirit*, tr. G. Bennington and R. Bowlby (University of Chicago Press, Chicago, 1989).

P *Positions* (Minuit, Paris, 1972).

PC 'La phénoménologie et la clôture de la métaphysique', *Epochēs*, 7 (1966), pp. 181–200; all page references are to an unpublished French version of the essay.

POS *Positions*, tr. A. Bass (Athlone Press, London, 1981).

PSY *Psyché: inventions de l'autre* (Galilée, Paris, 1987).

RMM 'Violence et métaphysique, essai sur la pensée d'Emmanuel Levinas', *Revue de Métaphysique et de Morale*, 69 (1964), no. 3, pp. 322–54); no. 4, pp. 425–73.

SP *Speech and Phenomena and Other Essays on Husserl's Theory of Signs*, tr. D. B. Allison (Northwestern University Press, Evanston, 1973).

TA *D'un ton apocalyptique adopté naguère en philosophie* (Galilée, Paris, 1983).

TP *The Truth in Painting*, tr. G. Bennington and I. MacLeod (University of Chicago Press, Chicago, 1987).

TT 'The Time of a Thesis: Punctuations', in *Philosophy in France Today*, ed. A. Montefiore (Cambridge University Press, Cambridge, 1982), pp. 35–50.

VP *La voix et le phénomène* (Presses Universitaires de France, Paris, 1967).

WD *Writing and Difference*, tr. A. Bass (Routledge and Kegan Paul, London and Henley, 1978).

WORKS BY LEVINAS

AE   *Autrement qu'être ou au-delà de l'essence* (Martinus Nijhoff, The Hague, 1974).

CPP   *Collected Philosophical Papers*, tr. A. Lingis (Martinus Nijhoff, The Hague, 1987).

DEE   *De l'existence à l'existant* (Vrin, Paris, 1986).

DL   *Difficile liberté*. Livre de poche edition (Albin Michel, Paris, 1976).

DQVI   *De Dieu qui vient à l'idée*, 2nd edn (Vrin, Paris, 1986).

EDE   *En découvrant l'existence avec Husserl et Heidegger*, 3rd edn (Vrin, Paris, 1974).

EE   *Existence and Existents*, tr. A. Lingis (Martinus Nijhoff, The Hague, 1978).

EeI   *Ethique et Infini* (Fayard/France Culture, Paris, 1982).

FF   *Face to Face with Levinas*, ed. R. A. Cohen (State University of New York Press, Albany, 1986).

H   *Humanisme de l'autre homme*. Livre de poche edition (Fata Morgana, Montpellier, 1972).

HS   *Hors Sujet* (Fata Morgana, Montpellier, 1987).

LR   *The Levinas Reader*, ed. Seán Hand (Blackwell, Oxford, 1989).

ND   'Le nom de Dieu d'après quelques textes Talmudiques', *Archivio di Filosofia*, 550 (1969), pp. 155–67.

NP   *Noms Propres* (Fata Morgana, Montpellier, 1976).

OB   *Otherwise than Being or Beyond Essence* (Martinus Nijhoff, The Hague, 1981).

PEQA   'La Pensée de l'être et la question de l'autre', *Critique*, 369 (1978), pp. 187–97.

QLT   *Quatre Lectures Talmudiques* (Minuit, Paris, 1968).

RRL   *Re-Reading Levinas*, ed. R. Bernasconi and S. Critchley (Indiana University Press, Bloomington, 1991).

TA   *Le temps et l'autre* (Presses Universitaires de France, Paris, 1989).

TeI   *Totalité et Infini* (Martinus Nijhoff, The Hague, 1961).

TH   'Transcendence et Hauteur', *Bulletin de la Société Française de la Philosophie*, 56, no. 3 (1962), pp. 89–113.

TI   *Totality and Infinity*, tr. A. Lingis (Duquesne University Press, Pittsburgh, 1969).

TO   *Time and the Other*, tr. Richard Cohen (Duquesne University Press, Pittsburgh, 1987).

OTHER WORKS

CD   Jean-Luc Nancy, *La communauté désœuvrée* (Christian Bourgois, Paris, 1986).
ER   J. Hillis Miller, *The Ethics of Reading* (Columbia University Press, New York, 1987).
FP   Philippe Lacoue-Labarthe, *La fiction du politique* (Christian Bourgois, Paris, 1987).
HAP   Philippe Lacoue-Labarthe, *Heidegger, Art and Politics. The Fiction of the Political*, tr. Chris Turner (Blackwell, Oxford, 1990).
LI   Edmund Husserl, *Logical Investigations*, 2 vols, tr. J. N. Findlay (Routledge and Kegan Paul, London, 1976).
LU   *Logische Untersuchungen*, 6th ed, 3 vols (Max Niemeyer, Tübingen, 1980).
RJ   Philippe Lacoue-Labarthe, Jean-Luc Nancy, *et al., Rejouer le politique* (Galilée, Paris, 1981).
RT   Philippe Lacoue-Labarthe, Jean-Luc Nancy, *et al., Le retrait du politique*; (Galilée, Paris, 1983).
SuZ   Martin Heidegger, *Sein und Zeit*, 15th ed (Max Niemeyer, Tübingen, 1984). All references give the German pagination, included in the margins of the English translation (Cf. *Being and Time*, tr. J. Macquarrie and E. Robinson, Blackwell, Oxford, 1962).

Prefatory Note and Acknowledgements

The argument of this book, which is formally laid out in chapter 1 and then fully exposed in chapters 2–4, is that Derridian deconstruction can, and indeed should, be understood as an ethical demand, provided that ethics is understood in the particular sense given to it in the work of Emmanuel Levinas. Levinas's work, whose full philosophical importance is only now beginning to be recognized, exerted a powerful and continuous influence on the development of Derrida's thinking, and by following the intricate textual dialogue between Levinas and Derrida, one can see how the question of ethics can be compellingly raised within deconstruction.

In the first chapter, after introducing the problematic of this book and the context within which it arose, I give a brief introduction to Levinasian ethics. I then show why Levinas's work should occupy a privileged place in discussions of the ethics of deconstruction, and respond to the Heideggerian objection (Heidegger is a constant point of reference in this book, occupying a central place in the argument of most chapters) that all discussion of ethics is philosophically anachronistic and at the very antipodes of Derrida's thinking. After showing how Derrida's remarks on ethics permit a Levinasian response to these Heideggerian objections, I go on to describe what takes place in deconstruction by delineating the concepts of double reading and closure. After focusing on some of Derrida's more recent remarks, I outline what I call an unconditional ethical imperative, which, I claim, is the source of the injunction that produces deconstruction and is produced through deconstructive reading, and show how the 'concepts' of the general text and *différance* can be articulated within an ethical problematic. I conclude the chapter by discussing the relation of my argument to Hillis Miller's claim for an ethics of reading.

My Ariadne's thread for the disclosure of the ethics of deconstruction is the concept of the closure of metaphysics (*la clôture de la métaphysique*). Taking this concept as an index, chapter 2 attempts to understand the logic that governs deconstructive reading through a scholarly genealogy of the concept of closure, and shows the extent of Derrida's debt to Husserl and, in particular, Heidegger. As a consequence of this analysis, I develop the hypothesis of *clôtural* reading, and briefly show how this hypothesis functions in relation to two of Derrida's texts: *Voice and Phenomenon* (*La voix et le phénomène*) and 'Violence and Metaphysics'.

In chapters 3 and 4, I go on to give two extended and, it is hoped, exemplary *clôtural* readings: of a text by Derrida on Levinas and a text by Levinas on Derrida. These readings will hopefully grant some insight into the novel and complex structures that govern Levinas's later philosophy. In ' "Bois" – Derrida's Final Word on Levinas', I carefully reconstruct the argument of Derrida's second, and hitherto largely ignored, essay on Levinas, 'At this very Moment in this Work here I am', analysing the way in which Levinas's work *works* and discussing the relation between ethical difference and sexual difference; whereas in 'Wholly Otherwise: Levinas's Reading of Derrida', I piece together Levinas's scattered but fascinating remarks on Derrida, where he reads deconstruction in terms of his own ethical problematic, giving a double reading of *Voice and Phenomenon*. I go on to discuss the theme of scepticism and its refutation, and look at the place of Husserl's theory of meaning in the dialogue between Levinas and Derrida, before concluding with a discussion of the non-verbal dimension to Levinasian ethics and its implications for the question of humanism.

The last chapter, 'A Question of Politics: The Future of Deconstruction', is the critical moment of the book, the moment of interruption, or ingratitude, that is essential to a *clôtural* reading. I argue that there is an impasse of the political in Derrida's work, and that deconstruction fails to offer a coherent account of the passage from ethical responsibility to political questioning and critique. I approach this impasse by focusing on Derrida's response to the question of Heidegger and politics in *Of Spirit*. Expanding the focus of my argument, I then show how this Derridian impasse of the political is deepened, complicated, and extended in the work of Philippe Lacoue-Labarthe and Jean-Luc Nancy. In a third moment, I outline what I call 'a Levinasian politics of ethical difference', which permits one to pass beyond this impasse and traverse the passage from ethics to politics. In conclusion, and by way of imagining a possible future for deconstruction, I re-evaluate the political function of philosophy, and assess its implications for democracy.

Having worked on this project for a few years, I have amassed a vast debt of gratitude: first and foremost to the staff and students of the Philosophy Department at Essex University, both past and present, especially Jay Bernstein, Barbara Crawshaw, Peter Dews, David Krell, William Large, Onora O'Neill, Mike Weston, and particularly Robert Bernasconi, *il miglior fabbro*, whose teaching and research provided the impetus for this book and who carefully supervised its first draft. A debt is owed to Dominique Janicaud for his help during my time as a student at Nice University. I would also like to thank my external examiner, David Wood, for his encouragement and comments. Much of the initial work on the book was done during a year as a Fellow at the Centre for Critical and Cultural Theory at Cardiff University, and particular thanks are due to Catherine Belsey and Christopher Norris. Teaching a Ph.D. seminar with Ernesto Laclau proved invaluable in sorting out my ideas for the final chapter. Parts of this book have appeared in a number of journals: *Textual Practice*, *Cahiers du Centre de Recherches Histoires des Idées*, and the *Journal of the British Society for Phenomenology*; and chapter 3 appeared in *Re-Reading Levinas*. Finally, I would like to thank Donna Brody for helping me with proof reading. I am also grateful to Faber and Faber Ltd and to Random House for permission to quote from 'September 1, 1939' by W. H. Auden.

S.C.

Colchester,
September 1991

1

The Ethics of Deconstruction: The Argument

> I can only describe my feeling by the metaphor, that, if a man could write a book on Ethics which really was a book on Ethics, this book would, with an explosion, destroy all the other books in the world.
>
> Wittgenstein, 'Lecture on Ethics'

1.1 Introduction

Why bother with deconstruction? Why read deconstructive writings? Why read texts deconstructively? Why should deconstruction be necessary, or even important? What demand is being made by deconstruction? These are questions which haunt the critical reader who has followed the work of Jacques Derrida. They are questions voiced by the reader who, in pleasure and patience, has read Derrida's work, but who now, perhaps impatiently, wants to question the demand that is placed on him or her by that work. They are questions, I shall claim, that demand an *ethical* response, that call deconstructive reading to responsibility, to be responsible. The urgency and necessity of providing such a response lies at the heart of this book. My claim, in a nutshell, is that the textual practice of deconstructive reading can and, moreover, *should* be understood as an ethical demand, and that such an understanding of deconstruction most fully responds to the concerns expressed in the above questions.

What do I mean by the ethics of deconstruction? As a way into this question, it is perhaps helpful to consider the reception of Derrida's work in the English-speaking world as having occurred in two waves: first, the earlier, literary reception of deconstruction in the middle to late 1970s through the work of the Yale school, particularly Paul de Man, J. Hillis Miller, Harold Bloom, and Geoffrey Hartman;[1] and second, the later, philosophical reception of deconstruction through the work of Rodolphe Gasché, Irene Harvey, John Llewelyn, and Christopher Norris.[2] However, what both these waves have in common, with the exception of Hillis Miller's recent work, is that they either overlook or relegate the importance of the relation of ethics to deconstructive reading. It is assumed that ethics, conceived of as a branch of philosophy, namely moral philosophy or practical reasoning, is a region of inquiry – like logic or physics – which presupposes the philosophical or metaphysical foundation that deconstruction deconstructs. Thus, if the relation between ethics and deconstruction is analogous to that between a branch, or region, of philosophical inquiry and that which puts all such inquiry into question, then, one would be entitled to ask, what could deconstruction possibly have to do with ethics, apart from radically putting into question the possibility of the latter?

In this book, I will attempt to respond to this question by arguing that an ethical moment is essential to deconstructive reading and that ethics is the goal, or horizon, towards which Derrida's work tends. This means that the conception of ethics employed in this book will differ markedly from the traditional conception of ethics *qua* region or branch of philosophy. I shall explain the former presently; but, in order to forestall any possible confusion, I should say now that when I speak of the ethics of deconstruction, I am not assuming that the genitive 'of' means that ethics has its origin, or foundation, in deconstruction and that the relation between deconstruction and ethics is one of inference or derivation. Nor am I claiming that the meaning of deconstruction has been so clearly established that one can now draw out its implications and applications: an applied deconstruction at work in the field of practical reasoning. My claim is not that *an* ethics can be derived from deconstruction, like an effect from a cause, a superstructure from an infrastructure, or a second critique from a first critique (while recognizing Kant's claim to the primacy of practical reason). Rather, I hope to demonstrate that the pattern of reading produced in the deconstruction of – mostly, but by no means exclusively – philosophical texts has an ethical structure: deconstruction 'is' ethical; or, to formulate the same thought less ontologically (as the primacy of the third person present indicative of the copula in predicative propositions – S is P – is one of the principal targets of deconstruction), deconstruction takes place (*a lieu*) ethically, or there is duty in deconstruction (*Il y a du devoir dans la déconstruction*).[3]

Thus, one might perhaps speak of a third wave in the reception of deconstruction, beyond its literary and philosophical appropriations, one in which ethical – not to mention political – questions are uppermost. Indeed, such a third wave corresponds to the concerns of Derrida's work on Heidegger, Paul de Man, friendship, racism, apartheid, and the debate with John Searle.[4] As part of this third wave, one might consider J. Hillis Miller's *The Ethics of Reading*, about which I shall have more to say below,[5] which sought precisely to challenge the prevailing prejudice that deconstruction, particularly in the form practised by Paul de Man, is a species of nihilistic textual free play which suspends all questions of value and is therefore, so the argument goes, immoral (such also, in essence, is Gadamer's objection to Derrida[6]). However, despite the success of Hillis Miller's argument – which is compelling for many reasons – he still works with a traditional conception of ethics as a 'region of philosophical or conceptual investigation' (*ER* 3).

So what is the meaning of the word 'ethics' in the locution 'ethics of deconstruction'? As will clear by now, this book is primarily concerned with the explication of Derrida's work, a work which has always been, and remains, highly sensitive to the ethical modalities of response and responsibility in reading. Yet the way in which the question of ethics will be raised within deconstructive reading will be through a *rapprochement* with the work of Emmanuel Levinas. I believe that one of the major reasons why Derrida's work has not been read as an ethical demand by his major commentators is because of an avoidance or ignorance of the novel conception of ethics at work in Levinas's thinking.[7] When I speak of ethics in this book, I will be referring to the Levinasian understanding of the term. In virtue of this, it will become clear that the relation of the ethics of deconstruction to conventional moral philosophy, or even applied ethics, will at best be oblique, and perhaps even critical. This is not at all to say that Levinasian ethics is unrelated to the tradition of moral philosophy or to concrete questions of the justifiability of human action. It is rather that, for Levinas, the construction of a system, or procedure, for formulating and testing the moral acceptability of certain maxims or judgements relating to social action and civic duty is itself derived and distinct from a primordial ethical experience that Levinas's work seeks to describe. Levinas sometimes speaks of this distinction in terms of the difference between the ethical and the moral (although he is not consistent on this point), where the latter refers to 'the socio-political order of organizing and improving our human survival', which is itself founded upon the *prima philosophia* of an ethical responsibility towards the other (*FF* 29). Rather than speaking of the moral, I shall employ the distinction between ethics and *politics* discussed in the final chapter of the book. On this topic, it is significant that Derrida refers to Levinasian ethics as 'an ethics of ethics' (*ED* 164/*WD* 111) and that when Levinas was asked in an interview how he would construct an ethics on the basis of his notion of ethical experience, he answered, 'My task does not consist in constructing ethics; I only try to seek its meaning (*sens*)' (*EeI* 85). As Levinas states in 'Signature', 'Moral consciousness is not an experience of values' (*DL* 409); it is rather the delineation of the essence or meaning of the ethical in a way that disrupts traditional moral thinking and all claims to good conscience. An alternative – although barbarous – title for this book might be 'The Ethics of Ethics of Deconstruction'.

1.2   Levinasian Ethics

What is this Levinasian conception of ethics? One might sketch the movement of Levinas's thinking – a movement that Derrida compares with the crashing of a wave on a beach, always the same wave returning and repeating its movement with deeper insistence (*VM* 124/*WD* 312) – by saying that ethics occurs as the putting into question of the ego, the knowing subject, self-consciousness, or what Levinas, following Plato, calls the Same (*le même; to auton*). It is important to note at the outset that the Same refers not only to the *res cogitans*, but also to its *cogitata*. In Husserlian terms, the domain of the Same includes not only the intentional acts of consciousness (*noeses*), but also the intentional objects which give meaning to those acts and which are constituted by consciousness (*noemata*). Or again, in Heideggerian terms, it includes not only *Dasein*, but the world which is constitutive of the Being of Dasein (*Dasein* as *in-der-Welt-Sein*). Thus, the domain of the Same maintains a relation with otherness, but it is a relation in which the 'I', ego, or *Dasein* reduces the distance between the Same and the Other, in which their opposition fades (*TeI* 99/*TI* 126). Now, the Same is called into question by the other (*l'Autre; to heteron*); or, to use Levinas's word, the 'alterity' (*altérité*) of that which cannot be reduced to the Same, that which escapes the cognitive powers of the knowing subject. The first time that Levinas uses the word 'ethics' in the text proper – that is, excluding the Preface – of 'the great work' (*VM* 137/*WD* 92) *Totality and Infinity*, he defines it as 'the putting into question of my spontaneity by the presence of the Other' (*On appelle cette mise en question de ma spontanéité par la présence d'Autrui, éthique*) (*TeI* 13/*TI* 43). Ethics, for Levinas, is critique; it is the critical *mise en question* of the liberty, spontaneity, and cognitive emprise of the ego that seeks to reduce all otherness to itself. The ethical is therefore the location of a point of alterity, or what Levinas also calls 'exteriority' (*extériorité*), that cannot be reduced to the Same. Thus, to complete the quotation from 'Signature' begun above, moral consciousness is not an experience of values, 'but an access to exterior being' (*DL* 409). This exterior being is named 'face' (*visage*) by Levinas, and is defined as 'the way in which the other [*l'Autre*] presents himself, exceeding the *idea of the other in me*' (*TeI* 21/*TI* 50). In the language of transcendental philosophy, the face is the condition of possibility for ethics. For Levinas, then, the ethical relation – and ethics is simply and entirely the event of this relation – is one in which I am related to the face of the Other (*le visage d'autrui*),[8] where the French word '*autrui*' refers to the other human being, whom I cannot evade, comprehend, or kill and before whom I am called to justice, to justify myself.

As such, Levinasian ethics bears a critical relation to the philosophical tradition. For Levinas, Western philosophy has most often been what he calls 'ontology', by which he means the attempt to comprehend the Being of what is, or beings (*das Sein des Seienden*) (*TeI* 13/*TI* 42), the most recent example of which is Heidegger's fundamental ontology, in which the elaboration of the question of the meaning of Being presupposes *ab initio* a comprehension of Being (*compréhension de l'être; Seinsverständnis*), albeit a vague and average comprehension (*SuZ* 5–6). But equally, for Levinas, epistemology in either its idealist or realist versions is an ontology in so far as the object of cognition becomes an object *for* consciousness, an object that can be internalized by consciousness or grasped through an adequate representation. The ontological event that defines and dominates the philosophical tradition from Parmenides to Heidegger, for

Levinas, consists in suppressing or reducing all forms of otherness by transmuting their alterity into the Same. Philosophy *qua* ontology is the reduction of the other to the Same, where the other is assimilated like so much food or drink – 'O digestive philosophy!' as Sartre exclaimed against French neo-Kantianism.[9] Taking up the analysis of separated existence in *Totality and Infinity*, ontology is the movement of comprehension which takes possession of entities through the activity of labour; it is the movement of the hand, the organ of grasping (as in the linguistic chain *greifen, Griff, begreifen, Begriff*), which takes hold of (*prend*) and comprehends (*comprend*) entities in the virility of its acquisition and digestion of alterity (*TeI* 131–2/*TI* 158–9).

In his 1962 paper 'Transcendence and Height', which provides the best précis of Levinas's philosophical project in the period immediately following the publication of *Totality and Infinity* in 1961,[10] Levinas outlines and criticizes this digestive philosophy. For Levinas, the Same is *par excellence* the knowing ego (*le Moi connaissant*), what he calls the melting pot (*le creuset*) of Being (*TH* 89). The ego is the site for the transmutation of otherness. Now, Levinas claims, the ego desires liberty and comprehension. The latter is achieved through the full adequation or correspondence of the ego's representations with external reality: truth. The ego comprehends and englobes all possible reality; nothing is hidden, no otherness refuses to give itself up. Liberty, therefore, is simply the assurance that no otherness will hinder or prevent the Same and that each *sortie* into alterity will return to self bearing the prize of comprehension. Philosophy is defined by Levinas as the alchemy whereby alterity is transmuted into sameness, by means of the philosopher's stone of the knowing ego (*TH* 92).

Non-ontological philosophy – one is tempted to write 'non-philosophy', but the meaning of the word 'philosophy' for Levinas must be nuanced in order to distance it from mere *doxa*, or religious dogma, on the one hand, and Heidegger's thesis on the end of philosophy on the other – would consist in the resistance of the other to the Same. It is this resistance, this point of exteriority to the philosophical *logos*, that Levinas seeks to describe in his work. In *Totality and Infinity*, such a point of exteriority is located in the face of the Other, but is still articulated in the language of ontology, as when Levinas writes that 'Being is exteriority' (*TeI* 266/*TI* 290). Thus, in Heideggerian terms, the meaning of the Being of beings (the basic question of metaphysics) is determined as exteriority, the latter being Levinas's word for Being.[11] However, in his later work, and by way of a sinuous self-critique, this description of exteriority assumes the title *Autrement qu'être ou au-delà de l'essence* (1974); here Levinas is preoccupied with the possibility of an ethical form of language, the Saying (*le Dire*), which would be irreducible to the ontological language of the Said (*le Dit*), in which all entities are disclosed and comprehended in the light of Being. The great innovation in *Otherwise than Being*, although present in the Preface to *Totality and Infinity* (*TeI* xviii/*TI* 30), is the model of the Saying and the Said as the way of explaining how the ethical signifies within ontological language. The Saying is my exposure – corporeal, sensible – to the Other, my inability to refuse the Other's approach. It is the performative stating, proposing, or expressive position of myself facing the Other. It is a verbal or non-verbal ethical performance, whose essence cannot be caught in constative propositions. It is a performative *doing* that cannot be reduced to a constative description. By contrast, the Said is a statement, assertion, or proposition (of the form S is P), concerning which the truth or falsity can be ascertained. To employ another model, one might say that the content of my words, their identifiable meaning, is the Said, while the Saying consists in the fact that these words are being addressed to an interlocutor. The Saying is the sheer radicality of human speaking, of the event of being in relation with an Other; it is the non-thematizable ethical residue (*AE* 23/*OB* 18) of language that escapes comprehension, interrupts philosophy, and is the very enactment of the ethical movement from the Same to the Other. In a psychoanalytic register, the distinction between the Saying and the Said perhaps corresponds to Lacan's demarcation, inherited from Benveniste, of the orders of *énonciation* (the subject's act of speaking) and *énoncé* (the formulation of this act of speech into a statement).

Given that philosophy *qua* ontology speaks the language of the Said – it is propositional; it fills books – the methodological problem facing the later Levinas, a problem that haunts every page of *Otherwise than Being*, is the following: How is the Saying, my exposure to the Other, to be Said, or given a philosophical exposition that does not utterly betray this Saying? In *Otherwise than Being*, Levinas's thinking and, more especially, his style of writing become increasingly sensitive to the problem of how the ethical Saying is to be thematized – and necessarily betrayed (*AE* 7/*OB* 6) – within the

ontological Said. One might call this Levinas's 'linguistic or deconstructive turn'. His 'solution' to this problem is found in the
method of *reduction*, discussed below in chapter 4. In brief, it is a question of exploring the ways in which the Said can be unsaid, or *reduced*,
thereby letting the Saying reside as a residue, or interruption, within
the Said (*AE* 8/*OB* 7). The philosopher's effort, Levinas claims,
consists in the reduction of the Said to the Saying and the disruption
of the limit that divides the ethical from the ontological (*AE* 56–
8/*OB* 43–5). Ethics is not the simple overcoming or abandonment of
ontology, but rather the deconstruction of the latter's limits and its
comprehensive claims to mastery. Thus, whereas *Totality and Infinity*
powerfully articulates the non-ontological 'experience' of the face of
the Other in the language of ontology (a gesture which, as Levinas
points out, is refutable in the same manner as philosophy's refutation
of scepticism – which, of course, does not prevent scepticism from
returning incessantly to haunt rational discourse after its refutation.
Levinas's later work might be described as the attempt to articulate
scepticism's refusal of philosophy in the language of philosophy) (*AE*
210–18/*OB* 165–71), *Otherwise than Being* is a performative disruption
of the language of ontology, which maintains the interruption of
the ethical Saying within the ontological Said. Whereas *Totality and
Infinity* writes about ethics, *Otherwise than Being* is the performative
enactment of ethical writing – that is, following my epigraph, a form
of writing that, with an explosion, destroys all other books in the
world.

The language of *Otherwise than Being* – and no attempt has yet
been made to appreciate this book's strangeness, the disturbance it
provokes within philosphical discourse – performs a kind of spiralling
movement (*un mouvement en vrille*) (*AE* 57/*OB* 44), between the inevitable language of the ontological Said and the attempt to unsay that
Said in order to locate the ethical Saying within it. *Otherwise than Being*
enacts the reduction of the Said to the Saying, a reduction which
nevertheless maintains a residue of the unsaid Said within the Saying.
Levinas's language maintains an ambiguity, or oscillation, between
differing registers of language, that ensures the interruption of ontology. I shall demonstrate this complex linguistic structure in chapters
3 and 4.

Thus, with what Blanchot sees as a continual refinement and an
increasingly rigorous reflection on the possibilities of philosophical

language (*FF* 45), Levinas articulates the primacy of the ethical – that is, the primacy of the interhuman relationship, 'an irreducible structure upon which all the other structures rest' (*TeI* 51/*TI* 79). For Levinas – excepting certain *instants merveilleux* (*H* 94) in the history of philosophy, notably the Good beyond Being in Plato's *Republic* and the idea of infinity in Descartes' *Meditations* – it is ethics that has been dissimulated within the philosophical tradition. Thus, rather than ethics being understood as a traditional and regional component of philosophical thinking, built upon the ground of an ontological or logocentric metaphysics, Levinasian ethics is a 'first philosophy' (*TeI* 281/*TI* 304) that disrupts ontology or logocentrism. Accordingly, the fundamental question for philosophy is not Hamlet's 'To be or not to be?' (*AE* 4/*OB* 3) or Heidegger's Leibnizian question 'Why are there beings at all and why not rather nothing?' but rather, 'How does Being justify itself?' (*LR* 86).

1.3   Derrida and Levinas: An Emerging Homology

But why should Levinas be given a privileged place in the discussion of the ethics of deconstruction? I should like to begin unfolding this question by looking at some remarkably candid comments that Derrida made about Levinas during a discussion transcribed in *Altérités*, which appeared in 1986. After explaining his approach to the question of ethics and responding to the charge that he rarely speaks on the subject (*A* 37, 70–2), matters that I shall take up below, Derrida is challenged by André Jacob to specify what intellectual distance he maintains with respect to Levinas's work. Jacob asks:

> I cannot believe that you could subscribe to everything in Levinas which rightly represents at once an important revolution in the meaning of alterity with respect to traditional morality, but without losing what was best in morality. (*A* 74)

Derrida responds with the following surprising remark:

> I don't know....Faced with a thinking like that of Levinas, I never have an objection. I am ready to subscribe to everything that he says. That does not mean that I think the same thing in the same way, but in this respect the differences are very difficult to determine; in this case,

what do differences of idiom, language or writing mean? I tried to pose a certain number of questions to Levinas whilst reading him, where it may have been a question of his relation to the Greek *logos*, of his strategy, or of his thinking with respect to femininity for example, but what happens there is not of the order of disagreement or distance. (*A* 74)

Derrida does not think the same thing in the same way as Levinas, but he is ready to subscribe to everything Levinas says; consequently, when Derrida writes on Levinas, he is only raising questions and not formulating objections or refutations. But André Jacob, unhappy with this happy homoiousis between Derrida and Levinas asks, almost incredulously:

But there is in Levinas a relation to two traditions which are fundamental, and I think that your relationship to these traditions is not the
same in either case. (*A* 75)

What Jacob is saying is, surely Derrida does not share or acquiesce in sharing the traditions of phenomenology and Judaism to the same extent as Levinas? But, in response, Derrida surprises his interlocutor once again:

Perhaps that's also true, but the difference cannot be translated into
a difference of content or of philosophical position. I would have
difficulty, especially in improvising like this, in stating this difference;
it must be tangible, but yet it is not situatable. The double tradition of
which you speak, like many others, I share it with Levinas, although
he is much more profoundly engaged in it than I; none the less, poten-
tially and in principle, we share the same traditional heritage, even
if Levinas has been engaged with it for a much longer time and with
greater profundity. Therefore, the difference is not there either. This
is not the only example, but I often have difficulty in placing these
discrepancies otherwise than as differences of 'signature', that is, of
idiom, of ways of proceeding, of history, and of inscriptions connected
to the biographical aspect, etc. These are not philosophical differences.
(*A* 75)

At this point the dialogue between Derrida and Jacob breaks off, leaving one to conclude that there are no philosophical differences between Derrida and Levinas, and that Jacob's attempt to drive a wedge between them has failed. They share the same double tradition of phenomenology and Judaism, even if Levinas possesses it more profoundly; and the only differences that Derrida seems willing to admit are those of writing, idiom, biography, and signature. However, I think Derrida is being a little disingenuous here; for is he not the thinker who, to an unprecedented extent, has shown the crucial role that idiom, signature, and especially writing play in the *textual* constitution of the philosophical *logos*? One should perhaps also be cautious about such remarks because they were transcribed from an oral, improvised debate and were given in response to some rather direct interrogation. However, they do make the point rather well that the privilege accorded to Levinas in the discussion of Derrida's work is not without foundation.

There are other, ultimately more powerful reasons for privileging Levinas, which will be demonstrated in the course of the following discussions. First, Derrida's 1964 essay – or rather, monograph – on Levinas, 'Violence et Métaphysique' (*RMM*),[12] shows the problematic of deconstructive reading preparing itself through a dialogue with Levinasian ethics. Indeed, this essay was the only extended analysis of Levinas's work to appear in either French or English during the 1960s, and it has largely determined the reception of Levinas's thinking, particularly in the English-speaking world. Derrida's essay might therefore be expected to provide clues as to the genesis of the deconstructive problematic; more specifically – and here it differs from, say, Derrida's early work on Husserl – it might show how that problematic arises out of a confrontation with a primarily ethical thinking. Second, Derrida's 1980 essay on Levinas, 'En ce moment même dans cet ouvrage me voici' (*ECM*), a text of major importance, which has hitherto gone largely undiscussed, allows one to judge whether Derrida's deconstructive problematic has developed as a whole, and in particular *vis-à-vis* the question of ethics.[13] However, the general theme of the influence of Levinas on Derrida and the question of the convergence between the two undergoes a reversal of intentionality in a third point: namely, that Levinas is, to my knowledge, the sole object of deconstructive reading who has responded *responsibly* to Derrida (unlike, say, Searle or Foucault). In the short but philosophically rich 1973 essay devoted to Derrida's work, 'Tout autrement', as well as in several other places, Levinas gives an ethical reading of deconstruction.[14] Although he is reluctant to mention

'Violence and Metaphysics' by name and instead focuses his attention on Derrida's reading of Husserl in *Voice and Phenomenon*, I shall claim, and hope to show, that Levinas's reading of Derrida provides a rare glimpse of what it might mean to respond ethically to deconstruction. Of course, it is an intriguing, although ultimately indeterminable, question as to what extent one might read Levinas's work after *Totality and Infinity*, particularly *Otherwise than Being*, as a response to the questions raised by Derrida in 'Violence and Metaphysics'.[15] Indeed, if one may speak of the influence of Derrida on Levinas, then it can best be seen perhaps in the way in which, in *Otherwise than Being*, Levinas is far more conscious of the linguistic and logocentric recoils that arise when the ethical Saying is thematized within the ontological Said. A third title for this book might be 'The Deconstruction of Ethics'.

If the textual dialogue between Derrida and Levinas is in any way exemplary, then its exemplarity consists in the way in which each moment of the dialogue, the succession of textual encounters, calls each of the two thinkers into question and leads him to a level deeper than the ontology of questioning (what is x?) – namely, responsibility for the Other. I shall claim that there exist certain thematic and strategic similarities between Derrida's and Levinas's thinking which allow both deconstruction to be understood as an ethical demand and ethics to be approached deconstructively. This does not mean that I wish to reduce the dialogue between Levinas and Derrida to a relation of identity. Despite Derrida's confessional protestations cited above, the two thinkers are evidently not identical; moreover, if Levinas's conception of ethics is conditional upon the respect for alterity and difference, perhaps they *should not* be identical. (Of course, they might well say the Same in the Heidegger's sense of Same, *das Selbe*, which he distinguishes from the identical, *das Gleiche*.[16]) The question of how one responds responsibly to the ethical demand described in Levinas's and Derrida's work is a problem that will haunt this book. It is the explosive problem of the writing of ethics noted above: namely, that if ethics is defined in terms of respect for alterity (*TeI* 279/*TI* 302), how is alterity respected in a discourse upon that alterity? Is not a book on ethics a denial of ethics, and must not ethics be a denial of the book? My ambition is spelt out by Levinas in the concluding paragraph of 'Wholly Otherwise', where he writes of Derrida:

Indeed the ridiculous ambition of 'improving' a true philosopher is not our intention. To meet him on his way is already very commendable and is probably the very modality of the philosophical encounter. In underlining the primordial importance of the questions posed by Derrida, we wished to express the pleasure of a contact made in the heart of a chiasmus. (*NP* 89)

I will not presume, ambitiously, to improve upon Derrida or Levinas; nor do I want to 'Derridianize' Levinas or transform Derrida into a Levinasian. My hope is simply to allow these two thinkers to meet on their way and to see such a meeting as an index for the more general problematic of the ethics of deconstruction. The figure that Levinas employs to explain this meeting, or dialogue, is that of a chiasmus, itself of course derived from the Greek letter χ, which denotes a crossing, or interlacing. Indeed, Derrida has employed the same trope to describe the double gesture of deconstructive reading.[17] If, in any chiasmic dialogue, the two lines of thought are bound to cross in what Levinas calls 'the heart of a chiasmus', then this should not blind one to the multiplicity of points where those lines of thought diverge. Ethical dialogue should not result in the annulment of alterity, but in respect for it.

1.4 Derrida's Double-Handed Treatment of Ethics

But is there not a real danger here of betraying the very subject that I am trying to elucidate? Could one not object to my argument by claiming that all discussion of the ethics of deconstruction – however cautiously and cleverly it might be formulated – is simply at the very antipodes of Derrida's work? More precisely, should one not recall that it is precisely Derrida himself who, in 'Violence and Metaphysics' and despite the undoubted generosity of his reading, demonstrated how Levinas's ethical overcoming of ontology is itself dependent upon the totalizing ontologies it sought to overcome – namely, Husserlian phenomenology, Hegelian dialectic, and Heidegger's thinking of the meaning or the truth of Being? Indeed, one must; but if this were all that Derrida had to say about Levinasian ethics, then there would be little reason for the *rapprochement* that is being attempted here. As Robert Bernasconi points out, to interpret 'Violence and Metaphysics' solely as a statement of the derivative and secondary character of ethics *vis-à-vis* phenomenology, ontology, and dialectics would be to read Derrida's essay simply as a *critique* of Levinas and not as a deconstructive reading.[18] To read Derrida's essay deconstructively (that is, with the same care and rigour with which Derrida reads Levinas) is to identify another strand of thought, perhaps at odds with the idea of critique.

In 'Ousia and grammē', Derrida writes that a deconstructive reading must operate with 'Two texts, two hands, two visions, two ways of listening (*écoutes*). Together at once and separately' (*M* 75/*MP* 65). A good example of this double-handed, double-stranded account of deconstruction with respect to Levinas concerns the question of empiricism. In the concluding pages of 'Violence and Metaphysics', Derrida 'accuses' Levinas of empiricism, a doctrine, he claims, whose only philosophical shortcoming is to present itself as a philosophy at all (*ED* 224/*WD* 151). This seemingly disparaging remark would lead one to believe that Derrida's own position is opposed to – or at least differs from – that of empiricism. Strangely, this is not at all the case. Three years after the first publication of 'Violence and Metaphysics', in *Of Grammatology*, Derrida makes the following remark about the style of deconstruction:

> From the interior of the closure, one can only judge its style in terms of received oppositions. One will say that this style is empiricist and, in a certain way, one would be right. The *exit* is radically empiricist. (*G* 232/*OG* 162; cf. *M* 7/*MP* 7)

Bearing in mind that this is a definition of deconstruction given from within the metaphysical closure – that is, from within the conceptual oppositions (e.g. the empirical versus the transcendental) that constitute metaphysics – it would appear that Derrida offers with one hand what he threatens to take away with the other. However, to interpret these two uses of empiricism as a contradiction is to miss the point. In 'Violence and Metaphysics', *Of Grammatology*, and throughout his work, Derrida is trying to explicate certain necessities within discourse which all philosophers, Levinas and Derrida included, are obliged to face. The questions that Derrida addresses to Levinas, then, are questions that address the whole field of philosophical language, within whose parameters the discourse of deconstruction is also inscribed. If there were any way in which deconstruction could circumvent the logic of palaeonymy, where all discourse is obliged to employ the 'old signs' (*VP* 115/*SP* 102) of metaphysics, then it would attempt to give expression to the *'unheard of* thoughts' (ibid.) which glimmer beyond the metaphysical closure. However, as the resources of metaphysical discourse are the only ones that are available, one must continue to use them even when trying to promote their displacement.

So, if the derivative character of Levinasian ethics might be said to be only one strand of Derrida's understanding of ethics, then is there another strand? In order to elaborate this question, I shall return to Derrida's remarks in *Altérités* (*A* 70–2). Early in the debate, Derrida is asked, once again by André Jacob, 'the reasons why he rarely speaks of ethics' (*A* 37). Although Derrida does not appear at all anxious to answer this question, he begins by saying that his reticence about the word 'ethics' is similar to that of Heidegger in his *Letter on Humanism*.[19] On Heidegger's reading, ethics and the whole question of the 'ought' (*Sollen*)[20] is a late-comer to thinking, with a status similar to that of logic and physics, one which arises in Plato's school after the birth of philosophy and science (*epistēmē*).[21] Heidegger's central point here is that, before the scholarly reification of thinking into philosophy and the tripartite demarcation of philosophy into ethics, logic, and physics, thinkers did not know ethics as a separate region of inquiry. This did not make their thinking unethical; on the contrary, Heidegger claims, the tragedies of Sophocles and the sayings of Heracleitus think the original notion of *ethos* even more fundamentally than Aristotle's *Ethics*.[22] Heidegger discusses Heracleitus' 119th fragment, *ethos anthropoi daimon*, which is usually translated as 'A man's character is his daimon', or even 'Character for man is destiny',[23] but which Heidegger renders: 'The (familiar) abode is for man the open region for the presencing of god (the unfamiliar one)' (*Der (geheure) Aufenthalt ist dem Menschen das offene für die Anwesung des Gottes (des Ungeheuren)*).[24] Heidegger interprets *ethos* as abode, or dwelling place (*ethos bedeutet Aufenthalt, Ort des Wohnens*); and thus the fundamental meaning of ethics is thought in terms of the abode of man – that is, the familiar and everyday place where the human being dwells and comes to stand out, to ek-sist, in the unfamiliar truth of Being (*die Wahrheit des Seins*). For Heidegger, original ethics (*die ursprüngliche Ethik*)[25] is human dwelling thought upon the horizon of the truth of Being – that is, thought non-metaphysically, in so far as metaphysics has never been capable of thinking Being itself (*das Sein selbst*) without regard for Being's determination in terms of beings or entities (*das Seiende*). Therefore, to make ethics a 'first philosophy' – that is, a metaphysics – and to oppose such an ethics to ontology (to create a metaphysical opposition), as Levinas attempts to do, is to continue the oblivion of the truth of Being that is presupposed and dissimulated by all ethico-metaphysical discourse. Since this oblivion of Being is what, for Heidegger, has characterized the entire onto-theological adventure of Western metaphysics, to insist upon the metaphysical priority and primacy of ethics over ontology is to repeat one of the most traditional of philosophical gestures: namely, Kantianism.

Such are Derrida's Heideggerian reservations about the use of the word 'ethics'. One must not simply 'do' ethics in the usual sense of the word; one must first engage in a deconstructive analysis of 'l'éthicité de l'éthique' or, in Nietzschean terms, a calling into question of the value of values.[26] And yet, Derrida continues, these Heideggerian and Nietzschean reservations are themselves displaced by the sense that Levinas gives to the word 'ethics':

> I believe that when Levinas speaks of ethics – I wouldn't say that this has nothing in common with what has been covered over in this word from Greece to the German philosophy of the 19th Century, ethics is wholly other (*tout autre*), and yet it is the same word. (*A* 71)

Ethics is wholly other and yet it is the same word. It is with this ambiguity in mind that one can begin a serious deconstructive, or double-handed, reading of Levinas's work. In Levinas's hands, the word 'ethics' becomes wholly other, thereby loosening itself from the traditional metaphysical determination criticized by Heidegger in the *Letter on Humanism*. In Levinas's anachronistic use of a word laden with specific and (following Nietzsche's genealogy) regrettable historical determinations, it seems as if he has found a new and hitherto hidden condition of possibility for ethics that was dissimulated in the Graeco-German philosophical tradition (*A* 71). Levinasian ethics no longer simply denotes a region of philosophical inquiry derived and secondary to the basic question of philosophy: the question of Being. And although in *Totality and Infinity* ethics is indeed described as a 'first philosophy' and as metaphysics (*TeI* 281/*TI* 304), one might claim that as Levinas's work develops in the direction of *Otherwise than Being*, he proposes the thought of the Good beyond Being as a third option that exceeds the ontological difference between Being and beings (*AE* 54–5/*OB* 42–3). Thus, as Derrida says, the word ethics undergoes a 'semantic transformation' (*A* 71) or reversal in Levinas's work. It is the same word, often apparently employed in the same way, but its meaning has been displaced. And, on the basis of this displacement of meaning in Levinas's use of the word 'ethics', Derrida finds its employment far less bothersome. 'Starting from that argument, I would find the word "ethics" much less restrictive', he says (*A* 71). Such ambiguity or displacement of meaning is also noted by Blanchot with respect to Levinas's use of the word 'responsibility': 'This banal word', he writes, 'that generally qualifies, in prosaic and bourgeois fashion, a man who is mature, lucid and conscious...one must try and understand how Levinas has renewed it, opened it up to the point of making it signify (beyond all sense) the responsibility of an other philosophy (*d'une philosophie autre*).'[27]

Fascinatingly, these Heideggerian and Nietzschean reservations about the word 'ethics' are also shared by Levinas himself, as he makes clear in the following remarks, which refer back explicitly to Derrida's discussion in *Altérités* and are transcribed from a debate also held at the Centre Sèvres in Paris:

> A second point now needs to be raised; it concerns the term ethics itself. I have recourse to it whilst fully fearing the moralistic reson-ances that it bears and which risk absorbing its principle meaning. It seems to me that Jacques Derrida underlined this with respect to my work in a meeting that was held in this very place. For me, the term ethics always signifies the fact of the encounter, of the relation of myself with the Other: a scission of Being in the encounter – without coincidence! (*Le terme éthique signifie toujours pour moi le fait de la rencontre, de la relation d'un moi à autrui: scission de l'être dans la rencontre – pas de coïncidence!*)[28]

The meaning of ethics for Levinas is found in the relation that I have with the Other and in the unique demand that is placed upon me by him or her. The Other who approaches me is a singular other who does not lose him or her self in a crowd of others. Similarly, the subject who is faced with obligation and who is prepared to expiate or substitute him or her self for the Other is an entity not immedi-ately subsumable under a universal concept of the ego, as something belonging in common to all human beings. Rather, at the moment of obligation, it is *I*, a singular self, who am obliged to respond to a particular other (*AE* 105/*OB* 84). 'The ego involved in responsibility is me and no one else' (*AE* 162/*OB* 126–7). This is what Levinas implies by his repeated citation of the biblical phrase '*me voici*' ('See me here!' or 'Here I am') (*AE* 190/*OB* 149). Here *I* am for the Other, and before the trace of the Wholly Other. Subjectivity is *my* subjection to the other all the way to substitution for him or her. Now, for Derrida (and also for Blanchot), it is precisely in this privilege accorded to the irreducible particularity of my obligations to the singular other, prior to procedures of universalization and legislation, in the anarchy of generosity or what Blanchot calls a 'prophetic singularity',[29] that the word 'ethics' is able to exceed its traditional determination.

> The respect for the singularity or the call of the other is unable to belong to the domain of ethics, to the conventionally and traditionally determined domain of ethics. (*A* 71)

Of course, one might object – and Derrida himself raises this objection – that such an ethics is no ethics at all and is not even worthy to bear the name. Indeed, Derrida himself wonders whether the title 'ultra-ethics' might not be a more fitting description of his own and Levinas's projects. However, whether one speaks of the *Ethics of Deconstruction* or, more barbarously, of the *Ethics of Ethics of Deconstruction* or the *Ultra-Ethics of Deconstruction* is of subsidiary importance. As Levinas is fond of saying in *Otherwise than Being*, the ethical Saying must proceed through an abuse of language (*AE* 30/*OB* 188). *Traduire c'est trahir*: to translate or express the Saying in the language of the Said is necessarily to betray that Saying, although the Said can always be reduced to its condition in the Saying. I have in these pages simply sought to demonstrate Derrida's double-handed treatment of ethics. Despite his clear reticence about employing the word 'ethics', Derrida sees in Levinas a deconstructive attempt to displace ethics and think it anew by locating its condition of possibility in the relation to the Other, the *Autrui*, the singular other.

However, working with both hands, a doubt still persists: ethics is wholly other for Levinas, and *yet it is the same word*. Is it henceforth forbidden to consider Levinas's thinking as an inverted Heideggerianism, a wilful and short-sighted inversion of Heidegger's account of metaphysics? As a polemic not so much against Heidegger as against 'the primacy of Heideggerian ontology' (*TeI* 15/*TI* 45)[30] in France after the Second World War? As a belated and retarded return to the ontic, the humanistic, the subjective? Not at all. One should rather see Levinas's inverted Heideggerianism as one strand in an irreducibly double reading. Levinas's proposition that 'Being is exteriority' (*L'être est extériorité*) (*TeI* 266/*TI* 290) – that is, that what it means to be a human being is to be open to the exteriority or, if one prefers, the alterity of the Other – is a metaphysical and humanistic determination of the truth or essence of Being. Such a determination of Being is metaphysical on a Heideggerian account, in the same way as the determination of the Being of beings as *eidos, ousia, causa sui*, self-consciousness, or will-to-power, the difference being that Levinas is a retarded metaphysician, who is still producing theses on Being at the moment when philosophy has ended and we have entered the completion of metaphysics.[31] Levinas fails to see the radicality of the *question* of Being as a question, and thus he is logically, if not chronologically, pre-Heideggerian.

The above is a plausible, if violent, reading of Levinas; just as plausible and just as violent as Heidegger's reading of Nietzsche and the entire metaphysical tradition. However, to anticipate what will be elaborated in detail in the following chapters, the Levinasian text is swept across by a double movement, what Jacques Rolland has called a 'logic of ambiguity',[32] between a metaphysical (in Heidegger's sense) or ontological (in Levinas's sense) language of Being as exteriority and the thought of the other than Being that decisively interrupts metaphysics or ontology. Levinas's writing is hinged or articulated around an ambiguous, or double, movement between the ontological Said and the ethical Saying. To read Levinas is to read with two hands; it is to render legible the ambiguity enacted in his writing. I shall claim that the very possibility of ethics is found in the articulation of this hinge, the activation of this ambiguity between what is said in a text, the language of ontological propositions, and the very ethical Saying of that text. This, of course, is also true of the text that I am writing at this very moment, a text that seeks to persuade the reader by presenting its argument as if in a 'final and absolute vision' (*TeI* 53/*TI* 81), but a vision which, paradoxically, is neither final nor absolute, but rather a particular address to an interlocutor, a reader. Books narrate their own explosions (*AE* 216–7/*OB* 170–1).

1.5   Deconstructive Reading and the Problem of Closure

My Ariadne's thread for the disclosure of the ethics of deconstructive reading in Derrida's work – which should also grant some under-standing of Derrida's relation to the philosophical tradition – is the concept of the closure of metaphysics (*la clôture de la métaphysique*). In 'Violence and Metaphysics', and with direct reference to Levina-sian ethics, Derrida defines closure as '*the problem of the relations between belonging and the breakthrough, the problem of closure*' (*le problème des rapports entre l'appartenance et la percée, le problème de la clôture*) (*ED* 163/*WD* 110). Broadly stated, the problem of metaphysical closure describes the duplicitous historical moment – *now* – when 'our' language, concepts, institutions, and philosophy itself show them-selves both to belong to a metaphysical or logocentric tradition which is theoretically exhausted, while at the same time searching for the breakthrough from that tradition. In Lacoue-Labarthe's formulation, the age is closed; philosophy is finished; and what is demanded is a certain modesty of thought (*FP* 13–21/*HAP* 1–7). The problem of closure describes the liminal situation of modernity out of which the deconstructive problematic arises, and which, as I shall show, Derrida inherits from Heidegger. Closure is the double refusal both of re-maining within the limits of the tradition and of the possibility of transgressing that limit. At the moment of historical and philo-sophical closure, deconstructive thinking occurs as the disruption and interruption of the limit that divides the inside from the outside of the tradition. From Derrida's earliest essay on Husserl, ' "Genesis and Structure" and Phenomenology', to his more recent work – for example, his 'Toward an Ethic of Discussion' (*LI* 281–2/*LItr* 152–3), the concept of closure (both *clôture* and *fermeture*) has remained a constant and essential gesture within the logic of deconstruction. A deconstructive reading shows both how a text is dependent upon the presuppositions of a metaphysics of presence or logocentrism – that is, for Derrida, any text which identifies truth with presence or *logos*, occurring in the voice and entailing the debasement of writing and all forms of exteriority (*G* 11–12/*OG* 3) – which that text might attempt to dissimulate, and how the text radically questions the metaphysics it presupposes, thereby entering into contradiction with itself and pointing the way towards a thinking that would be other to logocentrism. Closure is the hinge that articulates the double movement between logocentrism, or metaphysics, and its other. Ethics signifies in the articulation of this hinge.

Chapter 2 will provide an extended analysis of the sense, genesis, and development of the problem of closure in Derrida's writings, paying special attention to the place of this problem in his readings of Husserl and Heidegger. Such an analysis is important because, first, it permits some assessment of the relation between deconstruction, phenomenology, and the thinking of Being. Second, and with particular reference to Heidegger, the problem of closure relates Derrida's thinking to the history of metaphysics (*qua* the forgetfulness or oblivion of Being; *Seinsvergessenheit*), the context within and against which deconstruction works, which will thereby confront the claim that Derrida's work is a species of dehistoricized formalism. Third, and most important, it permits a notion of *clôtural* reading, which is the methodological tool needed to explicate fully the ethics of deconstructive reading.

However, before outlining my concept of *clôtural* reading, it is necessary to sketch the understanding of deconstruction that underpins this concept and which will guide the analyses of the following chapters. What is deconstruction? Or, since it is perhaps easier initially to give a negative response to this question, what is *not* deconstruction? (*Qu'est-ce que la déconstruction n'est pas?*) (*PSY* 387). Employing a short text of Derrida's written in 1983 and published in 1985, 'Letter to a Japanese Friend', which was written specifically in order to aid the possible translation of the word *déconstruction* into Japanese, one can quickly sketch some important caveats. First, Derrida insists that deconstruction is not something negative; it is not a process of demolition (which does not automatically entail that it is positive) (*PSY* 390). Furthermore, deconstruction needs to be sharply distinguished from analysis, which presupposes a reduction of entities to their simple, or essential, elements, elements which themselves would stand in need of deconstruction. Crucially, deconstruction is not critique, either in the general or the Kantian sense. Derrida writes: 'The instance of the *krinein* or of *krisis* (decision, choice, judgement, discernment) is itself, as is moreover the entire apparatus of transcendental critique, one of the essential "themes" or "objects" of deconstruction' (*PSY* 390). Similarly, deconstruction is not a method or way that can be utilized in the activity of interpretation. This is also to say that deconstruction cannot be reduced to a methodology (among competing methodologies) in the human or natural sciences or a technical procedure assimilable by academics and capable of being taught in educational institutions (*PSY* 390–1). Further, deconstruction is not an *act* produced and controlled by a subject; nor is it an *operation* that sets to work on a text or an institution. Derrida concludes the 'Letter' characteristically by writing, 'What deconstruction is not? But everything! What is deconstruction? But nothing!' (*PSY* 392). All ontological statements of the form 'Deconstruction is x' miss the point a *priori*; for it is precisely the ontological presuppositions of the copula that provide one of the enduring themes of deconstruction. Rather, carefully avoiding the verb 'to be', Derrida claims that deconstruction takes place (*a lieu*), and that it does so wherever there 'is' something (*où il y a quelque chose*). Such is the *enigma* (Derrida's word; *PSY* 391) of deconstruction: it cannot be defined, and therefore resists translation; it is not an entity, a thing; nor is it univocal or unitary. Derrida writes, paying careful attention to the reflexivity of the statement, *Ça se déconstruit* ('It deconstructs itself', the *Ça* being a translation of both Freud's *Es* – the Id, the unconscious – and a homophone for *Sa* – *savoir absolu*, absolute knowledge (*PSY* 391)). It deconstructs itself wherever something takes place.

But such a formulation, although subtle and accurate, risks being unhelpful because of its generality. Having taken on board the negative caveats in the problem of defining deconstruction, I would now like to assemble a more 'constructivist' account of deconstruction, by asking *how* deconstruction takes place. Derrida addresses this question concisely and lucidly in *Of Grammatology*, in a chapter entitled 'The Exorbitant. Question of Method'. The first essential point to make, however trivial it may seem, is that deconstruction is always deconstruction of a *text* (understood for the moment in the limited sense; I shall come to the notion of the general text presently). Derrida's thinking is always thinking *about* a text, from which flows the obvious corollary that deconstruction is always engaged in *reading* a text. The way of deconstruction is always opened through reading – what Derrida calls 'a first task, the most elementary of tasks' (*MPM* 35/*MPMtr* 41). Any thinking that is primarily concerned with reading will clearly be dependent upon the text that is being read. Thus Derrida's readings are parasitic, because they are close readings of texts that draw their sustenance from within the flesh of the host. What takes place in deconstruction is reading; and, I shall argue, what distinguishes deconstruction as a textual practice is *double reading* – that is to say, a reading that interlaces at leasts two motifs or layers of reading, most often by first repeating what Derrida calls 'the dominant interpretation' (*LI* 265/*LItr* 143) of a text in the guise of a commentary and second, within and through this repetition, leaving the order of commentary and opening a text up to the blind spots or ellipses within the dominant interpretation.

Now when Derrida reads Rousseau, he organizes his reading around the word *supplément*. It is claimed that this word is the 'blind spot' (*tâche aveugle*) (*G* 234/*OG* 163) in Rousseau's text, a word which he employs but whose logic is veiled to him.[33] Derrida's reading of Rousseau traces the logic of this supplement, a logic which allows Rousseau's text to slip from the grip of its intentions and achieve a textual position that is other than the logocentric conceptuality that Rousseau intended to affirm. Thus Derrida's reading of Rousseau occupies the space between the writer's intentions and the text, between what the writer commands and fails to command in a language. It is into this space between intentions and text that Derrida inserts what he calls the 'signifying structure' (*G* 227/*OG* 158) of the reading that constitutes Part 2 of *Of Grammatology*.

How does one perform a deconstructive reading? In 'The Exorbitant. Question of Method', Derrida pauses in his reading of Rousseau in order to justify his own methodological principles. The signifying structure of a deconstructive reading, he claims, cannot simply be produced through the 'respectful doubling of commentary' (*G* 227/ *OG* 158). Although Derrida is acutely aware of the exigencies of the traditional instruments of commentary as an 'indispensable guardrail' (*cet indispensable garde-fou*) in critical production, he claims that commentary 'has always only *protected*, it has never *opened*, a reading' (*G* 227/*OG* 158).

Here I would like to pause for a moment to consider what Derrida could possibly mean by the word 'commentary' in this context. Is he claiming, oblivious to the achievements of Heideggerian and especially Gadamerian hermeneutics, that there can be a pure commentary or literal repetition of a text that is not already an interpretation?

Derrida corrects and clarifies the above remarks from *Of Grammatology* in one of his responses to Gerald Graff in the 'Afterword' to *Limited Inc.*, where he writes: 'The moment of what I called, perhaps clumsily, "doubling commentary" does not suppose the self-identity of "meaning", but a relative stability of the dominant interpretation (including the auto-interpretation) of the text being commented upon.' He continues: 'Perhaps I should not have called it commentary' (*LI* 265/*LItr* 143). Thus, for Derrida, the moment of commentary refers to the reproducibility and stability of the dominant interpretation of a text: for example, the traditional logocentric reading (or misreading) of Rousseau. Commentary is always already interpretation, and Derrida does not believe in the possibility of a pure and simple repetition of a text. However – and this is a crucial caveat – there is an unavoidable need for a competence in reading and writing such that the dominant interpretation of a text can be reconstructed as a necessary and indispensable layer or moment of reading. 'Otherwise', Derrida writes, echoing a sentence from *Of Grammatology* effectively ignored by many of its opponents and proponents alike, 'one could indeed say just anything at all and I have never accepted saying, or being encouraged to say, just anything at all' (*LI* 267/*LItr* 144–5; cf. *G* 227/*OG* 158).

Derrida goes on to argue that the moment of 'commentary', or of the dominant interpretation, reflects a minimal *consensus* concerning the intelligibility of texts, establishing what a given text means for a community of readers. Although such a search for consensus is 'actively interpretative', Derrida adds, 'I believe that no research is possible in a community (for example, academic) without the prior search for this minimal consensus' (*LI* 269/*LItr* 146). Thus, although 'commentary' alone does not open a genuine reading, the latter is not possible without a moment of commentary, without a scholarly competence in reading, understanding, and writing, without a knowledge of texts in their original languages (for example, Rousseau's or Derrida's French), without knowing the corpus of an author as a whole, without knowing the multiple contexts – political, literary, philosophical, historical, and so forth – which determine a given text or are determined by that text. This is what one might call the deconstructive duty of scholarship. I would go further and claim that there is a hermeneutic principle of fidelity – one might even say 'an "ethico-political duty" ' (*un 'devoir éthico-politique'*) (*LI* 249/*LItr* 135) –

and a minimal working notion of truth as *adaequatio* underlying deconstructive reading, as its primary layer of reading. If deconstructive reading is to possess any demonstrative necessity, it is initially by virtue of how faithfully it reconstructs the dominant interpretation of a text in a layer of 'commentary'.

To choose an extreme example, in 'Limited Inc. a b c', every word of Searle's 'Reiterating the Differences: A Reply to Derrida' is repeated, or re-reiterated. Derrida clearly views this as a way of responding responsibly to the brutality of Searle's essay, which decides to 'insult' (*LI* 257/*LItr* 139) Derrida's work – for example, Searle writes of 'Derrida's distressing penchant for saying things that are obviously false'[34] – rather than engage in the necessary critical demonstration. Thus, bearing the above qualifications in mind, one might say that a reading is *true* in the first instance to the extent that it faithfully repeats or corresponds to what is said in the text that is being commented upon. This is perhaps the reason why Derrida quotes at such length and with such regularity in his writings, and it is also the basis for his accusation of falsity against Habermas's critique of his work in 'Excursus on Leveling the Genre Distinction between Philosophy and Literature', in which Derrida is not cited a single time (*LI* 244/*LItr* 156).[35]

Returning to *Of Grammatology*, it is clear that although the respectful repetition of the text which 'commentary' produces fails to open a reading, this in no way entails that one should then transgress the text by reductively relating it to some referent or signified outside textuality (such as historical material or the psychobiography of the author). To determine textual signifiers by referring them to a governing signified – for example, to read *A la recherche* in terms of Proust's asthma – would be to give what Derrida calls a transcendent reading (*G* 229/*OG* 160). The axial proposition of *Of Grammatology* is 'Il n'y a pas de hors-texte' ('There is no outside-text') (*G* 227/*OG* 158), or again, 'Il n'y a rien hors du texte' ('There is nothing outside of the text') (*G* 233/*OG* 163); and one should be attentive to the nuanced difference between these two sentences: the first claims that there is no 'outside-text', no text outside, whereas the second claims that there is *nothing* outside the text, that the text outside is nothing, implying by this that any reading that refers the text to some signified outside textuality is illusory. Within the logocentric epoch, the textual signifier (and writing, inscription, the mark, and the trace in general) has always been determined as secondary, as a fallen exteriority preceded by a signified. A deconstructive reading must, therefore, remain within the limits of textuality, hatching its eggs within the flesh of the host.

Thus, the 'methodological' problem for deconstruction becomes one of discovering how a reading can remain internal to the text and within the limits of textuality without merely repeating the text in the manner of a 'commentary'. To borrow the adverbial phrase with which Derrida describes his reading of Husserl, deconstructive reading must move *à travers* the text, *traversing* the space between a repetitive commentary and a meta-textual interpretation, '*traversing (à travers)* Husserl's text, that is to say, in a reading which cannot simply be that of commentary nor that of interpretation' (*VP* 98/*SP* 88). By opening up this textual space that is other to 'commentary' or interpretation, a certain distance is created between deconstructive reading and logocentric conceptuality. The signifying structure of a deconstructive reading traverses a space that is other to logocentrism and that tends, eccentrically, to exceed the orbit of its conceptual totality. In an important and explicit reference to the 'goal' or 'aim' of deconstruction, Derrida writes:

> We wanted to attain the point of a certain exteriority with respect to the totality of the logocentric epoch. From this point of exteriority a certain deconstruction of this totality (...) could be broached (*entamée*). (*G* 231/*OG* 161–2)

It is from such a point of exteriority that deconstruction could cut into or penetrate the totality, thereby displacing it. The goal of deconstruction, therefore, is to locate a point of otherness within philosophical or logocentric conceptuality and then to deconstruct this conceptuality from that position of alterity.

It is at this point that the concept of double reading can be properly understood. If the first moment of reading is the rigorous, scholarly reconstruction of the dominant interpretation of a text, its intended meaning (*vouloir-dire*) in the guise of a commentary, then the second moment of reading, in virtue of which deconstruction obeys a double necessity, is *the destabilization of the stability of the dominant interpretation* (*LI* 271/*LItr* 147). It is the movement of traversing the text which enables the reading to obtain a position of alterity or exteriority, from which the text can be deconstructed. The second moment brings the text into contradiction with itself, opening its intended meaning, its *vouloir-dire*, onto an alterity which goes against what the text wants to say or mean (*ce que le texte veut dire*). Derrida often articulates this double reading around a semantic ambivalence in the usage of a particular word, like *supplément* in Rousseau, *pharmakon* in Plato, or *Geist* in Heidegger. It is of absolutely crucial importance that this second moment, that of alterity, be shown to arise necessarily out of the first moment of repetitive commentary. Derrida ventriloquizes this double structure through the mouth of Heidegger in *De l'esprit*:

> That is why, without opposing myself to that of which I am trying to think the most matinal possibility, without even using words other than those of the tradition, I follow the path of a repetition which crosses the path of the wholly other. The wholly other announces itself within the most rigorous repetition. (*C'est pourquoi sans m'opposer à ce dont j'essaie de penser la possibilité la plus matinale, sans même me servir d'autres mots que ceux de la tradition, je suis le chemin du tout autre. Le tout autre s'annonce dans la répétition la plus rigoreuse.*) (E 184/OS 113)

Thus, by following the path of a repetition, the *Wiederholung* of a text or a tradition, one inevitably crosses the path of something wholly other, something that cannot be reduced to what that text or tradition wants to say. It is at this point that the similarities between Derridian deconstruction and Heideggerian *Destruktion* become apparent. Indeed, Derrida initially employed the term *déconstruction* as an attempt to render into French the Heideggerian notions of *Destruktion* (de-struction, or non-negative de-structuring) and *Abbau* (demolition or, better, dismantling) (*PSY* 388). For the Heidegger of *Being and Time*, the working out, or elaboration (*die Ausarbeitung*), of the question of the meaning of Being does not become truly concrete until the ontological tradition — that is, the tradition that has forgotten the question of Being, and more precisely the *temporal* dimension of this question — has been completely repeated (*wiederholen*) and deconstructed (*SuZ* 26). In the 1962 lecture 'Time and Being', *Abbau* is presented (and presented, moreover, as a synonym for *Destruktion*) as the progressive removal of the concealing layers that have covered over the first Greek sending of Being as presence (*Anwesenheit*). The repetition of the metaphysical tradition is a dismantling that reveals its unsaid as unsaid.[36] Returning to Derrida, it is the belonging together or interlacing of these two moments, or paths, of reading – repetition and alterity – that best describes the double gesture of deconstructive reading: the figure of the chiasmus.

What takes place in deconstruction is double reading – that is, a form of reading that obeys the double injunction for both repetition and the alterity that arises within that repetition. Deconstruction opens a reading by locating a moment of alterity within a text. In Derrida's reading of Rousseau, the concept of the supplement is the lever employed to show how Rousseau's discourse is inscribed within the general text, a domain of textuality irreducible to logocentric conceptuality. In this way one can see how a moment of blindness in a logocentric text grants insight into an alterity that exceeds logocentrism. As Derrida remarked once in an interview, 'Deconstruction is not an enclosure in nothingness, but an openness towards the other.'[37] What takes place in deconstruction is a highly determinate form of double reading which pursues alterities within texts, primarily philosophical texts. In this way, deconstruction opens a discourse on the other to philosophy, an otherness that has been dissimulated or appropriated by the logocentric tradition. Philosophy, particularly in its Hegelian moment, has always insisted on thinking of its other (art, religion, nature, and so forth) as its *proper* other, thereby appropriating it and losing sight of its otherness. The philosophical text has always believed itself to be in control of the margin of its proper volume (*M* 1/*MP* x). As Levinas points out in 'Transcendence and Height', philosophy might be defined as the activity of assimilating all otherness to the Same (*TH* 92). Such a definition would seem to be accurate in so far as the philosophical tradition has always attempted to understand and *think* the plurality and alterity of a manifold of entities through a reduction of plurality to unity and alterity to sameness. The same gesture (or gesture of the Same) is repeated throughout the philosophical tradition, whether it be in Plato, where the plurality of the instances of an entity (*phainomena*) are understood in relation to a unifying *eidos*; or whether it be in Aristotle, where *philosophia protē* (that is to say, metaphysics) is the attempt to understand the Being of a plurality of entities in relation to a unifying *ousia*, and ultimately a divine *ousia*: the god (*to theon*); or, indeed, whether it be in terms of Kantian epistemology, where the manifold or plurality of intuitions are brought into unity and sameness by being placed under concepts which are regulated by the categories of the understanding (and other examples could be cited).

The very activity of thinking, which lies at the basis of epistemological, ontological, and veridical comprehension, is the reduction of plurality to unity and alterity to sameness. The activity of philossophy, the very task of thinking, is the reduction of otherness. In seeking to think the other, its otherness is reduced or appropriated to our understanding. To think philosophically is to comprehend –*comprendre, comprehendere, begreifen*, to include, to seize, to grasp – and master the other, thereby reducing its alterity. As Rodolphe Gasché points out, 'Western philosophy is in essence the attempt to domesticate Otherness, since what we understand by thought is nothing but such a project.'[38] As the attempt to attain a point of exteriority to logocentrism, deconstruction may therefore be 'understood' as the desire to keep open a dimension of alterity which can neither be reduced, comprehended, nor, strictly speaking, even *thought* by philosophy. To say that the goal of Derridian deconstruction is not simply the *unthought* of the tradition, but rather that-which-cannot-be-thought, is to engage in neither sophistical rhetoric nor negative theology. It is rather to point towards that which philosophy is unable to say.

Derridian deconstruction attempts to locate 'a non-site, or a non-philosophical site, from which to question philosophy'.[39] It seeks a place of exteriority, alterity, or marginality irreducible to philosophy. Deconstruction is the writing of a margin that cannot be represented by philosophy. In question is an other to philosophy that has never been and cannot become philosophy's other, but an other within which philosophy becomes inscribed.

However – and this is crucial – the paradox that haunts Derrida's and all deconstructive discourse is that the only language that is available to deconstruction is that of philosophy, or logocentrism. Thus to take up a position exterior to logocentrism, if such a thing were possible, would be to risk starving oneself of the very linguistic resources with which one must deconstruct logocentrism. The deconstructor is like a tight-rope walker who risks 'ceaselessly falling back inside that which he deconstructs' (*G* 25/*OG* 14). Deconstruction is a double reading that operates within a double bind of both belonging to a tradition, a language, and a philosophical discourse, while at the same time being incapable of belonging to the latter. This ambiguous situation of belonging and not belonging describes the problem of *closure*.

Returning to my Ariadne's thread, why do I propose the concept of *clôtural* reading? *Clôtural* reading is double reading extended to include the analysis of closure and the question of ethics. A *clôtural* reading analyses a text in terms of how it is divided against itself in both belonging to logocentric conceptuality and achieving the breakthrough beyond that conceptuality. A text is read doubly, in the manner described above, the difference being, first, that a *clôtural* reading is specifically situated in relation to a logocentric epoch that is closed, whereas a deconstructive reading perpetually breaches this closure, disrupting its limit and allowing the movement of alterity to interrupt any unity of logocentric textuality and epochality; and second, following both Levinas's account of the history of Western philosophy in terms of the primacy of an ontology which seeks to enclose all phenomena within the closure[40] of comprehension and reduce plurality to unity (*TeI* 75–8/*TI* 102–4) and his critique of the ontological concept of history, which is always the history of the victors, never of the victims, and thus a history of barbarity, against which Levinas speaks in tones very similar to those of Walter Benjamin when the latter opposes historical materialism to objectivist history,[41] it will be argued that the notion of *clôtural* reading allows the question of ethics to be raised within deconstruction. *Clôtural* reading is history read from the standpoint of the victims of that history. It is, in a complex sense, *ethical* history.

Clôtural reading articulates the ethical interruption of ontological closure, thereby disrupting the text's claims to comprehensive unity and self-understanding, a procedure which, as I shall show in chapters 3 and 4 extends all the way to a reading of Derrida's and Levinas's texts. A *clôtural* reading of a text would consist, first, of a patient and scholarly commentary following the main lines of the text's dominant interpretation, and second, in locating an interruption or alterity within that dominant interpretation where reading discovers insights within a text to which that text is blind. My governing claim is that these insights, interruptions, or alterities are moments of *ethical transcendence*, in which a necessity other than that of ontology announces itself within the reading, an event in which the ethical Saying of a text overrides its ontological Said. This is very much the way in which

Levinas reads the idea of infinity in Descartes' *Meditations* or the Good beyond Being (*epikeina tes ousias*) in Plato's *Republic*, texts from the ontological tradition which resist claims to totality and comprehension and adumbrate an ethical structure irreducible to ontology. As I will show, this is also how Levinas reads Derrida. Paraphrasing Levinas, it is in exegesis, or rigorous commentary, that the passage to transcendence is produced, the transcendence of the Other.[42] In this sense, one might speak, as Robert Bernasconi has done, of a 'Levinasian hermeneutics',[43] whereby reading would reveal the ethical Saying at work within the Said of the text. The passage to transcendence that opens through a rigorous reading is neither contingent nor secondary, but rather articulates the unconditioned ethical conditions of possibility for the interruption of ontological or logocentric closure. It is precisely this ethical unconditionality that I would now like to explore.

1.6 From Text to Context: Deconstruction and the Thought of an Unconditional Ethical Imperative

It is this thought of unconditionality as 'the opening of another ethics' (*l'ouverture d'une autre éthique*) (*LI* 221/*LItr* 122) that, I believe, constitutes the horizon for Derrida's work. In an interview with Jean-Luc Nancy which appeared in 1989, Derrida speaks thus of the unconditional affirmation which motivates deconstruction: 'The affirmation that motivates deconstruction is unconditional, imperative and immediate.'[44]. But such a position is most forcefully proposed in the concluding pages of Derrida's 'Afterword' to *Limited Inc.*, where he writes:

> This leads me to elaborate rapidly what I suggested above concerning the question of context, of its *non-closure* [*non-fermeture*] or, if you prefer, of its irreducible opening [*ouverture*]....In the different texts I have written on (against) apartheid, I have on several occasions spoken of 'unconditional' affirmation or of 'unconditional' 'appeal' [*appel*]. This has also happened to me in other 'contexts' and each time that I speak of the link between deconstruction and the 'yes'. Now, the very least that can be said of *unconditionality* (*a word that I use not by accident to recall the character of the categorical imperative in its Kantian form*) is that it is independent of every determinate context, even of the

determination of a context in general. It announces itself as such only in the *opening* of context. Not that it is simply present (existent) elsewhere, outside of all context; rather it intervenes in the determination of a context from its very opening, and from an injunction, a law, a responsibility that transcends this or that determination of a given context. Following this, what remains is to articulate this unconditionality with the determinate (Kant would say, hypothetical) conditions of this or that context; and this is the moment of strategies, of rhetorics, of ethics, and of politics. The structure thus described supposes both that there are only contexts, that nothing *exists* outside context [*qu'il **existe** rien hors contexte*], as I have often said, but also that the limit of the frame or the border of the context always entails a clause of *non-closure* [*non-fermeture*]. The outside penetrates and thus determines the inside. (*LI* 281–2/*LItr* 152–3; my emphasis)

*Nothing **exists** outside a context*: I want to interrupt the quotation at this point and try to unravel the presuppositions and implications of this complex and compact passage. There *is* nothing outside context – that is to say, there is no entity, no thing, that has existence outside of context. One might say that the context is not commanded by a dominant referent, a transcendental signified: God, self-consciousness, or whatever. Yet – and this is the central point – the context itself contains a clause of non-closure; that is, in the terms of my argument, context obeys a *clôtural* logic according to which the limit that bounds, frames, encloses, and determines any context is necessarily interrupted by that which exceeds context. Pursuing Derrida's argument, what interrupts the closure of a determinate context, making that context an open structure, is an unconditional affirmation that intervenes in this context and motivates deconstruction. Such, I would claim, is the ethical moment in Derrida's thinking.

Yet what does the word 'context' mean in this context? Opening a dictionary, one might define context as those parts of a discourse which immediately precede or follow any particular passage or text and which can determine its meaning. One can think of the real context of somebody – in this context, me – writing a text with the intention of communicating a given, determinate idea: for example, to demonstrate once and for all that Derridian deconstruction has overriding ethical implications. However, in order to understand properly what is at stake here, it is necessary to return to 'Signature, Event, Context', the *Ur*-text to which the above quote is responding. The latter was presented as a paper in the context of a Congrès International de Philosophie de Langue Française in 1971 on the theme of communication. Derrida there asks: Are the conditions or limits of a context ever absolutely determinable? His response is negative, claiming that a context can never be absolutely determined or saturated. For Derrida, this response has a double consequence: first, that the current concept of context is inadequate, and second, that a generalized concept of context would entail an enlargement or displacement of the traditional concept of writing, which could no longer be seen simply as a means of communication for the transmission of meaning. Using the example of Condillac's account of writing in the *Essay on the Origins of Human Knowledge*, an example that typifies the logocentric treatment of writing, Derrida goes on to show how the determination of the function of writing in terms of the communication of meaning is a model which governs both common sense and philosophy, 'I would even go so far as to say that it is the interpretation of writing that is peculiar and proper to philosophy' (*LI* 21/*LItr* 3). Condillac represents a philosophical tradition dominated by the privilege of the Idea; that is, the essence, or idea, of a real, perceived, or ideal object is represented by the sign. The linguistic sign represents both the idea of an object and the object itself, its meaning or referent. Within this classical semiology, the privileged medium for the communication of the sign is the voice. The essential link of the *logos* to the voice, or *phonē*, has never been broken in this tradition: logocentrism is phonocentrism. Writing, therefore, is merely a species of general communication which is employed in the absence of the addressee, when he or she is no longer present within earshot. Thus absence is structurally bound up with the event of writing, for it is only the absence of the addressee that prompts one to write. If the addressee were present, then we could speak face to face. However, in contrast to the presence and evanescence of speech, written communication must be 'repeatable – iterable – in the absolute absence of the receiver (*destinataire*)' (*LI* 27/*LItr* 7). And, of course, what is true for the addressee is also true for the addressor or author of writing: namely, that the iterative structure of writing ensures that a text can continue to be read after its author has disappeared or died – which is why Socrates condemns writing in the *Phaedrus*.[45] Writing breaks with the context of communication, if by the latter one understands the intersubjective communication of conscious, co-present subjects. Writing also breaks with the limited concept of context, because the written sign always exceeds its context; for it must, by virtue of its iterability, perdure beyond the present moment of its inscription and even after the death of its author. Furthermore, a text can be quoted in other contexts, and enter into new contexts. These sentences might be quoted – for good or ill or even after my death – in another context, regardless of my present intentions.

Derrida then wants to extend this account of the written sign – in terms of its breaking with the horizon of communication, presence, meaning, and a narrowly defined concept of context – to the 'entire field of what philosophy would call experience, even the experience of Being: so-called "presence" (*l'expérience de l'être: ladite "présence"*)' (*LI* 29–30/*LItr* 9). What is valid for the written sign is also valid for spoken language and the possibility of any linguistic sign,

> This structural possibility of being weaned from the referent or from the signified (hence from communication and from its context) seems to me to make every mark, including those which are oral, a grapheme in general; which is to say, as we have seen, the non-present *remainder* [*restance*] of a differential mark cut off from its putative 'production' or origin. And I shall even extend this law to all 'experience' in general if it is conceded that there is no experience consisting of *pure* presence but only of chains of differential marks. (*LI* 32/*LItr* 10)

In order to elucidate Derrida's argument at this point, and in particular what is meant by a chain of 'differential marks', it is necessary to recall Derrida's radicalization of Saussure's linguistic theory. But first, as a proviso, it should be noted that Derrida is not denying the empirical fact of our speech, consciousness, self-presence, and intersubjective co-presence. Rather, he is engaging in an argument as to the priority or originality of these phenomena. Derrida is not denying the existence of ordinary spoken language or of the affection of being present to myself and to the other when I speak (a denial that would lead to some absurd form of linguistic idealism); the claim is rather that these phenomena cannot systematically or consistently exclude what is opposed to them: that is, writing or absence. Derrida asks the transcendental question, What are the conditions of possibility for presence, speech, meaning, and so forth? He argues that these conditions of possibility include precisely what presence, speech, and meaning attempt to exclude, which consequently renders the priority of these phenomena and the entire system of logocentrism impossible. The conditions of possibility for logocentrism are also its conditions of impossibility. The written sign, constituted by iterability, delay, and difference and characterized by exteriority, *restance*, and the transgression of every closed structure, comes to function as a model for the conditions of possibility for experience in general. Therefore, experience is not to be understood simply as the perception or intuition of phenomena that are present to self-consciousness; rather, experience is *produced* by chains of differentially ordered signs, or 'marks', which precede and produce meaning and exceed any determinate structure (a position which, incidentally, Derrida considers to be consistent with Husserl's project for a pure logical grammar in the *Logical Investigations* (LI 32.–6/*LItr* 10–12 and 22, n. 4)).

Derrida's 1968 paper, '*La Différance*', articulates the conditions of possibility and impossibility for logocentric conceptuality through a confrontation with Saussurian linguistics. As Derrida makes clear in the discussion following the paper, the choice of Saussure is strategic, and for two reasons. First, Saussurian linguistics exerted a hegemony in the human sciences at that time, functioning as a general model for research in anthropology (Lévi-Strauss), psychoanalysis (Lacan), political theory (Althusser), and other disciplines.[46] Second, Saussure's discourse can be employed to produce a wider notion of strategy, in the sense that all discourse is strategic, because no transcendental truth or point of reference is present outside the field of discourse which would govern that field (*M* 7/*MP* 7). All deconstructive discourse is strategic and adventurous; which is to say that it cannot be justified absolutely. For Derrida, the thought of *différance* is most appropriate to thinking through the present epoch (and it, too, has only a strategic justification). As is now well known, the verb *différer* has a double sense in French, which is rendered into English by the separate verbs 'to differ' and 'to defer'. *Différer* in the sense of 'to differ' means that something is different from something else; it has a spatial sense, and refers to the non-identical relations pertaining between phenomena. *Différer* in the sense of 'to defer' means to postpone the completion of an act; it thus has a temporal meaning, conveyed by the verbs 'to temporize', 'to delay', or 'to put off'. The neologism *différance* refers polysemically to both these meanings, the temporal and the spatial. By spelling *différance* with an *a*, not an *e*,

Derrida demonstrates both that there is a difference between *différence* and *différance* that is inaudible when spoken and also that the resultant gerund, the differing/deferring, gives an active sense to *différance*, which is implied when Derrida writes, as he often does, of the *movement* of *différance* (*VP* 75, 92, 94/*SP* 67, 82, 84).

As has already been shown, within the classical semiological problematic, ideas are represented by signs, which themselves represent or stand for things. The sign thus represents the presence of the thing which it stands for or supplements but is itself different from the sign. The concept of the sign is premised on a deferral, or difference, between it and what it is a sign for. As Derrida writes, 'The sign represents the present in its absence. It takes the place of the present. When we cannot grasp or show the thing, state the present…we go through the detour of the sign.… The sign, in this sense, is deferred presence' (*M* 9/*MP* 9). Thus the sign is traditionally seen as secondary, as derived from a lost presence. Now Derrida simply wants to put into question the secondariness of the sign, which is the secondariness of deferral, and to postulate in its place an 'originary' *différance* that is constitutive of presence. This has two consequences: first, *différance* can no longer be contained within the classical theory of the sign, and second, and more significantly, it puts into question the authority of presence, and consequently the metaphysical demand to formulate the meaning of Being as presence. The second consequence thus opens a questioning of the Heideggerian type into the value of presence (even if Derrida will want to question the Heideggerian problematic at its very source). It is in the context of this questioning of the sign that Derrida introduces Saussure's semiology, and particularly the determination of the sign as *arbitrary* and *differential*. For Saussure, the linguistic sign is the unity of concept (signified) and sound-image or phoneme (signifier) and not the unity of name and thing. In breaking the bond that ties meaning to reference, Saussure breaks with the classical theory of the sign, and introduces the thesis of arbitrariness; namely, that the bond between the signifier and the signified is not natural, but instituted, or conventional. If the sign is arbitrary, then the manner of its signification is differential; that is, signs do not signify through their intrinsic plenitude (the sign 'dog' does not refer to the fully present entity of the 'dog-in-itself'). Rather, signs signify through their relative position in a chain of differences. For Saussure, 'in language there are only differences'; furthermore, difference is not a difference between positive terms (that is, the difference between the really present dog and the really present cat), for in language there are only differences *without positive terms*.[47] Language has neither ideas nor sounds that existed prior to the linguistic system, but only phonic or conceptual differences that issue from the system.

Derrida then teases out the consequences of Saussure's semiology. The signified concept is never present in and of itself; it signifies only in so far as it is inscribed in a chain or systematic play of differences. This play of differences that is constitutive of meaning 'is' *différance* itself. That is why *différance* is neither a word nor a concept, but rather the condition of possibility for conceptuality and words as such. *Différance* is the playing movement that produces the differences constitutive of words and conceptuality. There is no presence outside or before semiological difference. Retaining the framework of the Saussurian problematic, Derrida sees all languages or codes as constituted as and by a weave of differences. This is what Derrida means when he claims that 'It is because of *différance* that the movement of signification is possible' (*M* 13/*MP* 13). If this is the case, then each 'present' element in a linguistic system signifies in so far as it differentially refers to another element, and thus is not itself present. The sign is rather what Derrida – borrowing from Levinas – calls a 'trace', a past that has never been present (*M* 12, 22/*MP* 12, 21). The present is constituted by a differential network of traces. In order for the present to be present, it must be related to something non-present, something *différant*, and so not be present. As Derrida writes,

> An interval must separate the present from what it is not in order for the present to be itself, but this interval that constitutes it as present must, by the same token, divide the present in and of itself, thereby also dividing, along with the present, everything that is thought on the basis of the present, that is, in our metaphysical language, every being, and singularly substance or the subject. (*M* 13/*MP* 13)

As one can see, the effects of Derrida's radicalization of Saussure are by no means merely local. The presence of the present is constituted by a network of traces whereby the interval between elements is described as spacing (*espacement*) and the temporal relation among elements is one of irreducible temporization (*temporisation*). It is this time–space structure that Derrida names with the term 'archi-writing' (*archi-écriture*), a structure within which presence – which, as Heidegger has shown, is the very ether of metaphysics (*M* 17/*MP* 16) – is but an effect.

It is this archi-writing, with its radically extended concept of writing, that will constitute the field for the new science of writing, *grammatology*. With this generalized concept of writing in mind, one can begin to understand the bold theses put forward in the opening of *Of Grammatology* in 1967: namely, that what has been determined for the last twenty or so centuries under the name of language is, for reasons of historical or epochal necessity, now letting itself be gathered under the name of writing (*G* 15–16/*OG* 6); that writing comprehends language (*G* 16/*OG* 7), the latter being a species of the former (*G* 18/*OG* 8); that there is no linguistic sign before writing (*G* 26/*OG* 14); that writing – the *grammē*, the *grapheme*; differentially ordered inscription in general – determines the element through which something like experience becomes possible (*G* 20/*OG* 9); that the 'rationality' of writing no longer issues from a *ratio* or *logos*, and that this is what provides the 'rationale' for the *dé-construction* (this is the form in which the word appears for the first time in *Of Grammatology*) of the *logos* (*G* 21/*OG* 10); and that the meaning of Being can no longer be thought upon the horizon of presence, but rather in terms of a determined signifying trace (*G* 38/*OG* 23). The grammatological space of a general writing, that in virtue of which experience is possible, is the space of what Derrida calls 'le texte en général' (*G* 14/*OG* 26). The general text is a limitless network of differentially ordered signs which is not preceded by any meaning, structure, or *eidos*, but itself constitutes each of these. It is here, upon the surface of the general text, that there 'is' deconstruction ('*Il y a de la déconstruction*'), that deconstruction takes place (*a lieu*). It is this general textuality that Derrida seeks to deploy performatively in many of his readings, most notably and extensively in *Glas*.[48] My claim here is that the words 'context' and 'general text' say exactly the same.

Returning to the context of Derrida's 'Afterword' to *Limited Inc.*, one can now better understand how the concepts of 'context' and 'general text' are equated and are articulated with the thought of unconditionality as the opening of another ethics. Some pages before the long quote from the 'Afterword' cited above, Derrida offers as one possible definition of deconstruction 'the effort to take this limitless context into account' (*la prise en compte de ce contexte sans bord*) (*LI*

252/*LItr* 136). He then proceeds to redefine the axial proposition of deconstructive method discussed above: namely, '*Il n'y a pas de hors-texte*' (*G* 227/*OG* 158), as '*Il n'y a pas de hors contexte*' (*LI* 252/ *LItr* 136). This redefinition is required because the word 'text', despite Derrida's many corrections,[49] is still understood empirically and thereby reduced to a refutable slogan. To say it once again, the text is not the book, if by the idea of a book one understands a material object which is commanded by a horizon of meaning and maintains the priority of the *phonē* through a system of phonetic writing. A generalized concept of the 'text' does not wish to turn the world into some vast library; nor does it wish to cut off reference to some 'extra-textual realm'. Deconstruction is not bibliophilia. Text *qua* context is glossed by Derrida as 'the entire "real-history-of-the-world"' (*LI* 252/*LItr* 136); and this is said in order to emphasize the fact that the word 'text' does not suspend reference 'to history, to the world, to reality, to being *and especially not to the other*' (*à l'histoire, au monde, à la réalité, à l'être, **et surtout pas à l'autre**) (*LI* 253/*LItr* 37; my emphasis). All the latter appear in an experience which is not an immediate experience of presence – the text or context is not present, for reasons set out above – but rather the experience of a network of differentially (or *différantially*) signifying traces which are constitutive of meaning. *Experience or thought traces a ceaseless movement of interpretation within a limitless context.*

> What I call 'text' implies all the structures called 'real', 'economic', 'historical', socio-institutional, in short: all possible referents. Another way of recalling once again that 'there is nothing outside the text'. That does not mean that all referents are suspended, denied, or enclosed in a book, as people have claimed, or have been naïve enough to believe and to have accused me of believing. But it does mean that every referent and all reality has the structure of a différantial trace (*d'une trace différantielle*), and that one cannot refer to this 'real' except in an interpretative experience. The latter neither yields meaning nor assumes it except in a movement of différantial referring (*de renvoi différantiel*). That's all*. (*LI* 273/*LItr* 148; * in English in the original text)

If that's all Derrida would appear to mean by the words 'text' and 'context', then what of the unconditioned? Returning to the first, long quote from the 'Afterword' to *Limited Inc.* cited above, if the word 'context' articulates the conditions of possibility for experience in general, then this context is itself conditioned or motivated by the unconditioned; that is, by that which is independent of 'a context in general' (*LI* 281/*LItr* 152). Derrida's argument is not that the unconditioned is present or existent somewhere outside all context, but rather that it arises as the interruption, or non-closure, of any determinate context; it is an injunction, or law, that 'transcends this or that determination of a given context' (*LI* 281/*LItr* 152). Thus, there are only contexts; nothing *exists* outside context; and yet, Derrida claims, the context contains a clause of non-closure whereby an unconditioned injunction comes to interrupt the conditioned context. Derrida then translates this claim into the language of Kantian ethics, and in particular into the relation between *hypothetical* and *categorical* imperatives. For Kant, all imperatives command the will of a rational being either hypothetically or categorically. A hypothetical imperative is good only in so far as it is a means to an end; in this way, the will produces prudential maxims, namely that my desire for happiness is conditional upon the pursuit of some 'good' – for example, riches, knowledge, long life, or health. Hypothetical imperatives are conditioned, that is, a person counts this or that maxim as belonging to his or her happiness. By contrast, categorical imperatives command actions that are entirely good in themselves and are not performed for some ulterior end. Thus a categorical imperative is limited by no condition; it is simply and wholly the law that must be obeyed unconditionally and which possesses universal, objective necessity.[50]

Ethics, properly speaking, is restricted to imperatives that are categorical; and for Derrida, the ethical moment is the interruption of the general context of conditioned hypothetical imperatives by an unconditional categorical imperative. *Ethics arises in and as the undecidable yet determinate articulation of these two orders.* As Derrida writes, this moment of unconditional appeal is revealed in the link that connects deconstruction to the 'Yes', the moment of affirmation that one finds repeatedly in Derrida's writings. It is Nietzsche's 'vast and boundless Yes and Amen saying' (*das ungeheure unbegrenzte Ja- und Amen- sagen*)[51] that resounds at the end of *Glas*. It is the doubly affirmative 'Yes, Yes' of Molly Bloom's soliloquy that punctuates *Ulysse Gramophone*, which must be distinguished from the braying 'Ja, Ja' or 'I – A' of Nietzsche's Christian ass.[52] It is, as I shall show in the final chapter, the affirmation of the *Zusage*, the grant or pledge, that provides the horizon for Derrida's reading of Heidegger in *De l'esprit*. It is the 'Yes, to the stranger' (*Oui, à l'étranger*) (*PSY* 639) that opens and sustains Derrida's text on Michel de Certeau. But what is being affirmed here? To whom or to what does one say 'Yes'? In the final pages of *La Différance*, Derrida claims that there is no essence to *différance*, and that the latter itself 'remains a metaphysical name' (*M* 28/*MP* 26). *Différance* is not a master name or unique word for Being; rather, '*différance* has no name in our language'. There is no name for that which *différance* names, which is not simply to claim that it is existent yet ineffable, like the God of the negative theologians (although one might, audaciously, want to follow Angelus Silesius in linking the affirmative 'Yes' to the name of God: *Ja* and *Jahveh*; *PSY* 640–1). *Différance* is the unnameable; it is that which 'makes possible nominal effects'. The unnameable must be thought without 'nostalgia', but also without the other side of nostalgia, what Derrida calls 'Heideggerian hope' (*M* 29/*MP* 27). 'On the contrary', Derrida adds, 'we must *affirm* this' – that is, deconstruction must affirm and say 'Yes' to the unnameable. The ethical moment that motivates deconstruction is this Yes-saying to the unnameable, a moment of unconditional affirmation that is addressed to an alterity that can neither be excluded from nor included within logocentric conceptuality. In this book, I shall simply endeavour to point out some of the possible Levinasian resonances suggested by these formulations.[53]

My argument is that *an unconditional categorical imperative or moment of affirmation is the source of the injunction that produces deconstruction and is produced through deconstructive reading*. Thus there is a duty in deconstruction which both prompts the reader to the rigorous and ascetic labour of reading and produces a reading that commands respect in so far as it opens an irreducible dimension of alterity. In short – and the formality of this claim will have to be supplemented by the concrete analyses given in this book – this is why one should bother with deconstruction. Rejoining the main quotation from the 'Afterword' to *Limited Inc.* a few lines further on, Derrida concludes his discussion in the following way:

This unconditionality also defines the injunction that prescribes deconstruction. Why have I always *hesitated* to characterize it in Kantian terms, for example, or more generally in ethical or political terms, when that would have been so easy and would have enabled me to

avoid so many critiques, themselves all too facile? Because such
characterizations seem to me essentially associated with philosophemes
that themselves call for deconstructive questions. Through (*à travers*)
these difficulties, another language and other thoughts seek to make
their way. This language and these thoughts, which are also new
responsibilities, arouse in me a respect which, whatever the cost, I
neither can nor will compromise. (*LI* 282/*LItr* 153; my emphasis)

Derrida's hesitance about speaking without hesitation on ethics and
politics – one might even say his *avoidance* of these matters – is essential to the deconstructive enterprise in so far as it must deconstruct
the philosophemes that underpin ethical and political discourse. I
have already discussed the reasons for Derrida's hesitance *vis-à-vis* the
word 'ethics', but a similar hesitation must govern the deconstructive
employment of the notions of responsibility, obligation, duty, respect,
right, law, community, power, and so forth. As I shall demonstrate at
the end of the next chapter, *deconstruction is a 'philosophy' of hesitation*,
although it must be understood that such hesitation is not arbitrary,
contingent, or indeterminate, but rather, a rigorous, strictly determinate hesitation: the 'experience' of undecidability. As Derrida notes,
what has always interested him the most is the 'strictest possible
determination of the figures of play, of oscillation, of undecidability'
(*LI* 268/*LItr* 145). I have already begun to show the ethical implications of this deconstructive hesitance.

However, the crucial question that must be taken up (and which
will be the theme of the concluding chapter) is the following: What
is the *political* moment in deconstruction? Or, more precisely, what is
the relation between the rigorous undecidability of deconstructive
reading and the necessity for *political* decisions and *political* critique? Is
politics the moment of decision – that is to say, of judgement, action,
beginning, risk, commitment, of crisis in its etymological sense? And
if so, how and in virtue of what may one take a decision on an
undecidable terrain of *différance*? What exactly does Derrida mean
when he notes that 'there can be no moral or *political* responsibility
without this trial and this passage by way of the undecidable'? (*LI*
210/*LItr* 116; my emphasis). (Parenthetically, it is interesting to note
how this undecidable hesitation is itself avoided in the decisive
formulations of the 'Afterword' to *Limited Inc*. This might lead one
to ask about the status of the latter text and those of its genre –

interviews, transcribed debates and conversations – upon which much of my argument has relied. Are they properly speaking deconstructive? Are they not rather *political* or critical texts, which make an intervention and take a decisive risk? And why does Derrida *say* in a non-deconstructive mode that which cannot be *said* deconstructively, but which is the very *Saying* of deconstruction, that is, its ethico-political responsibility?)

Indeed, what about *this* text and the argument it sets forth? Is it deconstructive? Doubtless my argument has already shown too little hesitation, or avoidance, and too much decidedness, which is a result of my precipitous use of a series of philosophemes that are necessarily open to deconstructive interrogation: ethics, transcendence, truth, duty, unconditionality. Yet this decidedness, the madness of a decision which *always* slips back into the language of the tradition – in this case the anachronistic terminology of Levinas or Kant – is also necessary. This book is a response to what I believe to be an impasse in Derrida's work and in discussions of that work. It is a response to the serious and sincere question 'Why bother with deconstruction?' It asks after the *demand*, or *necessity*, for deconstruction. Yet, of course, the madness of the decision to speak without hesitation of the ethics of deconstruction itself calls for a deconstructive reading. This is true. I accept it unreservedly. As Levinas would say, '*Voilà des objections bien connues!*' ('These are familiar objections!') (*AE* 198/*OB* 155). However, this in no way minimizes the necessity of the gesture attempted here. Despite the anachronism of my philosophical vocabulary – or perhaps because of it, it is difficult to say – it is towards an unconditional injunction and towards a language that describes urgent ethical and political responsibilities that I will make my way in this book. Perhaps one should concur with Wittgenstein when he defines ethical language as the endless attempt to run up against the limits of language, a form of astonishment that cannot be expressed in a question and for which there is no answer.[54] Ethical Saying is precisely nothing that can be said; it is rather the perpetual undoing of the Said that occurs in running against its limits. One does not comprehend the ethical Saying within the Said; the Saying can only be comprehended in its incomprehensibility, in its disruption or interruption of the Said. Such, perhaps, is the limit of human reason described in the paradoxical final sentence of Kant's *Grundlegung*.[55] By speaking the language of philosophy, even by employing philosophemes that call for deconstruction, one prepares the ground for an explosion within that language. This, at least, invites a respect that should not be compromised.

1.7   The Ethics of Reading: Hillis Miller's Version

By way of conclusion, I would like to discuss J. Hillis Miller's *The Ethics of Reading*, whose general orientation would appear to be similar to the concerns outlined above. Miller has two targets in his book: first, he argues against the tendency, as he sees it, in Marxist, psychoanalytic, and hermeneutic theories of textual interpretation to reduce a literary text to its political, social, historical, religious, or psychological conditions. Second, he wants to refute the charge that the deconstructive analysis of texts is *immoral*. With regard to the first, Miller opposes any reading of a text that determines the latter's meaning by reference to what lies outside that text: its socio-political, historical, or psychobiographical context. Such interpretative tendencies are undermined in the name of a 'vigilant and sophisticated rhetorical analysis' (*ER* 7), which, as soon becomes clear, is what Miller understands by deconstructive reading. Miller's central claim is that 'there is a necessary ethical moment' in the act of reading, a moment which is 'neither cognitive, nor political, nor social, nor interpersonal, but properly and independently ethical' (*ER* 1). Ethics, for Miller, is simply the presence of an imperative, an 'I must', articulated within certain texts, which demands a response from and responsibility on the part of the reader. The claim is that this ethical imperative cannot 'be accounted for by the social and historical forces that impinge upon it' (*ER* 8), and that, furthermore, such an ethical moment, although not reducible to the political realm, 'leads to an act' (*ER* 4) – that is, it enters into 'the social, institutional, political realms' (*ER* 4). Thus, the argument here would seem to be that ethics derives from a response to the concrete situation of reading a book, and awakens a responsibility that leads to political action. Simply expressed, the study of literature makes a difference to how we act; 'the rhetorical study of literature has crucial practical implications for our moral, social, and political lives' (*ER* 3). This claim, so reminiscent of New Criticism, and one which I do not necessarily want to contest, is then articulated through a defence of deconstruction, which introduces Miller's second target in *The Ethics of Reading*: the claim that deconstructive reading is an immoral and nihilistic form of textual free play. Miller argues – convincingly, I believe – that such a claim is based upon a triple misunderstanding of deconstruction. He maintains that Derrida and Paul de Man do not and never have argued for any form of textual free play; second, that such a claim rests on a misunderstanding of the nature of nihilism (that properly defined, and in line with Nietzsche and Heidegger, it is the attackers of deconstruction, not its proponents, who are nihilistic); and third, that such a claim misunderstands the precise nature of the ethical moment in deconstructive reading. It is this moment that Hillis Miller then demonstrates in a series of concrete examples.

The precise nature of Miller's claim for an ethics of reading begins to become clear in his discussion of de Man, which in many ways is the central chapter of the book and should perhaps be read before the opening chapter on Kant. Miller's argument is that in de Man's work there is an imperative which has ethical force with respect to reading practice: namely, quoting de Man's luminous remarks in his Preface to Carol Jacobs's *The Dissimulating Harmony*, 'Reading is an argument...because it has to go against the grain of what one would want to happen in the name of what has to happen' (*ER* 52 and 116). What *has* to happen, for de Man, is described with the word 'allegory'; thus the nature of any act of reading is to be allegorical, impossible or unreadable. For de Man, on Miller's reading, the failure to read, or the impossibility of reading, 'is a universal necessity' (*ER* 51). Therefore, being true to what happens in the act of reading means obeying the law of unreadability, or letting the text shape 'the reader's evasions' (*ER* 52). In this version of the ethics of reading, getting it right means getting it wrong; and we do not – indeed, it is assumed that we *cannot* – know why we get it wrong, for we cannot see into the hidden workings of language. Thus, a de Manian ethical reading is the reading of unreadability; it is 'to commit again and again the failure to read which is the human lot' (*ER* 59). Or again, 'each reading is, strictly speaking, ethical, in the sense that it *has* to take place, by an implacable necessity, as the response to a categorical demand, and in the sense that the reader *must* take responsibility for it and for its consequences in the personal, social, and political worlds' (*ER* 59). So, for Miller, becoming a good reader, doing ethical readings, implies genuflecting before unreadability as the universal law of language. Indeed, the pathos of Miller's prose becomes almost apocalyptic at this point: 'I would even dare to promise that the millennium would come if all men and women became good readers in de Man's sense' (*ER* 58).

Nevertheless, Miller's thesis emerges most forcefully and persuasively in his final chapter on Henry James and Walter Benjamin. At the end of an elegant discussion of James's New York Preface to *The Golden Bowl*, Miller offers the following formulation of the ethics of reading:

> the strange and difficult notion that reading is subject not to the text as its law, but to the law to which the text is subject. This law forces the reader to betray the text or deviate from it in the act of reading, in the name of a higher demand that can yet be reached only by way of the text. (*ER* 120)

Thus, an ethical reading is a responsible response which violates the text in order to preserve the text's matter – what I would call its ethical *Saying*. One reads against what is *said* in the text in order to remain faithful to what the text *says*. The imperative of reading is not simply (but is it ever simple?) fidelity to the text as if it were one's law, but rather a *fidelity to the law to which the text is subject*. This law is the matter or *Sache* of reading, which entails that the reader *should* betray the text that is being read in the name of the law to which that text is subject. This notion of law, matter, or Saying is finally illuminated with reference to Benjamin's 'The Task of the Translator', and in particular to what Benjamin means by 'that pure language' (*jene reine Sprache*) which it is the task of the translator to release from the original text into the medium of another language. The *reine Sprache* is the *Sache* of reading. Miller reformulates the ethics of reading as a subjection to this law or matter, this categorical demand that cannot be expressed directly but can only be given in figures. Benjamin uses the figure of a tangent touching the circumference of a circle to illustrate the relation between a translation and the original, or the reading and the law which governs that reading (*ER* 126).

The book ends at this point, with the formulation of this imperative in reading, this 'I must', about which Miller remains perplexed as to whether its necessity is linguistic or ontological, whether it is a fact of language or a thesis on the Being of entities. Miller adds the promise that he will continue his thoughts in another book (*ER* 127), it is to be hoped that my book will take up Miller's fascinating, but finally aporetic, formulation of the ethics of reading and deepen it philosophically with specific reference to Levinas, in order to show that this necessity is ethical in a sense not so far discussed by him. It seems to me that Miller's agnosticism as to whether the necessity or law to which reading is subject is linguistic or ontological is due to his metaphysical agnosticism – that is, his failure or refusal to investigate the meaning of necessity at sufficient metaphysical depth. Miller tends to assume de Man's minimal ontology of language, so brilliantly exposed by Gasché,[56] as the metaphysical basis of his reading practice. Although the concerns of my book are not the same as those underlying Miller's, because they do not grow directly out of debates within contemporary literary theory – for example, it is clear that Miller's real target is the so-called politics of interpretation that, he claims, has recently come to dominate literary studies and which he considers to be 'vague and speculative' (*ER* 4[57]) – but rather have their provenance in the Continental philosophical tradition, there are none the less a number of points of convergence. I too will attempt to address the charge of immorality levelled at deconstructive reading, and also wish to distinguish ethics from politics, although in a quite different formulation to that of Miller. Finally, the pattern of reading established by Miller, especially in the chapter on James and Benjamin, prefigures much of what I include under the heading of *clôtural* reading.

Yet, there are a number of questions and objections that I would want to address to *The Ethics of Reading*. First, Miller's understanding of the concept of text is limited – namely to books – and thus quite distinct from the Derridean notion of the general text *qua* context and archi-writing discussed above. Second, as already pointed out, Miller understands ethics in its traditional determination as a region of philosophical inquiry and not in the more radical Levinasian sense; which, of course, leaves him open to the Heideggerian objections to an ethics of deconstruction outlined above. Third, Miller's notion of ethics is explicitly and narrowly textual; the ethical moment, the 'I must', arises as a response to a text, and the paradigmatic concrete ethical situation is that of a man or a woman reading a book in a literature class. Thus the horizon of *The Ethics of Reading* is *pedagogical*, and refers specifically to the highly determined pedagogical context of the North American university. For me, by contrast, the paradigmatic ethical moment is that of being pre-reflectively addressed by the other person in a way that calls me into question and obliges me to be responsible. This is the concrete context for ethics; or rather, it is the context in which ethics interrupts the context of the world. Hence the problem, on a Levinasian view, is not so much 'Is there an ethical structure or law of reading?' as 'How is the ethical relation to the other person to be inscribed in a book without betraying it immeasurably? How does the ethical relation to the Other enter into the textual economy of betrayal? And how is that text to be read so as to preserve its ethical Saying?' Fourth, the passage from ethics to politics is insufficiently elaborated by Miller, and the precise nature and intended context of political action are not adequately specified. Is Miller referring exclusively to the ethical status of the teaching of literature in the United States and its relation to liberal democratic politics conceived on the American model? If so, he ought to say so. Further, I would want to ask if it is possible to say precisely in what direction – the *doxai* of left, right, or centre – one's political action might be transformed after one has put down a book that has been read ethically? Finally, ethics in Miller's sense, far from being concrete, may be said to lead to an empty, formal universalism which, although inspired by Kant's ethics, is not even properly Kantian (Miller seems to have no place for Kant's formula of the end in itself, which guarantees respect for persons[58]). For Miller, ethics is simply and entirely a formal, universal command to respect, an 'I must' or moment of sublimity derived from a text and then somehow translated into political action. But on the Levinasian view for which I shall be arguing, ethics is not immediately derived from a consciousness of respect for the universal law – a position that is always open to Hegel's critique of Kant's formalism.[59] Rather, ethics is first and foremost a respect for the concrete particularity of the other person in his or her singularity, a person who is not merely an example of the law, in the way that Miller claims that a text, analogous to a person, can be an example of the law (*ER* 18[60]), but rather the condition of possibility for an experience of the law. Ethics begins as a relation with a singular, other person who calls me into question and then, and only then, calls me to the universal discourse of reason and justice. Politics begins as ethics.

NOTES

1 This initial reception of deconstruction in the English-speaking world is perhaps best exemplified by Bloom *et al.*, *Deconstruction and Criticism* (Seabury, New York, 1979), which contains essays by Bloom, de Man, Derrida, Hartman, and Miller.

2 Rodolphe Gasché, *The Tain of the Mirror. Derrida and the Philosophy of Reflection* (Harvard University Press, Cambridge, Mass., and London, 1986); Irene E. Harvey, *Derrida and the Economy of Différance* (Indiana University Press, Bloomington, 1986); John Llewelyn, *Derrida on the Threshold of Sense* (Macmillan, London and Basingstoke, 1986); Christopher Norris, *Derrida* (Fontana, London, 1987). Crucial to the debate between the literary and philosophical receptions of Derrida's work is Gasché, 'Deconstruction as Criticism', in *Glyph*, 6 (1979), pp. 177–215.

3 See ' "Il faut bien manger" ou le calcul du sujet. Entretien (avec J.-L. Nancy)', in *Après le sujet qui vient, Cahiers confrontation*, 20 (Winter 1989), p. 103. This sentence is cited in the above text as an implicit allusion to Jean-Luc Nancy's reading of Derrida in 'La Voix libre de l'homme', a paper given originally at the 1980 conference *Les Fins de l'homme. A partir du travail de Jacques Derrida* and reprinted in *L'Impératif catégorique* (Flammarion, Paris, 1983). Nancy's innovative and decisive analysis prefigures much of the analysis carried out in this book; see esp. pp. 115–26.

4 See *E/OS; LSS/MPM* 147–232; 'Le dernier mot du racisme', in *PSY* 353–62 ('Racism's Last Word', tr. Peggy Kamuf, *Critical Inquiry*, 12 (1985), pp. 291–329); 'Admiration de Nelson Mandela: ou Les lois de la réflexion', in *PSY* 453–75; 'The Politics of Friendship', *Journal of Philosophy*, 85, no. 11 (1988), pp. 632–44; and especially; 'Vers une éthique de la discussion', in LI 201–85. ('Afterword: Toward an Ethic of Discussion', in *LItr* 111–16).

5 For two interesting discussions of this text, see Geoffrey Galt Harpham, 'Language, History and Ethics', *Raritan*, 7, no. 2 (1987), pp. 128–46; and Christopher Norris, 'The Ethics of Reading and the Limits of Irony: Kierkegaard among the Postmodernists', *Southern Humanities Review*, 22, no. 1 (Winter 1989), pp. 1–35. For a related approach, see Tobin Siebers, *The Ethics of Criticism* (Cornell University Press, Ithaca and London, 1988). Unfortunately, I became aware of Siebers's work only after I had completed the bulk of the writing of this book.

6 Gadamer claims that Derrida's work – he is thinking of a text like *Spurs*, rather than the earlier work on Husserl's phenomenology – is not ethically serious. Of course, at the centre of this *Auseinandersetzung* is the

figure of Heidegger, and more specifically, the question of the validity of Heidegger's reading of Nietzsche. In an interview given in 1985, Gadamer remarked, 'As to deconstruction, however, this does not seem to me to be a serious enterprise. Derrida's *Éperons*, for example, is a literary game. It cannot be situated with respect to our human, religious, moral interests and demands' (Roy Boyne, 'Interview with Hans-Georg Gadamer', *Theory, Culture and Society*, 5 (1988), p. 25). For a full discussion of the Gadamer–Derrida debate, see *Dialogue and Deconstruction. The Gadamer – Derrida Encounter*, ed. D. Michelfelder and R. Palmer (State University of New York Press, Albany, 1989), which contains a complete translation of the debate, as well as Gadamer's responses to the encounter and a series of commentaries. On the ethical stakes of this debate, see D. Michelfelder, 'Derrida and the Ethics of the Ear', in *The Question of the Other*, ed. A. B. Dallery and C. E. Scott (State University of New York Press, Albany, 1989), pp. 47–54. Of course, the substantive question to be examined here is whether deconstruction is the only way of reading that answers an ethical demand. This in turn depends on the definition of ethics that one employs. As will become clear, the concept of ethics employed in this book is not assimilable to Gadamer's hermeneutic model of dialogue, which implies the notions of understanding, mutuality, agreement, conversation, and reciprocity. On my definition of ethics, it is indeed only a deconstructive approach that is capable of upholding an ethical demand.

7 The notable exception to this is the work of Robert Bernasconi, who, more than anyone else, has established the philosophical proximity of Derrida's and Levinas's work in a series of important essays. See R. Bernasconi, 'The Trace of Levinas in Derrida', in *Derrida and Différance*, ed. D. Wood and R. Bernasconi (Parousia Press, Coventry, 1985), pp. 17–44; *idem*, 'Levinas and Derrida: The Question of the Closure of Metaphysics', in *FF* 181–202; *idem*, 'Deconstruction and the Possibility of Ethics', in *Deconstruction and Philosophy*, ed. J. Sallis (University of Chicago Press, Chicago and London, 1987), pp. 122–39; *idem*, 'Levinas, Philosophy and Beyond', *Continental Philosophy*, vol. 1, ed. H. Silverman (Routledge, London and New York, 1988), pp. 232–58. Also important in this regard is the work of John Llewelyn; see Llewelyn, 'Levinas, Derrida and Others vis-à-vis', in *Beyond Metaphysics* (Macmillan, London and Basingstoke, 1985), pp. 185–206; and *idem*, 'Jewgreek or Greek-jew', in *The Collegium Phaenomenologicum*, ed. J. Sallis, G. Moneta, and J. Taminiaux (Kluwer, Dordrecht, 1988), pp. 273–87.

8 Throughout this book I shall follow the standard translation of Levinas's *autre/Autre* by 'other' and *autrui/Autrui* by 'Other'.

9 See Jean-Paul Sartre, 'Intentionality: A Fundamental Idea of Husserl's

Phenomenology', *Journal of the British Society for Phenomenology*, 1, no. 2 (May 1970), p. 4.

10 This text marks a moment in the development of Levinas's work similar to that of 'La Différance' in Derrida's development. Indeed, both papers were originally delivered to the Société Française de la Philosophie.

11 Levinas remarks on his attempt after *TI*, to distance himself from the language of ontology in a number of places. In an interview contained in *The Provocation of Levinas*, ed. R. Bernasconi and D. Wood (Routledge, London and New York, 1988), he says: '*Totality and Infinity* was my first book. I find it very difficult to tell you, in a few words, in what way it is different from what I've said afterwards. There is the ontological terminology: I spoke of being. I have since tried to get away from that language' (p. 171).

He makes a similar remark at the end of the autobiographical essay 'Signature': 'The ontological language which is still used in *Totality and Infinity* in order to exclude a purely psychological signification of the proposed analyses is henceforth avoided' (*DL* 412).

As a final example, in the 1987 Preface to the German edition of *TI*, reprinted in the Livre de Poche edition (Kluwer, Dordrecht, 1990), Levinas writes: '*Otherwise than Being or Beyond Essence* already avoids the ontological – or, more precisely, eidetic – language to which *Totality and Infinity* ceaselessly returns, in order to avoid the consequence that the analyses that place in question the *conatus essendi* of Being be considered to repose upon some psychologistic empiricism' (pp. i–ii).

12 'Violence et métaphysique' was subsequently reprinted with a number of modifications in *ED* in 1967. I shall discuss an important modification of it in 2.4.

13 'En ce moment même dans cet ouvrage me voici' was subsequently reprinted in *PSY* 159–202, and a translation by R. Berezdivin appears in *RRL* 11–48.

14 'Tout autrement' first appeared in a 1973 issue of *L'Arc* (no. 54, pp. 33–7) consisting entirely of papers on Derrida's work. It was reprinted in *NP* 81–8, and my translation of it appears in *RRL* 3–10. A brief but detailed discussion of Derrida appeared in the essay 'La pensée de l'être et la question de l'autre', which was originally given as a paper in 1975 and was published in 1978 in *Critique*, 34, no. 369, pp. 187–97. It was republished in *DQVI* 173–88. Four other references to Derrida are contained in footnotes of Levinas: first in *Otherwise than Being* (*AE* 46/*OB* 189), where it is a question of Derrida's translation of Husserl's *Bedeutung* by *vouloir-dire*; second in the 1974 essay 'De la conscience à la veille', where it is a reference to Derrida's term 'logocentrism' (*DQVI* 58); third with respect to Derrida's work on Husserl, in the 1965 article

'Intentionalité et sensation' (*EDE* 157); and fourth, also in 1965, in the important essay 'Enigme et phénomème' (*EDE* 206), in which Levinas gives a bibliographical reference to Derrida's Introduction to Husserl's *Origin of Geometry*. Other references by Levinas to Derrida are given in interviews – for instance, in a conversation with Richard Kearney (*FF* 22, 33) and the interview contained in *Provocation of Levinas*, p. 179. The remarks in the latter interview were expanded in a most interesting fashion in a discussion contained in Levinas's *Autrement que savoir* (Osiris, Paris, 1987, pp. 68–70), where he talks frankly about how he had been '*tourmenté*' by Derrida's questions. There are also essays, notably 'God and Philosophy', originally given as a paper in 1973, then published in *Le Nouveau Commerce*, nos 30–1 (1975), pp. 97–128, and republished in *DQVI* 93–127, which show clear traces of a developing dialogue with Derrida's work. Finally, there is evidence from private correspondence that Levinas knew of and had assimilated Derrida's 'Violence and Metaphysics'. In Francis Guibal's *...et combien de dieux nouveaux: Levinas* (Aubier-Montaigne, Paris, 1980), pp. 51 and 79, the author cites a letter that Levinas sent to P. Decloux concerning Derrida's essay. Also, in Bernard Forthomme's *Une Philosophie de la transcendance. La métaphysique d'Emmanuel Levinas* (La Pensée Universelle, Paris, 1979), there is mention of Levinas's correspondence with Jan de Greef on the subject of the latter's doctoral dissertation. The discussion appears to touch on Derrida's essay, and, in particular, the question of the philosophical status of empiricism (cf. pp. 388 and 259). On all questions of Levinas's reception of Derrida, see Bernasconi's essays, listed in n. 7.

15   The possibility of maintaining such a thesis has been established by Roland Paul Blum in 'Deconstruction and Creation', *Philosophy and Phenomenological Research*, 46, no. 2 (1985), pp. 293–306, and is all too briefly outlined in Etienne Féron's excellent article 'Ethique, langage et ontologie chez Emmanuel Levinas', *Revue de Métaphysique et de Morale*, 82, no. 1 (1977), pp. 63–87.

16   See e.g. Heidegger, *Lettre sur l'humanisme*, 3rd, bilingual edn (Aubier-Montaigne, Paris, 1983) p. 168; English translation by Frank A. Capuzzi, in *Martin Heidegger. Basic Writings* (Routledge and Kegan Paul, London and Henley, 1978), p. 241.

17   'Everything goes through this chiasmus, all writing is caught in it – practices it. The form of the chiasmus, of the χ, interests me a great deal, not as the symbol of the unknown, but because there is in it, as I underline in "La dissémination", a kind of fork (the series *crossroads, quadrifurcum, grid, trellis, key*, etc.) that is, moreover, unequal, one of the points extending its range further than the other: this is the figure of

the double gesture, the intersection, of which we were speaking earlier' (*P* 95).

For other references to the figure of the chiasmus in Derrida's work, see *AF* 14; *E* 84; *D* 403; *VP* 189–92; and 'Le retrait de la métaphore', *Analecta Husserliana*, 14 (1985), p. 290.

18 Derrida, 'Deconstruction and the Possibility of Ethics', p. 124.

19 Heidegger, *Lettre sur l'humanisme*, pp. 138–56; *Basic Writings*, pp. 231–7.

20 The relation between Being and the 'ought' is discussed as the fourth limitation of Being in Heidegger, *Einführung in die Metaphysik* (Max Niemeyer, Tübingen, 1958), pp. 149–52 and 72; tr. R. Mannheim as *Introduction to Metaphysics* (Yale University Press, New Haven and London, 1959), pp. 196–9 and 92.

21 Heidegger, *Lettre sur l'humanisme*, p. 142; *Basic Writings*, p. 232.

22 Heidegger, *Lettre sur l'humanisme*, p. 144; *Basic Writings*, pp. 232–3.

23 See Kathleen Freeman, *Ancilla to the Pre-Socratic Philosophers* (Harvard University Press, Cambridge, Mass., 1948), p. 32.

24 Heidegger, *Letter sur l'humanisme*, p. 150; *Basic Writings*, p. 234.

25 Heidegger, *Letter sur l'humanisme*, p. 151; *Basic Writings*, p. 235.

26 See Nietzsche, *Zur Genealogie der Moral, in Werke in Drei Bänden*, ed. K. Schlechta (Carl Hanser Verlag, Munich, 1966), p. 768; tr. W. Kaufmann as *On the Genealogy of Morals* (Vintage, New York, 1967), p. 20. I would simply like to register my conviction that there is an urgent need for a full, scholarly comparison of Levinas's account of the formation of ethical subjectivity with Nietzsche's genealogical account of morality. Does the latter necessarily contradict and undermine the former? So it would seem. The Nietzschean genealogy shows how morality is founded on a hostility to life – reaction and *ressentiment*, a slave revolt against aristocratic values – that begins in Judaism and reaches a pinnacle of perverse perfection in Christianity. Systems of morality and religion are systems of cruelty for Nietzsche; their origins are soaked in blood. On this account, Levinas would indeed seem to be some kind of latter-day ascetic priest. What follows from this? Is one then, in the most naïve and pre-Nietzschean manner, going to base a negative value judgement of Levinas's work on Nietzsche's genealogy? This would presuppose the very moral vocabulary that Nietzsche's polemic undermines, as well as suppose that there is some position outside the genealogy, some neutral ground from which one could speak. Surely this is denied by Nietzsche. Let us imagine, more perversely but more engagingly, that Nietzsche and Levinas were in accord: yes, morality is soaked in blood, it is an experience of suffering, of self-torture. This is what Levinas suggests by his allusions to the cloak of Nessus, a garment dipped in poisoned blood and fatal to Hercules, in his attempt to find a metaphor that

would adequately describe the experience of ethical subjectivity. Ethics is traumatic and painful for Levinas, but is this a ground from which one can proceed to reject it? Levinasian ethics is not some uncritical appeal to good conscience or to conventional morality. I am here imagining the perverse profile of some future work in which Levinas and Nietzsche might be seen as co-genealogists of morality.

27   Blanchot, *L'Ecriture du désastre* (Gallimard, Paris, 1980), p. 45.

28   In Levinas, *Autrement que savoir*, p. 28.

29   In one of only two footnotes to *L'Ecriture du désastre*, Blanchot writes:

> What is enunciated or rather announced with Levinas, is a surplus, some-thing beyond the universal, a singularity that we might call Jewish and which still *waits* to be thought. To this extent, it is prophetic. Judaism as that which overcomes the thinking of the always in order to have always already been thought, but which however bears the responsibility of the thinking that is to come. This is what the other philosophy of Levinas *gives* us, a burden and a hope, the burden of hope. (*Ce qui s'énonce ou plutôt s'annonce avec Levinas, c'est un surplus, un au-delà de l'universel, une singularité qu'on peut dire juive et qui* attend *d'être encore pensée. En cela prophétique. Le judaïsme comme ce qui dépasse la pensée de toujours pour avoir été toujours déjà pensé, mais porte cependant la responsabilité de la pensée à venir, voilà ce que nous donne la philosophie autre de Levinas, charge et espérance, charge de l'espérance.*) (p. 45n.)

30   The phrase '*le primat de l'ontologie heideggerienne*' is translated by Alphonso Lingis as 'the primacy of ontology for Heidegger', thereby losing the reference to the Heideggerian context that was prevalent in many philosophical circles in France at the time of composition of TI. For some evidence of this, see the correspondence between Levinas and José Etcheveria that is appended to *TH* (112–13), in which Levinas deals with Heideggerian objections to his thinking and rejects as 'impious' (*impie*) the thought that philosophy is henceforth bound to Heideggerian teachings.

31   For an explanation and discussion of these terms, see below, 2.5.

32   See Jacques Rolland, 'Une Logique de l'ambiguïté', in *Autrement que savoir*, pp. 35–54.

33   This formulation implies, of course, a certain delusion on Rousseau's part: namely, that he did not mean to say what he actually said, and that what he actually meant to say is in contradiction with what is said in his text. Such a line of thought recalls Paul de Man's objections to Derrida in 'The Rhetoric of Blindness: Jacques Derrida's Reading of Rousseau', in *Blindness and Insight. Essays in the Rhetoric of Contemporary Criticism*, 2nd ed (Methuen, London, 1983), pp. 102–41, where de Man goes so

far as to claim that 'Rousseau's text has no blind spots' (p. 139). Consequently, 'there is no need to deconstruct Rousseau' (ibid.). However, de Man continues, there is a profound need to deconstruct the established tradition of Rousseau interpretation, which has systematically misread his texts. Thus, although de Man claims that Derrida is Rousseau's 'best modern interpreter' (p. 135), one who has restored 'the complexities of reading to the dignity of a philosophical question' (p. 110), he also maintains that Derrida is blind to the necessarily ambivalent status of Rousseau's *literary* language (p. 136). Derrida fails to read Rousseau as *literature. Of Grammatology* is therefore an exemplary case of de Man's thesis on the necessary interaction of blindness and insight in the language of criticism.

In defence of Derrida, let me say briefly that despite de Man's many insights, *his* blindness to *Of Grammatology* consists in his reading the latter as a *critique* of Rousseau, and not as a double reading. Derrida is no more speaking *against* Rousseau than he is speaking *for* him. Indeed, one might go so far as to say that the proper name 'Rousseau', whose texts Derrida comments on, simply signifies the dominant reading (or, for de Man, misreading) of Rousseau: that of the 'époque de Rousseau' (*G* 145/*OG* 97), which sees Rousseau simply as a philosopher of presence and ascribes to him the fiction of logocentrism, a fiction that extends even to modern anthropologists like Lévi-Strauss, whose structuralism, it must be remembered, is Derrida's real target for so much of Part 2 of *Of Grammatology.*

34 John Searle, 'Reiterating the Differences: A Reply to Derrida', in *Glyph*, 2 (1977), p. 203.

35 Jürgen Habermas, *The Philosophical Discourse of Modernity*, tr. Frederick Lawrence (Polity Press, Cambridge, 1987), pp. 185–210.

36 Cf. Heidegger, *Zur Sache des Denkens* (Max Niemeyer, Tübingen, 1969), p. 9; tr. J. Stambaugh as *Time and Being* (Harper and Row, New York, 1972), p. 9.

37 Richard Kearney, *Dialogues with Contemporary Continental Thinkers* (Manchester University Press, Manchester, 1984), p. 124.

38 Gasché, *Tain of the Mirror*, p. 101.

39 Kearney, *Dialogues with Contemporary Continental Thinkers*, p. 108.

40 Levinas seems to prefer the word *fermeture to clôture* (cf. *AE* 22, 222, 227/*OB* 20, 176, 180), although he uses *clôture* when describing the society of the couple in 'Phenomenology of Eros' (*TeI* 243/*TI* 265) and in the Talmudic reading 'Vieux comme le monde', in *QLT* 171. He also writes of 'le cercle clos de la totalité' (*TeI* 146/*TI* 171), and in the haunting final pages of *Otherwise than Being* of *claustration* (*AE* 224/*OB* 180), *dé-claustration* (*AE* 227/*OB* 180), and the *jeu clôturant* of essence (*AE*

222/OB 176).

41   On the question of history in Levinas, see his 'Commerce, the Historical Relation and the Face' (*TeI* 201–8/*TI* 226–32). For Benjamin, see his 'Theses on the Philosophy of History', in *Illuminations*, tr. H. Zohn (Fontana/Collins, London, 1973), pp. 255–66, esp. pp. 258–9. I believe it makes little sense to claim that Levinas is anti-historical and that the face-to-face relation takes place *beyond* history, as Derrida appears to claim in 'Violence and Metaphysics' (*ED* 139/*WD* 94). Rather, Levinas stands opposed to the ontological, or *economic* (*TeI* 203/*TI* 228), concept of history that reduces and reifies individuals, determining them in terms of the sum of their works or products – that is, in terms of economic relations of exchange and commerce. The task, after Benjamin, is to criticize history in the name of what history excludes, to brush history against the grain. Levinas's work is a history for those without works or texts; it is a history of interiority (*TeI* 203/*TI* 227).

42   See a short, recent text on this topic: Levinas, 'Ecrit et Sacré', in *Introduction à la philosophie de la religion*, ed. F. Kaplan and J.-L. Vieillard-Baron (Les Editions du Cerf, Paris, 1989), pp. 353–62. Levinas writes: 'It is in exegesis – interpolating itself between the obvious and the non-immediate meaning, but which *teaches* – that the passage to transcendence is produced' (*C'est dans l'exégèse – que s'intercale entre le sens obvie et le sens non immédiat, mais enseignant – que se produit le passage à l'au-delà ou transcendance*) (p. 357).

43   See 'Bernasconi, "Failure of Communication" as a Surplus: Dialogue and Lack of Dialogue between Buber and Levinas', in *Provocation of Levinas*, p. 101.

44   ' "Il faut bien manger" ou le calcul du sujet', in *Cahiers Confrontation*, p. 112. To do justice to this passage, let me give the context:

> 'Deconstructive explication, with its provisional prescriptions can demand the indefatigable patience of recommencement; but the affirmation that motivates deconstruction is unconditional, imperative and immediate – in a sense which is not necessarily or simply Kantian and even if this affirmation, because it is double, as I have tried to show, always remains threatened' (*L'explication déconstructive avec les prescriptions provisoires peut demander la patience infatigable du re-commencement mais l'affirmation qui motive la déconstruction est inconditionelle, impérative et immédiate – en un sens qui n'est pas nécessairement ou seulement kantien et même si cette affirmation, parce qu'elle est double, comme j'ai tenté de le montrer, reste sans cesse menacée*).

45   'Besides, once a thing is committed to writing it circulates equally among those who understand the subject and those who have no business with it; a writing cannot distinguish between suitable and unsuit-

able readers. And if it is ill-treated or unfairly abused it always needs its parent to come to its rescue; it is quite incapable of defending or helping itself' (Plato, *Phaedrus*, 275e, tr. W. Hamilton (Penguin, Harmondsworth, 1973), p. 97).

46 The original discussion that followed '*La Différance*' is reprinted in *Derrida and Différance*, pp. 129–50. The reference to Saussure is on p. 149.

47 Ferdinand de Saussure, *Course in General Linguistics*, tr. Wade Baskin (Fontana/Collins, London, 1974), p. 120.

48 For a discussion of *Glas*, see S. Critchley, 'A Commentary on Derrida's Reading of Hegel in *Glas*', *Bulletin of the Hegel Society of Great Britain*, 18 (Autumn/Winter 1988), pp. 6–32.

49 See e.g. 'Living On: Border Lines', in Bloom *et al.*, *Deconstruction and Criticism*, p. 84, and *P* 82/*POS* 59–60.

50 Immanuel Kant, *Grundlegung zur Metaphysik der Sitten* (Reclam, Stuttgart, 1984), pp. 414–17; tr. H. J. Paton as *The Moral Law* (Hutchinson, London, 1948).

51 Friedrich Nietzsche, *Also sprach Zarathustra* (Alfred Kröner Verlag, Leipzig, 1930), p. 181; tr. R. J. Hollingdale as *Thus Spoke Zarathustra* (Penguin, Harmondsworth, 1961), p. 185. It is quoted by Derrida in *Glas* (*GL* 365b/*GLtr* 262b), and again with reference to Michel de Certeau in 'Nombre de oui' (*PSY* 642).

52 Cf. Nietzsche, 'Die Erweckung', in *Also sprach Zarathustra*, pp. 343–7; tr. pp. 319–22.

53 See e.g. the final words of *Otherwise than Being* (a passage that will be analysed in chapter 3): 'After the death of a certain god inhabiting the world behind the scenes, the substitution of the hostage discovers the trace – unpronounceable writing – of that which, always already past – always "he/it" ["*il*"] – does not enter into any present, and to whom neither the names designating beings nor the verbs where their essence resounds are suitable – but who, Pro-noun [*Pro-nom*], marks with his seal everything that can bear a name' (*AE* 233/*OB* 185). It should be noted that the later Levinas's meditation on the trace is an attempt to keep open an irreducible dimension of transcendence that supports the alterity of the Other and resists any appropriation of its otherness. Levinasian ethics is addressed to the unnameable, to that which precedes all names, a pro-noun, or fore-name that comes before all names, the trace of an unpronounceable, inaudible writing which does not enter into any present.

54 'Man has the urge to thrust against the limits of language. Think for instance about one's astonishment that anything exists. This astonishment cannot be expressed in the form of a question, and there is no

answer to it' (*Der Mensch hat den Trieb, gegen die Grenzen der Sprache anzurennen. Denken Sie z.B. an das Erstaunen, daß etwas existiert. Das Erstaunen kann nicht in Form einer Frage ausgedrückt werden, und es gibt auch kein Antwort*) (Notes on talks with Wittgenstein, transcribed by Friedrich Waismann, in 'Lecture on Ethics', *Philosophical Review*, 74 (1965), p. 12.

55   'And thus, while we do not comprehend the practical unconditioned necessity of the moral imperative, we do comprehend its *incomprehensibility*. This is all that can fairly be asked of a philosophy which presses forward in its principles to the very limit of human reason' (*Und so begreifen wir zwar nicht die praktische unbedingte Notwendigkeit des moralischen Imperativs, wir begreifen aber doch seine* Unbegreiflichkeit, *welche alles ist, was billigermaßen von einer Philosophie, die bis zur Grenze der menschlichen Vernunft in Prinzipien strebt, gefordert werden kann*) (Kant, *Grundlegung zur Metaphysik der Sitten*, p. 463).

56   See Rodolphe Gasché, 'In-difference to Philosophy', in *Reading de Man Reading*, ed. L. Waters and W. Godzich (University of Minnesota Press, Minneapolis, 1989), pp. 259–94.

57   Miller is thinking specifically of the whole gamut of political approaches to literary interpretation contained in W. J. T. Mitchell (ed.), *The Politics of Interpretation* (University of Chicago Press, Chicago, 1983).

58   '*Act in such a way that you always treat humanity, whether in your own person or in the person of any other, never simply as a means, but always at the same time as an end*' (Kant, *Grundlegung*, p. 429). Levinas makes a favourable remark on this subject in an interview given to *Le Monde* in 1980: 'I like the second formulation of the Categorical Imperative, the one which says, "respect man in myself and in the Other." In this formulation we are not in the element of pure universality, but already in the presence of the Other' (*J'aime la seconde formule de l'impératif catégorique, celle qui dit de 'respecter l'homme en moi et en autrui'. Dans cette formule, nous ne sommes pas dans la pure universalité, mais déjà dans la présence d'autrui*) (in *Entretiens avec 'Le Monde'. 1. Philosophies* (Editions la Découverte, Paris, 1984), p. 146).

59   See Hegel, 'Reason as Lawgiver' and 'Reason as Testing Laws', in *Phenomenology of Spirit*, tr. A. V. Miller (Oxford University Press, Oxford, 1977), pp. 252–62.

60   See Kant, *Grundlegung*, p. 402.

2

The Problem of Closure in Derrida

It is decreed by divine law that Being shall not be without boundary....

There is a Limit (*peiras*), it is complete on every side, like the mass of a well-rounded (*eukukleou*) sphere. It is all the same to me from what point I begin, for I shall return again to this same point.

Parmenides

(Spirit) is in itself the movement which is cognition – the transformation of that in-itself into that which is for itself, of Substance into Subject, of the object of *consciousness* into an object of self-consciousness, i.e. into an object that is just as much superseded (*aufgehobenen*), or into the *Concept* (*Begriff*). The Movement is the circle that returns into itself (*zurückgehende Kreis*), the circle that presupposes its beginning and reaches it only at the end.

Hegel, *Phenomenology of Spirit*

Aletheia, unconcealment is named here. It is called well-rounded (*gutgerundete*) because it is turned in the pure sphere of the circle in which beginning and end are everywhere the same. In this circle there is no possibility of twisting, distortion and closure (*Verschließens*)....

In what circle are we moving here, indeed, inevitably? Is it the *eukukleos Alētheie*, well-rounded unconcealment (*die gut gerundete Unverborgenheit*) itself, thought as the opening (*Lichtung*)?

Heidegger, 'The End of Philosophy and the Task of Thinking'

2.1 Introduction

The goals of this chapter are both scholarly and exploratory; my primary concern is to give a thorough account of the concept of closure (*clôture*) in Derrida's work.[1] Secondly, and only on the basis of

that account, I propose and explore the hypothesis of *clôtural* reading, which, I believe, best describes what takes place in Derridian
deconstruction.

Following the introductory first part, I delineate in the second part
the sense and usage of the word 'closure', while, in the third part I
trace the genesis of the concept of closure in Derrida's work to his
early readings of Husserl. The fourth part comprises an extended
analysis of the closure of metaphysics, which develops Derrida's reading of Husserl and the relation of deconstruction to phenomenology,
and goes on to show how the concept of metaphysical closure
functions more generally in Derrida's work. In the fifth part, I offer
an extended discussion of the relation between the closure of metaphysics and the end of philosophy, and compare Derrida and
Heidegger. I try to assess the debt that the concept of metaphysical
closure owes to Heidegger's analysis of the history of metaphysics
and examine whether Derrida's reading of Heidegger has developed
or altered in some of his more recent texts. In the final part, I develop
the hypothesis of *clôtural* reading, which relates deconstruction to a
metaphysical closure that it ceaselessly seeks to interrupt. In the concluding pages I offer two examples of such a reading, of Derrida's
Voice and Phenomenon and 'Violence and Metaphysics'.

In the following analysis, I run the continual risk of enclosing
Derrida's work within a philosophical context, a historical or biographical chronology, and even a 'deconstructive methodology', which, I
believe, would reduce the dimension of alterity so carefully delineated
by deconstructive reading.[2] *Betrayal is the fate of all commentary.* For
commentary is never neutral; it employs a meta-language which
always derives from a *choice* or a *decision* – in short, a critical judgement which focuses upon certain texts, themes, and authors to the
exclusion of others. All work on Derrida must negotiate an irreducible economy of betrayal, where the non-philosophical interruption
of the philosophical *logos* is continually denied by the commentary on
that interruption. Perhaps the task of philosophy itself consists in this
act of betrayal, this indiscretion with regard to non-philosophy (*AE*
8/*OB* 7). However, working within this economy, it is necessary to
state axiomatically that deconstruction is not simply a form of philosophical critique, a discourse which, etymologically and historically,
depends upon concepts of decision and choice and which places the
philosopher-author in a position of knowing mastery. The horizon on

which this chapter continually seeks to open itself is that of the suspension of choice, decision, and critical judgement through the undecidability of an 'act' of reading. It is my belief that the patience, care, and supreme scholarly rigour of deconstructive reading maintain an interruption or alterity irreducible to both philosophy and critique. Yet, within the suspension of choice, within the undecidability of a double reading, a certain decision or event announces itself, a heteronomous moment of alterity that interrupts the text of philosophy and maintains itself as an interruption or blind spot within philosophical or critical discourse. This event is the ethics of deconstructive reading.

2.2 The Sense of Closure

The word 'closure' appears in many contexts; one speaks of the closure of a college, a hospital, or a university department, the closure of a debate or a parliamentary session, a kangaroo closure, the closure of a mathematical set or the principle of closure in logic, the closure of a body of propositions or a set of axioms, the astronomical closure of the solar system, the closure of a poem or work of literature, the closure of a language or a linguistic system, the closure or confinement of the 'mad' and the poor, the closure of the book and the closure produced by the advent of print, the closure of the private realm, the closure of the American mind, the closure of the political universe or of the universe of discourse, the closure of the critical project, the closure of the well-rounded circle of Being or Absolute Knowledge, and the closure of metaphysics.

What strands of sense can be delineated in this word? It is initially helpful to make a distinction between two senses of closure: a *spatial* and a *temporal* sense.[3] Spatially, closure is that which encompasses and encloses all the co-ordinates or constituent parts appertaining to a given, finite territory; this can be better understood if one thinks of the spatial closure described by the circumference of a circle or the enclosure of an area through the construction of a fence, frontier, or fosse. Temporally, closure is the activity or process of bringing something to its conclusion, completion, or end. However – and this is crucial in what follows – if closure describes the activity of bringing something to its end, then closure must be rigorously distinguished from the concept of end; for an end signifies the completion of the act and not the act of completion. Thus, on a temporal level, closure signifies a state of being prior to the end, the bringing of a process to its conclusion.

The word 'closure' is more commonly employed in its spatial sense. In English, closure is directly derived from the medieval French *closure*, and appears in Chaucer with the spatial meaning of an enclosure.[4] The French word *clôture*, deriving from the same source as the English word, is still employed in American English to describe the closure of a debate in the United States Senate. Indeed, *clôture* was earlier employed in the House of Commons for the same purpose.[5] *Clôture* appears in French from the sixteenth century onwards; thus Malherbe writes, 'Beaux jardins qui dans votre clôture/Avez toujours des fleurs.'[6] As the circumflex over the first vowel makes clear, the word *clôture* is itself a truncation of *closture*, which was still in use in the first half of the sixteenth century; for example, Montaigne writes, 'Il y a nation où la closture des jardins et des champs qu'on veult conserver se faict d'un filet de coton.'[7]

In French, the word *clôture* has several particular uses, of which I shall discuss three, the first two being spatial, the final one temporal. First, it means *enceinte*, a surrounding wall or fence which produces a *clôture*, or area of enclosed space. To erect a closure is literally to build a *mur de clôture*, an enclosing wall which acts as a barrier, palisade, or trellis, dividing the inside of a circumscribed territory from the outside and often functions in the defence of a property, dwelling, or fortification. Second, one can speak of a religious obligation to keep a closure, where the space of a monastery or convent is a *clôture* which is off limits to the laity, but within which monks or nuns live a *cloîtré*, or cloistered, existence. In French, one can speak of a *voeu de clôture*, a 'vow of closure', based on Canon Law,[8] which forbids or limits the coming and goings in a monastery or convent. In this sense, to violate the closure (*violer la clôture*) is to enter a convent unlawfully and breach its barriers; thus Molière's Don Juan says, 'Je vous ai dérobé à la clôture d'un couvent.'[9] The obligation to keep a closure also has a wider, secular significance; Voltaire speaks of 'la clôture de la princesse Sophie'[10] as a complete obedience or withdrawal within a severe self-imposed discipline. Closure can also be associated with reclusion and withdrawal, the desire to become enclosed within a retreat. Third, closure is the act of terminating a process, of definitively ending a state of affairs. For example, one can speak of *la clôture d'une séance* ('the closure of a meeting or session'), *la clôture d'un compte* ('the closure of an account'), or *la clôture d'un débat* ('the closure of a debate'). In this temporal sense, closure is always associated with the process or activity of completion.[11]

Understood temporally or spatially, it is necessary to understand *clôture* as a limit, a moment in time or points in space which delimit a given area and seek to circumscribe it. When the limit has been drawn, one not only sees the delimited area inside the closure; one has also delimited the outside of the closure, the *outre-clôture*. Thus, the event of closure is a delimitation which shows the double appartenance of an inside and an outside, of *la clôture* and its string of antonyms: *ouverture*, *percée*, *commencement*, *début*. In what follows it is precisely the failure of complete delimitation or circumscription that will be of interest; and I shall pay special attention to the opening, or breakthrough, that occurs within the closure, violating its vows and breaching its barriers, thereby offering the *promise* of a new beginning.

2.3   The Genesis of Closure in Derrida's Reading of Husserl

To locate the genesis of the concept of closure in Derrida's work, one is obliged to turn to the genesis of his philosophical problematic in what appears to be his earliest published essay, ' "Genèse et structure" et la phénoménologie', which, although originally given as a paper in 1959, was not published until 1965.[12] Even at this early stage of Derrida's development, it can be shown that a concept of closure governs his philosophical strategy and organizes his relation to Husserlian phenomenology.

On the opening page of the essay, Derrida notes that Husserl always had a marked aversion to the philosopher's wish to close (*clore*) debate by offering conclusions, solutions, or decisions (*ED* 229/*WD* 154). A decision implies that a choice has been made, and thus closes down the continuous process of comprehension or faithful description. Thus Husserl could be said to reject 'speculative closure' (*la clôture spéculative*) (*ED* 230/*WD* 155) and also, by implication, the idea that philosophy can bring itself to a conclusion, or *Schluß* (syllogistic closure) by postulating a closed system or structure. It is already clear that Derrida is employing Husserlian phenomenology as a foil for engaging in a critique of structuralism and the closure that the idea of structure implies.[13] In the same context, Derrida introduces the term *ouverture*, claiming that the Husserlian denial of structural closure implies the 'structurality of an opening' (*ED* 230/*WD* 155). It is by means of the conceptual pair *clôture/ouverture* that Derrida will articulate the tension within Husserlian phenomenology, a tension which articulates the very possibility of philosophy.

> The difference between the minor structure – necessarily closed (*close*) – and the structurality of an opening (*ouverture*), such is perhaps the unsituated place where philosophy enroots itself. (*ED* 230/*WD* 155)

However, in addition to employing Husserl as a foil for a critique of structuralism, he also borrows Husserl's critique of Dilthey's *Weltanschauungsphilosophie* as a veiled critique of geneticist historicism. According to Derrida, Husserl criticizes Dilthey for attempting to understand 'pure truth' – that is, the truths of reason and not factual truths (*ED* 237/*WD* 160) – from within a finite historical totality. Now, for Husserl, the idea of truth – that is, the idea of philosophy – is an infinite idea, or 'Idea in the Kantian sense'. As such, no finite totality or *clôture* can account for the infinite *ouverture* to truth, to philosophy.

> Now the idea or the project which animates and unifies every *determinate* historical structure, every *Weltanschauung*, is *finite*: on the basis of the structural description of a *world view*, one can account for everything except the infinite opening to the truth, that is to say, philosophy. (*ED* 237–8/*WD* 160)

Philosophy is the idea of infinity, the *ouverture* which can never be comprehended within a finite, closed historical structure. (One can perhaps begin to see why Derrida was working simultaneously on Husserl and Levinas.) A schema can be discerned here, whose gesture will remain constant throughout Derrida's early work: the concept of closure designates a *finite totality* which is continually breached by a movement of infinitization. One of the virtues that Derrida finds in Husserlian phenomenology is that, by defining the *telos* of philosophical activity in the infinity of the 'Idea in the Kantian sense', it continually breaches the finite circle of closure. To summarize, then, Derrida's approach to the problem of genesis and structure employs the resources of Husserlian phenomenology in an uncritical and sympathetic way in order to focus ultimately on 'un problème de *clôture* ou d'*ouverture*' (*ED* 240/*WD* 162) which displaces both geneticism and structuralism.

In order to deepen this analysis and elicit a similar problematic to the one at work in 'Genesis and Structure', I will now take a brief detour into Derrida's Introduction to Husserl's *Origin of Geometry*. In Derrida's translation of *Vom Ursprung der Geometrie*, there are two occurrences of the word *clôture*: first, as a translation of *Geschlossenheit* (*ORG* 200[14]) which is rendered as 'closed character' in the English translation;[15] second, on the facing page of Derrida's translation (*ORG* 201), as a rendering of *Beschränkung*, which is translated as 'limitation' in the English version.[16] It is the first instance that is of interest here.

In the *Origin of Geometry*, Husserl seeks to address the problem of how the discipline of geometry first originated – that is to say, how geometrical ideality and, by implication, the objective ideality of the sciences in general arose from within the consciousness of its first inventor, the 'proto-geometer' (*ORG* 181). For Husserl, such a problem cannot be addressed scientifically, for the place in which the origin of geometry arises is precisely the pre-scientific cultural world (*ORG* 199). Geometry arises within the historical horizon of humanity, a world (for example, that of Thales – an example also favoured by Kant[17]) which possesses its own *Lebenswelt* and mode of being (*ORG* 199). The question of the origin of geometry is consequently enclosed within the pre-scientific world, and cannot transgress those pre-scientific materials. This is why Husserl claims that questions like that of the origin of geometry have the character of *Geschlossenheit*, of closure within a limited, finite domain.

In his commentary on Husserl's text, after citing the passage that has just been discussed, Derrida describes the Husserlian institution or investiture of geometry as a *philosophical* act (*ORG* 127). The philosopher is the one who inaugurates a *géométrie platonisante* (*ORG* 137), thereby generating the radical freedom of the theoretical attitude which permits the 'overcoming' (*dépassement*) (*ORG* 137) of finite knowledge based on sensible or factual data. The overcoming of the finite is achieved through the conception of philosophy as an infinite task. The constitution of mathematical, geometrical, or philosophical idealization is located in the transcendence of the infinite over the finite, the 'Idea in the Kantian sense', the *telos* of reason.

However, the linear movement from the origin of geometry to the *telos* of reason is not the work of a single act of infinitization. Derrida delineates two infinities which must be distinguished. (1) *First infinity*: the originary infinitization of the Greeks permitted the overcoming of finite, sensible knowledge and an opening onto an infinitely fecund mathematics and geometry. However, for Husserl, this originary infinitization, exemplified by Euclidean geometry, ancient mathematics, and the Aristotelian syllogism, is an *a priori* system which, nevertheless, remains 'finitely closed' (Derrida renders this as '*clos dans sa finitude*') (*ORG* 139). Thus, the originary infinitization of the Greeks constitutes a totality, bound within a finite closure. (2) *Second infinity*: at the dawn of modernity, notably, for Husserl, in the work of Galileo, there arose a new infinitization, which came to overturn the original one. This new infinitization arises from within the closure of the original infinity, but differs from it in so far as it conceives of science and philosophy as an infinite task which cannot be limited by any finite closure.

The distinction between antiquity and modernity could be said to be drawn between two notions of infinity: the finite infinity (*l'infinité finie*) (*ORG* 140) of antiquity's creation, where the flowering of mathematics and geometry overcomes the closed finitude of the empirical, and constitutes an *a priori* system which is itself a finite closure; and the infinite infinity (*l'infinité infinie*) (*ORG* 140) of the Copernican revolution of modernity, which arises from within the finite closure of antiquity, but overcomes that closure, and opens it to the infinite task of scientific knowledge.

A final example from Derrida's Introduction will allow us to rejoin the commentary on 'Genesis and Structure'; it concerns the problem of intra-mathematical closure. The problem, broadly stated, is whether there is a closure of the mathematical domain; that is, whether mathematical idealization and infinitization take place within a field that is finite and closed. In a footnote to the Introduction (*ORG* 141), Derrida engages in a brief discussion of mathematical closure, and alludes (as he does so often in the Introduction) to Suzanne Bachelard's *A Study of Husserl's Formal and Transcendental Logic*,[18] in which she discusses the question of the completion (*Vollständigkeit*), or closure, of an axiom system like mathematics or geometry. Husserl adopted Hilbert's 'axiom of completeness' (*Vollständigkeitsaxiom*), which claimed that both numbers and elements of geometry 'form a system of things which, if one retains the group of axioms, are not subject to any extension'.[19] Husserl called such an axiom system, capable of enclosing mathematical infinitization within a finite domain, a 'definite' (*definit*)[20] system. For Husserl, axiom systems like mathematics and geometry were de-finite domains, de-limited closures, 'an infinite yet self-enclosed world of ideal objectivities as a field for study'.[21] Hence it is precisely the possibility of closure that characterizes sciences like mathematics and geometry.

In relation to the above, it is worth pointing out, as Derrida does in both 'Genesis and Structure' (*ED* 241–2/*WD* 162) and 'The Double Session',[22] that subsequent developments in axiom theory – namely, Gödel's theorem, expressed in his 'On Formally Undecidable Propositions of *Principia Mathematica* and Related Systems'[23] – have serious consequences for Husserl's conception of definite axiom systems. Gödel demonstrated that meta-logical statements concerning the completeness or closure of axiom systems can neither be demonstrated nor refuted within those axiom systems. This entails that there is an undecidable statement within each axiom system which refutes Hilbert's 'axiom of completeness' and, by implication, the Husserlian conception of logic, mathematics, and geometry as closed, or definite, systems. The closure is exceeded by Gödel's undecidable proposition, a notion which Derrida adopts when trying to decide upon the semantic status of the word 'hymen' in Mallarmé.[24]

If undecidability is the excess over the closure, or the transcendence over the definite system, then although this contradicts Husserl's conception of exact sciences like mathematics and geometry, it paradoxically offers a description of the function of a rigorous science like phenomenology.[25] In 'Genesis and Structure', Derrida discusses Husserl's distinction between exact and rigorous science. An exact science, as has already been shown in the discussion of geometry and mathematics, is characterized by the possibility of closure. The closure of an exact science is the completion of a finite totality, within which all the propositions, hypotheses, and concepts of that science are contained and '*nothing further remains open*' (*ED* 241/*WD* 322). On the other hand, a rigorous science like philosophy or phenomenology possesses the 'structural impossibility' (*ED* 242/*WD* 162) of closure. Philosophy, defined in relation to the infinite *telos* of the Idea in the Kantian sense, is the infinite opening beyond the closure.

It is the infinite opening of the lived experience (*vécu*), which is signified at several moments of (Husserlian) analysis by reference to an *Idea in the Kantian sense*, the irruption of the infinite into (*auprès de*) consciousness. (*ED* 242/*WD* 162)

Philosophy is the irruption of infinity into the finite totality of exact science or, indeed, into finite consciousness. Philosophy opens onto the alterity of an infinity whose 'étrange *presénce*' (*ED* 242/*WD* 162) is *within* finite closure as its condition of both possibility and impossibility.[26] Derrida writes:

> In any case, the transcendentality (*transcendantalité*) of the opening is at once the origin and the undoing, the condition of possibility and a certain impossibility of every structure and every systematic structuralism. (*ED* 243/*WD* 163)

The essential novelty of Husserlian phenomenology consists in the transcendentality of an opening, or 'overflowing' (*débordement*) (*ED* 250/*WD* 167) which exceeds the borders of the closure and 'deconstructs', *avant la lettre*, the very possibility of structuralism. Thus, in his earliest published works, the strategy which governs Derrida's relation to Husserlian phenomenology is apparent: he employs the resources of phenomenology and puts on the mask of the phenomenologist in order to make a veiled attack on structuralism and the notion of finite totality which it presupposes. Phenomenology is the overcoming of structural closure.

2.4   The Closure of Metaphysics

In Derrida's early texts, 'closure' is a technical term designating a finite totality, which the infinitist gesture of phenomenology continually exceeds. By articulating and repeating this gesture in a sympathetic manner, Derrida is able to advance masked, and engage in a subversive critique of the contemporary French intellectual scene. Thus far, one would be correct in claiming that Derrida simply continues the theoretical position of Husserl, and at no point makes a decisive break with phenomenology. The announcement of this break or, more precisely, the articulation of a position that at once constitutes a continuation *and* a break with Husserl, is expressed through a crucial displacement of the concept of closure itself. The word *clôture* shifts from being part of a technical vocabulary to becoming a key term in the conceptual terminology with which Derrida will engage in a deconstruction of the metaphysics of presence.

This shift from technical to terminological usage can be clearly delineated with reference to Derrida's 'Violence and Metaphysics'. In the first version of this essay, which appeared in *Revue de Métaphysique et de Morale* in 1964, the word *clôture* appears twice: first, in a discussion of the Heideggerian conception of metaphysics, where Derrida writes that, for Heidegger, it is metaphysics itself 'which remains a closure of the totality' *'qui reste clôture de la totalité'* (*RMM* 460/*ED* 209/*WD* 142); and second in a footnote on Schelling's response to empiricism, where Derrida mentions the *clôture finie* (*RMM* 471/*ED* 225/*WD* 320). Both these uses of closure seem to compound its meaning as a finite, bounded totality discussed above.[27] However, in the second version of 'Violence and Metaphysics', which appeared in *Writing and Difference* three years later, Derrida made a number of additions to the text. Among these was a long insertion on the subject of what had become, between 1964 and 1967, the *problem* of closure:

> And if you will, *traversing* the philosophical discourse from which it is impossible to uproot oneself totally, to attempt a breakthrough towards what is beyond it (*une percée vers son au-delà*), the only chance of reaching it *within language* (Levinas recognizes that there is no thought before or outside it) is by *formally* and *thematically* posing the *problem of the relations between belonging and the breakthrough, the problem of closure* (*le problème des rapports entre l'appartenance et la percée, le problème de la clôture*. (*ED* 163/*WD* 110)

The claim implicit in this passage is that Levinas's ethical rupture with the ontological and phenomenological tradition can only be through renunciation of the linguistic resources of that tradition. The contradiction that is at work in Levinas (and which applies to the work of any philosopher, Derrida included) is that he can only accomplish such a rupture by employing the very resources of the tradition that he wishes to overcome: that is, the language of metaphysics (even an ethical metaphysics) and the discourse of ethics itself. Levinas's discourse is consequently caught in a double bind, between belonging to the tradition and achieving a breakthrough that goes beyond the tradition. Ethical discourse – and, as I argued in chapter 1, deconstructive discourse – is confined to the movement of *traversing* the philosophical *logos* between two points of tension: between belonging and the breakthrough, philosophy and non-philosophy. Now it is precisely this situation, in which the space of philosophy is criss-crossed by the crab-like traversals of the non-philosophical, which describes the *problem* of closure.

The above addition to 'Violence et métaphysique' adds a new dimension to the concept of closure; it is no longer simply a technical term designating a finite totality, but rather the terminological name for a problematic that describes the relations between logocentrism and its other, a problematic that is perhaps the major preoccupation of the works of Derrida published in book form in 1967. With this in mind, Derrida's relation to Husserlian phenomenology needs to be reassessed. The concept of structural closure exceeded by a phenomenology whose orientation is employed uncritically by Derrida gives way to the concept of the *closure of metaphysics*, a relation of belonging and not belonging to the metaphysical tradition within whose parameters phenomenology is ultimately inscribed. For Derrida, the dominant and distinctive tension within the Husserlian text resides in the way in which it both belongs to metaphysics and seeks to overcome metaphysics. This tension is most clearly evinced in certain passages from the *Cartesian Meditations*, which Derrida cites, to my knowledge, in no less than four separate texts devoted to Husserl.[28] In the *Cartesian Meditations*, Husserl sees transcendental phenomenology as, on the one hand, the 'universal overthrow' (*allgemeine Umsturz*)[29] or 'overcoming' (*Überwindung*)[30] of degenerate metaphysical speculation and, on the other hand, as the new *philosophia protē*,[31] the reawakening of the Cartesian impulse[32] – phenomenology as authentic metaphysics. The problem of closure is the hinge that articulates the two movements of this tension, this double metaphysics.

The relation between phenomenology and the problem of metaphysical closure is most clearly and succinctly evoked in Derrida's elegant Introduction to Husserl, 'La phénoménologie et la clôture de la métaphysique', which appeared in the Greek journal *Epochēs* in 1966 and has never been reprinted.[33] Derrida begins his Introduction by emphasizing Husserl's dogged mistrust of metaphysical speculation. Husserl opposes the concrete, apodictic, but non-empirical description of the things themselves to the speculation which reasons only from probable and uncertain premises. To return to the things themselves, 'le motif fondamental de la phénoménologie' (*PC* 1), is to describe everything that appears to consciousness as it is in its original nudity, prior to being clothed in speculative interpretation. Consequently, for Husserl, the word 'metaphysics' denotes the speculative dissimulation of the things themselves. However – and here the tension within phenomenology is broached – this return to the things themselves is itself metaphysical in so far as phenomenology seeks to rediscover the first principles of philosophy, natural science, and the humanities, which have been perverted by a 'degenerate' (*VP* 4/*SP* 5) metaphysics. Transcendental phenomenology is thus caught in the tension between a descriptively authentic metaphysics and a speculatively degenerate metaphysics – a double metaphysics.

Phenomenology, therefore, appears as *both* a transgression or breakthrough from the metaphysical tradition *and* a restoration of that tradition (*PC* 2). Phenomenology transgresses degenerate metaphysics in order to restore the Platonist conception of philosophy as *epistēmē* or the Aristotelian *philosophia protē*. For Derrida, the tension, or ambiguity, of a double metaphysics marks the entirety of Husserlian phenomenology, and places it within the problem of closure.

> The whole Husserlian itinerary is affected by this ambiguity: it holds us back within the field and within the language of metaphysics by the very gesture that carries it beyond metaphysical closure and the limits of all that is in fact called metaphysics. (*PC* 3)

The problem of closure at the heart of Husserl's project is that the very gesture that carries it beyond the metaphysical closure reinscribes it within the limits of closure. The closure of metaphysics is bound in a double gesture, one of transgression and restoration, a transgression of the closure that can proceed only by employing the metaphysical language and conceptuality that restores metaphysics to itself. Phenomenology is a double metaphysics that can proceed only with the novelty of its overcoming of metaphysics by employing an ancient metaphysical language – that is to say, by employing a logic of palaeonymy.

Derrida adopts a very similar strategy in his reading of Condillac *L'Archéologie du frivole*. Condillac's *Essai sur l'origine des connaissances humaines* distinguishes between 'two sorts of metaphysics' (*AF* 11).

First there is the traditional metaphysics of essences and causes, 'the metaphysics of the hidden' (*la métaphysique du caché*), which Condillac (after Locke) wished to overcome. Secondly, there is the new metaphysics based on phenomena and relations, described in terms which echo Derrida's reading of Husserl: 'A metaphysics of the open, one might say. *A phenomenology of the things themselves and a critical science of limits*' (*AF* 11). Such a metaphysics of the open would found itself upon the evidence of intuited, apodictic phenomena. For Derrida, Condillac's double metaphysics, like that of Husserl, can proceed only by way of palaeonymy (*AF* 12), in which the language of metaphysics is preserved in its overcoming and restored in its transgression. However, the difference between Condillac and Husserl consists in the fact that, for the former, the establishment of a new metaphysics does not represent a novel *philosophia protē*; it is rather a *second* philosophy which, 'through a chiasmus effect' (*AF* 14), criticizes the presuppositions of the traditional metaphysics which believes itself to be a first philosophy. Degenerate, or *mauvaise* (*AF* 15), metaphysics is to be supplemented by the authentic, or *bonne* (*AF* 16), metaphysics which displaces the former while inheriting its name.

The concept of metaphysical closure that has been detected in relation to Husserlian phenomenology as the play of belonging and non-belonging, of transgression and restoration, can also be said to govern many of Derrida's readings in *Writing and Difference*. Generated from within the reading of Husserl, the problem of closure assumes a more general terminological function within the deconstruction of logocentrism (indeed, the same might be said of many other of Derrida's key concepts). In his essay on Foucault's *History of Madness*, Derrida argues that to write a history of madness in the language of reason demands a writing that will not let itself be contained (*ne saurait se laisser contenir*) (*ED* 59/*WD* 36) in the metaphysical closure. In his essay on Freud, Derrida focuses on 'the Freudian opening or breach' (*la trouée freudienne*) (*ED* 337/*WD* 228) which 'uneasily lets itself be contained within logocentric closure' (*se laisse mal contenir dans la clôture logocentrique*) (*ED* 296/*WD* 198). A similar logic is at work in 'From Restricted Economy to General Economy', where Bataille is obliged to employ Hegelian discourse while engaging it in a 'slippage' (*glissement*) (*ED* 387/*WD* 263) of meaning so as to allow Bataille's discourse of *souveraineté* to move 'beyond the closure or the horizon of absolute knowledge' (*au-delà de la clôture ou de l'horizon du savoir absolu*) (*ED* 393/*WD* 268). The entire tension of these essays lies in the way in which the act whereby the closure is transgressed is accompanied by the restoration of the closure, leaving each text *on the limit* between belonging and not belonging to the tradition.

However, it must now be asked, what is the form of this limit? How is the closure of metaphysics to be represented? Derrida insists that the form of metaphysical closure cannot be represented as a circle with a linear, unbroken boundary surrounding a homogeneous space. In his 1978 paper 'Le retrait de la métaphore', in the context of his highly corrective reading of Paul Ricoeur's interpretation of 'White Mythology', he states that he does not hold with the interpretation of metaphysics as a homogeneous unity or believe in the existence of a unitary concept of metaphysics.[34] He adds, rather programmatically:

> I have also very often...advanced the proposition according to which there would never be 'the' metaphysics ['*la*' *métaphysique*], the 'closure' is not here the circular limit bordering a homogeneous field, but a more twisted [*retorse*] structure, I would be tempted to say today according to another figure: 'invaginated'. The representation of a linear and circular closure surrounding a homogeneous space is rightly, such is the theme of my greatest insistence, an auto-representation of philosophy in its onto-encyclopaedic logic.[35]

Recalling the spatial sense of closure delineated above, it can now be seen that closure is not an unbroken boundary, or circle, which encloses all the co-ordinates or constituent parts of a finite totality or homogeneous territory. The closure of metaphysics has a more twisted and devious limit that is 'invaginated' – that is to say, ensheathed within itself, or folded back upon itself. For Derrida, the representation of closure as a linear, circular boundary is a philosophical auto-representation or auto-intention, whereby philosophy justifies itself as a body of *paideia* that can be encircled within its own *kuklos*, master its own limits, and assume an encyclopaedic self-knowledge. As the epigraphs to this chapter indicate, certain dominant moments of the metaphysical tradition have assigned a limit (*peiras*) to what is, and represent truth and Being as a well-rounded sphere which attains a flawless closure within which there is no possibility of twisting or distortion. The dialectical movement of the Concept (*der Begriff*) is such that Hegelian *Aufhebung* traces the interior limit of a circle whose circumference comprises the totality of Absolute Knowing. As Hegel remarks in the Introduction to the *Aesthetics*, the whole, or the organic totality, of philosophy is the coronet, or crown (*der Krone*) within whose sphere revolve the circles of the various disciplines, such as art.[36] Philosophy is the circle of circles and maintains an encyclopaedic development. For Derrida, logocentrism always desires to attain a unitary closure, where the distinction between the inside and the outside, philosophy and non-philosophy, can be rigorously maintained. The philosophical enterprise is 'the mastery of the limit' (*la maîtrise de la limite*) (*M* i, *MP* x), the desire to command one's frontiers and thereby regulate the traffic that moves in and out of one's territory. Philosophy is the territorial desire for totality and closure.

The deconstruction of logocentrism proceeds by showing how the limit, or closure, of a logocentric text is irreducibly flawed. The closure with which a text's dominant interpretation surrounds itself is shown to possess certain faults, or breaks, which are the marks of an alterity which the text is unable to reduce. Thus, the deconstructive 'representation' of a text – for example, the Hegelian text (*P* 103/*POS* 77) – is not the circular closure of its auto-representation; rather, the text that is deconstructively read possesses a surface that is fissured and flawed by the traces of an alterity which it can neither reduce nor expel. In *Positions*, Derrida speaks of the philosophical text bearing the scar (*cicatrice*) (*P* 77/*POS* 57) of exteriority or alterity. Deconstructive reading leaves the logocentric text as a scarred, flawed body which is unable to demarcate its inside from its outside and which is divided within itself between belonging and not belonging to the logocentric tradition.

Circling back to Husserl, an illuminating example of the deconstructive representation of closure can be seen in Derrida's 1968 essay on *Ideas*, 'Form and Meaning' (*M* 187–207/*MP* 157–73). Indeed, the opening sentence of the essay distils the central thesis of Derrida's reading of Husserl: 'Phenomenology only criticized the state of metaphysics in order to restore it' (*La phénoménologie n'a critiqué la métaphysique en son fait que pour la restaurer*) (*M* 187/*MP* 157). The guiding thread employed by Derrida to elaborate this play of critique and restoration is the concept of form. The question is whether the Husserlian concept of form is able to leave the horizon of the determination of Being as presence (*parousia*), and consequently the closure of metaphysics (*M* 202/*MP* 169), which conceives of form on the basis of the Platonic *eidos* or the Aristotelian *morphē*. In the long, final footnote to the essay, Derrida suddenly (and characteristically) enlarges the horizon of his investigation. After speculating as to whether the concept of form is exhausted by the closure of presence, he introduces the theme of the *trace*:

> Form would already be in itself the *trace* (*ikhnos*) of a certain non-presence, the vestige of the un-formed, announcing-recalling its other, as perhaps Plotinus did to the whole of metaphysics. (*M* 206/*MP* 172)

The trace, in this context in the form of the Plotinian *ikhnos*,[37] is a vestigial 'memory' of non-presence within the concept of form, an irreducible excess that precedes both the concept of form and the determination of Being as presence. The trace constitutes the possibility of an exit beyond the closure of metaphysics.[38] Continuing the footnote, Derrida writes:

> Consequently, the closure of metaphysics, which the audacity of the *Enneads* seems to indicate in transgressing it (but we can accredit this to other texts), would not proceed *around* a homogeneous and continuous field of metaphysics. (*M* 206/*MP* 172)

The closure of metaphysics is in this case indicated through the transgression effected by the trace, a transgression that is discovered within the metaphysical concept of form. Within this epoch of metaphysics, within the texts of the metaphysical tradition – and 'doubtless already in Plato's text' (*M* 206/*MP* 172) – are discerned the scars, or traces, of an irreducible alterity which disturbs the unity of the concept of epoch and denies the construction of a unitary closure or totality. Thus the concept of closure does not bound a homogeneous totality; rather, it fissures the unified structure of metaphysics.

The concept of closure divides the concept of metaphysics along the irreconcilable yet inseparable axes of transgression and restoration, of belonging and not belonging, of the break and the continuation. The pattern that deconstructive reading continually finds at work within texts is one of dislocation, where two inassemblable readings or lines of thought open up within each text. One of these readings repeats the internal exigencies or dominant interpretation of the text, while the other, which only arises out of the repetition implicit in the first, transgresses the order of 'commentary' and shows how the text is divided against its own auto-representation.

As Derrida remarks, it is probably not a question of deciding or choosing between two lines of thought or two readings (*on n'a donc probablement pas à choisir entre deux lignes de pensée*) (M 207/MP 173). A choice implies a decision, a conclusion (*Schluß*) to reading and thinking, whereas deconstruction provokes 'an infinite and infinitely surprising reading' (*une lecture infinie et infiniment surprenante*) (M 206/MP 172) that shows the shortcomings of any unitary, finite notion of the tradition or totality and the absence of any *end* to the historico-metaphysical epoch within which reading is undertaken. I shall call such reading *clôtural*.

2.5   Heidegger and Derrida: Closure and the End of Philosophy

Much of the previous discussion of the concept of closure has concerned itself with an elaboration and complication of the spatial sense of closure introduced in the first part of the chapter. However, I should now like to turn to the *temporal* sense of closure, which was defined as the activity or process of bringing something to its end. Defined thus, the concept of closure was to be distinguished from the concept of end, for an end signifies the completion of an act or process, and not the activity or process of completion implicit in closure.

This distinction of closure from end echoes Derrida's by now famous declaration in the 'Exergue' to *Of Grammatology*:

> For essential reasons, the unity of all that which lets itself be caught sight of today across the most diverse concepts of science and writing is, in principle, always more or less secretly determined by a historico-metaphysical epoch of which we only catch a glimpse of the *closure*. We do not say *end*. (G 14/OG 4)

The claim here is that the unity derived from the concepts of science and writing is covertly, yet continually, determined by a historico-metaphysical epoch. The closure of this epoch can be caught sight of, a closure which, as was shown above, does not *enclose* an epochal totality, but which rather disrupts and fissures the concept of epoch and any homogeneous notion of metaphysics that such a notion presupposes. To catch a glimpse of the closure of the metaphysical epoch is already to have engaged in the latter's deconstruction.

Now, it is of vital importance to Derrida that this conception of the closure of metaphysics is distinguished from the notion of end, notably the end of philosophy. Some of Derrida's commentators (and, I imagine, many of his readers) assume that this distinction of closure from end is Derrida's self-conscious differentiation of his own project from that of Heidegger, in particular the latter's notion of the end of philosophy.[39] On this view, Derrida's avoidance of the concept of end could be seen as an implicit critique of Heidegger, a critique that might *appear* to be confirmed by certain passages in 'Being written' (*L'être écrit*) (*G* 31–41/*OG* 18–26), where Derrida offers a stern re-appraisal of Heidegger's reading of Nietzsche.[40] However, I should here like to ask: Does the Derridian concept of the closure of metaphysics necessarily stand in opposition to the Heideggerian notion of the end of philosophy? This will allow the more difficult question to be raised concerning the extent of Derrida's assimilation of Heidegger's analysis of the history of metaphysics. But first, what does Heidegger understand by the end of philosophy?

For Heidegger, the notion of the end of philosophy, like that of the overcoming of metaphysics (*Überwindung der Metaphysik*), gives rise to many misunderstandings,[41] a state of affairs he recognizes in his 1964 essay 'The End of Philosophy and the Task of Thinking'.

> What is meant by the talk about the end of philosophy (*Ende der Philosophie*)? We understand the end of something all too easily in the negative sense as a mere stopping, as the lack of continuation, perhaps even as decline and impotence. In contrast, what we say about the end of philosophy means the completion of metaphysics (*die Vollendung der Metaphysik*).[42]

Heidegger does not understand the end of philosophy as a full stop, or conclusion, to the metaphysical tradition; rather, it is necessary to think *das Ende* in terms of *die Vollendung*, as a completion, or fulfil-ment, of metaphysics, a term which Heidegger is careful to distinguish from perfection (*die Vollkommenheit*) (*SD* 62/*BW* 374). The *Vollendung* is the place (*der Ort*) (*SD* 63/*BW* 375) where the history of metaphysics is gathered and brought to completion. Thus, the Heideggerian notion of the end of philosophy does not mean that philosophy is *fin-ished* or that we have finished doing philosophy; rather, the completion of metaphysics means that, with Nietzsche's reversal of Platonism, all the essential possibilities of metaphysics have been exhausted. The exhaustion of the possibility of any novel theoretical advance in metaphysics does not mean that metaphysics will disappear. According to Heidegger, metaphysics dissolves into the empirical and technologized sciences which perform a scientific and methodological study of human beings and all that pertains to them. Although forgetful of their foundation in metaphysics, the sciences continue the metaphysical project, and carry it forward to its ultimate and total global domination.

> The end of philosophy proves to be the triumph of the manipulable arrangement of a scientific-technological world and of the social order proper to this world. The end of philosophy means the beginning (*Beginn*) of the world civilization based upon Western European thinking. (*SD* 65/*BW* 377)

The end of philosophy implies a beginning. The completion of metaphysics shows both how much metaphysics has accomplished and how much it will accomplish in the future. This point is confirmed in Heidegger's fragmentary essay 'Overcoming Metaphysics' (to which I will return in chapter 5), where he writes: 'The epoch of completed metaphysics (*vollendeten Metaphysik*) stands before its beginning (*Beginn*)' (*VA* 72/*EOP* 93). Indeed, certain sentences from the same essay suggest that the ending (*Verendung*) of metaphysics 'will last longer than the previous history of metaphysics' (*VA* 63/*EOP* 85). The epoch of the ending of completed metaphysics entails a domination by metaphysical modes of thinking for an indefinite duration. As Michel Haar points out, it is precisely this indefinite prolongation of the epoch of completed metaphysics that represents the danger (*die Gefahr*) for Heidegger.[43]

Thus, Heidegger's understanding of the concept of end as *Vollendung* entails a rethinking of the notion of the end of philosophy.[44] If this is granted, then, returning to the question raised above, would the distinction of closure from end be the condition for the separation of Derrida and Heidegger? In his essay 'Levinas and Derrida: The

Question of the Closure of Metaphysics', Robert Bernasconi discusses the relation of closure to end, and suggests that Heidegger's word *Verendung* might correspond to Derrida's *clôture*.[45] In a footnote appended to this remark, Bernasconi continues:

> It would seem therefore that when Derrida pointedly uses the word *closure* rather than *end*, he is addressing only a certain reading of Heidegger popular among some Heideggerians and so it is ironic that it has now been adopted by some readers of Derrida.[46]

The claim here is that the introduction of the thesis of the closure of metaphysics was not intended to oppose Heidegger, but rather to remedy the apocalypticism of certain of his readers who misunderstood the notion of the end of philosophy. This phenomenon is documented by Vincent Descombes in his history of twentieth-century French philosophy, *Le même et l'autre*, where he notes that 'The expression "end of philosophy" was borrowed from Heidegger, but it was in fact utilized in the most diverse senses.'[47] The concept of the end of philosophy, Descombes remarks, was often employed in 'un sens bien peu heideggerien'[48] to mean either the transition from philosophical theory to political praxis or to buttress the accusation that philosophy is nothing but the ethnocentric ideology of the West. A less controversial, but nonetheless indicative, example of this apocalypticism can be seen in Gilles Deleuze's *Différence et répétition*, where, in a discussion of Heidegger, he states that the turning of thinking towards the ontological difference takes place 'beyond metaphysics' (*au-delà de la métaphysique*);[49] he thus sees the overcoming of metaphysics as an exit from the metaphysical domain. Of course, to adopt such a position would be to misrepresent a principle element of Heidegger's thought. In 'Overcoming Metaphysics', Heidegger stresses that the path of an *Überwindung* of metaphysics can proceed only by way of a *Verwindung*, or appropriation, of the essence of metaphysics (*VA* 71/*EOP* 91). It should not be imagined that one is outside metaphysics simply because its end can be postulated: 'metaphysics overcome does not disappear' (*die überwundene Metaphysik verschwindet nicht*) (*VA* 64/*EOP* 85).

Derrida adopts this Heideggerian stance in *Positions*. When asked whether he believes the overcoming of metaphysics to be possible, he replies emphatically: '*There is not* a transgression if we understand by that the pure and simple installation in a beyond of metaphysics (*un au-delà de la métaphysique*)' (P 21/*POS* 12). It is therefore as an antidote to this apocalyptic transgression of metaphysics that Derrida introduces the concept of metaphysical closure. 'Every transgressive gesture re-encloses us...within the interior of the closure' (ibid.). The closure of metaphysics is a moving limit that restores each transgression and transgresses each restoration. Like the *Verendung* of completed (*vollendeten*) metaphysics, the duration of closure is without end, in-fin-ite, inde-fin-ite. 'That which is caught in the de-limited closure can continue indefinitely' (P 23/*POS* 13).

The Derridian concept of metaphysical closure is not postulated in opposition to a Heideggerian notion of the end of philosophy; it is introduced in order to correct certain apocalyptic misrepresentations of the latter. When closely examined, the concept of metaphysical closure has much in common with the end of philosophy *qua* completion of metaphysics. This claim can perhaps be more clearly understood with reference to Derrida's unpublished introduction to Husserl, 'La phénoménologie et la clôture de la métaphysique', which has already been partially discussed. In the final paragraph of that essay, Derrida attributes the concept of metaphysical closure directly to Heidegger.

> Heidegger...says that the thinking of Being was lost...when, at the birth of philosophy, Being was determined by metaphysics as presence, as the proximity of the being (*étant*) before the glance (*eidos*, phenom-enon, etc.) and consequently as ob-ject. This determination of Being as *pre-sence* (*pré-sence*) and then of presence as the proximity of the being to itself, as self-consciousness (from Descartes to Hegel) would outline the closure of the history of metaphysics. (*PC* 14)

Thus, for Derrida, the epoch of Being's forgottenness in its ancient determination as the presence of the *eidos* to the intellect or as the modern representation of the ob-ject (*der Gegen-stand*) to a self-present, self-conscious subject delimits the boundary of the historico-metaphysical closure. It is this sense of metaphysical closure in terms of the epoch of Being's oblivion and the unitary concept of metaphysics that such a history of Being presupposes that would ultimately seem to guide Derrida's early analyses of Husserl and Heidegger (not to mention Rousseau and others). For Derrida, each of these thinkers establishes a certain transgression and restoration of the closure of metaphysics.

> Husserl perhaps accomplished an admirable, modern, metaphysical revolution: an exit from metaphysics, outside of the entirety of its history, in order to come back finally to the purity of its origin. (*PC* 15)

The same double gesture is attributed to Heidegger in *Of Grammatology*,

> The ambiguity of the Heideggerian situation with regard to the metaphysics of presence and logocentrism. Heidegger's situation is at once contained within it and transgresses it. But it is impossible to separate. The very movement of transgression sometimes retains it on this side of the limit. (*G* 36/*OG* 22)

The movements of transgression and restoration cannot be separated. Their irreducibly double gesture provides the rhythm of deconstructive, or *clôtural*, reading. The peculiarity of Derrida's reading of Heidegger (which makes the latter's situation more acute than that of any other thinker whom Derrida reads) is that the problem of metaphysical closure with which the deconstruction of logocentrism gets under way is a resource that Derrida finds within the Heideggerian text. The thesis of the closure of metaphysics, on this reading, does not represent Derrida's break with Heidegger, but rather indicates the massive scale of Derrida's assimilation of Heidegger's analysis of the history of metaphysics.

It is therefore ironic that the distinction between closure and end should be seen as an implicit critique of Heidegger and not as a corrective to certain apocalyptic readings of the latter. It is doubly ironic that Derrida himself should be accused of apocalypticism, a charge to which he responds in his 1980 paper 'Of an Apocalyptic Tone Recently Adopted in Philosophy' by specifically *reintroducing* the concept of closure.

> That I have multiplied the distinctions between closure and end (*la clôture et la fin*), that I was aware of speaking of discourses *on* the end (*sur la fin*) rather than announcing the end, that I intended to analyse a genre rather than practice it, and even when I would practice it, to do

so with this genre clause of irony, which, I tried to show, never belongs to the genre itself... (*TA* 84/*AT* 30)

For Derrida, to adopt an apocalyptic tone in philosophy is to participate in a *fin-ite* discourse that focuses upon the end and becomes complicit with eschatology – that is, a project that teleologically relates its activity to a postulated end, that deals with the last things (death, judgement, the end of the world), and that adopts a tone that presages the revelation (*apokalypsis*) that will come at the end. Derrida speculates as to whether the entirety of philosophy is dominated by a complicity with apocalyptic or eschatological discourse. If this were the case, then the history of philosophy would consist in the diverse intonations of differing eschatologies. Philosophy as eschatology would perpetuate its life through the permanent proclamation of its death: Kantian, Hegelian, Marxian, or Nietzschean eschatology, the end of philosophy, the end of history, the death of God, the death of 'man', or the end of morality – 'That was the most serious *naïveté*' (*TA* 59/*AT* 21). Derrida claims that what is excluded from this apocalyptic discourse upon the end is the discourse on *the end of the end* (*la fin de la fin*) (*TA* 60/*AT* 21); and it is precisely for this reason that 'It is still necessary to distinguish between closure and end' (*Il faut encore distinguer entre la clôture et la fin*) (ibid.). The word *encore* in this sentence refers the reader back to the distinction between closure and end that Derrida made some 13 years prior to 'Of an Apocalyptic Tone', in *Of Grammatology*.

Of course, Derrida is obliged to adopt an apocalyptic tone, in the same way as he is obliged to employ the resources of logocentrism in the latter's deconstruction – but with the difference that Derrida ironizes *upon* the end and *on* apocalypse, and establishes a discourse which tries to think the end of the end and the apocalypse of apocalypse. Yet – and here my reading confronts both a closure and an opening – if the entirety of philosophy is complicit with an eschatological project, then is not Heidegger party to this contract? Although my reading of the Derridian concept of closure has attempted to show its filiation with the concept of the end of philosophy in Heidegger, is there not an eschatology implicit in the unitary conception of metaphysics as the epoch of Being's oblivion that informs Heidegger's conception of an *Überwindung* of metaphysics? Derrida explicitly makes this point in 'Of an Apocalyptic Tone', with an oblique reference to

Heidegger's 'The Anaximander Fragment' (*TA* 61/*AT* 21), where the latter discusses the gathering (*die Versammlung, logos*) of Being at the outermost point (*eskaton*) of its essence, and writes, 'Being itself is inherently eschatological.'[50] However, if one can speak of a Heideggerian eschatology that would presuppose a unitary conception of the history of metaphysics, which, as has been shown, informs the Derridian concept of metaphysical closure, then is not Derrida also party to the eschatological contract? Must a break between Heidegger and Derrida not be situated at this point?

The exposition of such questions must be governed by the patience of the double or *clôtural* gesture. *On the one hand*, in Derrida's early work, as the quotation from his unpublished introduction to Husserl shows, he inherits a unitary Heideggerian notion of the history of metaphysics which has attained its closure, *Verendung* or *Vollendung*. Similar Heideggerian resonances with respect to the theme of the completion of metaphysics as technology can be found in *Voice and Phenomenon*, where Derrida discusses the epoch of phonocentrism as the technical mastery of the being-object (*l'être-objet*), which presupposes the unity of *technē* and *phonē* (*VP* 84/*SP* 75). In the 'Exergue' to *Of Grammatology*, Derrida discusses *the* history of metaphysics as a unitary logocentric epoch characterized by the determination of Being as presence and the reduction of the trace (*G* 11–13/*OG* 3–4). In the same work, Derrida discusses the 'époque de Rousseau', which occupies a pivotal place in a phonocentric epoch whose moments of antiquity and modernity are Plato's *Phaedrus* and Hegel's *Encyclopaedia* respectively (*G* 145–8/*OG* 97–100). *On the other hand*, although Heidegger, more effectively than any other thinker, delineates the closure of metaphysics and what remains unthought within that closure, Derrida critically interrogates certain crucial aspects of Heidegger's thinking: for example, his reductive reading of Nietzsche; the relations between the onto-theo-logical privilege of the present (*die Gegenwart*), the thought of Being as presence (*Anwesenheit*), and the written trace, or *grammē*; the residual humanism at work in the nearness of *Dasein* to Being, compounded through Heidegger's emphasis upon the proper (*eigen, eigentlich*), authenticity (*Eigentlichkeit*), and the appropriative event of the truth of Being (*das Ereignis*). More recently, Derrida has investigated the relation of ontological difference to sexual difference in Heidegger, the logocentric privilege of the metaphor of the hand as that which is 'proper to man', and the subordination of animality and writing to humanity and speech. Finally, in the context of *L'affaire Heidegger* Derrida has taken up the sensitive issue of Heidegger's politics by tracing the latter's ambivalent employment of the word *Geist* from *Being and Time*, through the 1933 Rectoral Address, to his 1953 essay on Trakl, 'Language in the Poem'.[51] Indeed, a certain distance from Heidegger's analysis of the history of metaphysics is already announced in 'La différance' in 1968, where Derrida argues that the thought of *différance* cannot be contained within the concepts of epoch and epochality, which always belong to history *qua* history of Being (*M* 23/*MP* 22). Is it then possible to understand the concept of closure as the disruption of any unified notion of epochality, the deconstruction of Heidegger's version of the history of metaphysics?

Pursuing the second path of this double gesture, in Derrida's later work any question of eschatological complicity with Heidegger would seem to disappear. Derrida's doubts about Heideggerian conceptions of metaphysics and the history of Being are theoretically set out in the 1980 paper 'Envoi', and performatively practised in the 'Envois' to *La carte postale*, a text whose very plurality ('Envois', not 'Envoi') grotesquely parodies Heidegger's history of Being, in which 'the original sending of Being as presence' (*die anfängliche Schickung von Sein als Anwesenheit*)[52] among the Greeks becomes increasingly obscured in the successive epochs of the history of Being. The nucleus of Derrida's deconstruction in these texts is 'the presumed unity of a history of metaphysics or of the West' (*l'unité présumée d'une histoire de la métaphysique ou de l'Occident*) (*EN* 25). What is being challenged by Derrida is the unilateralism of Heidegger's claim that there is a sending (*envoi*; *Schickung*) of Being from the Greeks through epochs of increasing oblivion, which is gathered into the destiny or destination of Being (*das Seins-Geschick*) at the end of philosophy.[53] The epoch of metaphysics is addressed by the Greeks, and destined for 'us'; the sending of Being is always assured of reaching its destination.

Derrida claims that the history of Being is a teleology (*EN* 24) or eschatology, and hence 'a postal idea' (*une idée postale*) (*CP* 205), where the letter or postcard that the sender (*envoyeur*) addresses is sure to reach its addressee (*destinataire*). In an 'envoi' dated 9 May 1979, Derrida writes:

I no longer know to whom I said that 'epoch' – which is why I question myself on this subject – remains, because of the resting place (*la halte*), a postal idea which is contaminated beforehand by *postal différance*. (*CP* 205)

The eschatology of the history of Being depends upon the postcard that Parmenides sends to Heidegger or Socrates sends to Freud not getting lost in the post. Derrida wonders how this eschatology can hold itself together and whether the sending of Being might not be threatened by a 'dissension' or 'dissemination' (*EN* 25) which would divert the destining and gathering (*Versammlung*) of Being and 'deconstruct' (*EN* 25) Heidegger's text. To the 'grande époque' of Being's oblivion, which divides and unites Parmenides and Heidegger, Derrida opposes a plurality of 'sous-époques' (*CP* 205). To the original 'Envoi' of Being, Derrida opposes a plurality of 'envois', inassemblable singularities, postcards, which are not assured of reaching their destination and which cannot be gathered into a unitary history (*Geschichte*) of the destining (*Geschick*) of Being. Thus, for Derrida, the eschatology of Being does not arrive at its end (*CP* 207) or achieve its apocalypse; rather, it is continually breached by a postal *différance*, which is older (*M* 23/*MP* 22) than ontological difference and is no longer capable of being represented as a unitary history.

In the concluding paragraph to 'Envoi', Derrida spells out the ultimate orientation of his thinking on this matter, spiralling back, once again, to the concept of closure.

Towards what, towards whom, towards where have I ceaselessly referred in the course of this introduction, in a way that is at once insistent and elliptical? I dare say towards sendings (*envois*) and towards returnings (*renvois*) which may no longer be representative. Beyond a closure of representation (*Au-delà d'une clôture de la représentation*) of which the form could no longer be linear, circular, encyclopaedic or totalizing, I have attempted to retrace an open way on a thinking of the sending which, in order to be, like the *Geschick des Seins* of which Heidegger speaks, of a structure still foreign to representation, did not yet even gather with itself as a sending of Being across *Anwesenheit*, presence and then representation. (*EN* 29)

It is towards this difficult thought of 'sendings' that would have the form neither of presence (*Anwesenheit*) nor of representation (*Vorstellung*) that Derrida is heading. The plurality of such sendings – postcards, voices, events – would construct a structure that is incapable of being structured, rather like the architectural thinking of Bernard Tschumi, a moment of which is frozen in Parc de la Villette in Paris.[54] 'Sendings' would be an infinite web or general text of singularities, of events that would be pre-ontological (*EN* 29) and incapable of being gathered into Being or represented as a unitary epoch possessing a sender, an address, and a destination. To approach this thought of 'sendings', Derrida says that one must think 'tout autrement' (*EN* 30), in a manner that cannot be presented or represented in terms of a closure of presence or representation. Sendings are a self-deferring, differing web of traces that do not originate in the self; they *do not* originate (*Tout commence par le renvoi, c'est à dire ne commence pas*) (*EN* 29) but arise from the other, from others (*des envois de l'autre, des autres*) (*EN* 25). It is towards the thought of this delicate web of sendings, or singular alterities, a general textuality that would be otherwise than Being, such as was discussed in the previous section, that Derrida is trying to make his way in his later work.

It would indeed seem to be at this moment of stepping beyond or beneath the history of Being, the project of eschatology, and the unity of the history of metaphysics that Derrida's break with Heidegger could be situated. There would seem to be a development from the historico-metaphysical epochality of closure that informs much of his early work to the deconstruction or interruption of epochality that is outlined in a paper like 'Envoi'. Is there, then, a development in Derrida's position here? Derrida I and Derrida II?

The response to this question must, once again, be governed by the double gesture or logic of closure. *On the one hand*, a notion of development can illuminate the discussion of the concept of closure; for although the word *clôture* appears with some regularity in the essays which open *Margins of Philosophy* (see, for example, 'La différance', 'Ousia and grammē', 'The Ends of Man', and 'Form and Meaning')[55] and which date from the late nineteen-sixties, *clôture* appears with much less frequency in the essays that conclude the book and which date from the early nineteen-seventies. The *terminological* use of closure, which dates essentially from 1966, does not survive long after the end of that decade. Might one not speculate that the disappearance of closure from Derrida's conceptual vocabulary reflects his growing distance from the Heideggerian conception of the history of metaphysics which underpins the concept of metaphysical closure? Might not the disappearance of closure be linked to Derrida's renunciation of the history of Being?

On the other hand, to adopt this hypothesis would be to go too far, for it would ignore Derrida's protestations against Paul Ricoeur in 'Le retrait de la métaphore', where he explicitly denies both that the concept of metaphysical closure ever entailed a unitary conception of metaphysics and that there was or is a 'common theoretical nucleus' (*noyau théorique commun*) to his own work and that of Heidegger.[56] It would also overlook the fact that although the word *clôture* disappears from Derrida's conceptual vocabulary, this does not entail that the *problem* of closure ceases to be central to Derrida's work. In a text like 'Tympan', which dates from 1972, the word *limite* appears to bear the same conceptual force as *clôture*. Similarly, in *Spurs*, which was originally given as a paper in 1972, the concept of *limite* usurps the place of *clôture* while the latter term does not appear in the text (*EP* 93–6). It would also be to ignore the fact that the ultimate orientation of texts like 'Envoi' or the 'Envois' is no different from that of Derrida's earlier work. The step beyond the closure towards a thinking that would be wholly other recalls the gesture of an early text like *Voice and Phenomenon*, where, in the closing pages, it is a question of going beyond the closure of Absolute Knowing towards 'the *unheard of* thoughts' (*des pensées* inouïes (*VP* 115/*SP* 102) that cannot be signified or represented. Or again, in *Of Grammatology*, Derrida points towards the glimmer of the *outre-clôture* (*G* 25/*OG* 14), which functions like a flaw in the fabric of logocentric closure. Finally, in a text like 'Ellipsis', which concludes *Writing and Difference*, it is precisely through the repetition of the closed epoch of the book that there awakens both *écriture* and the *outre-clôture* (*ED* 429/ *WD* 295).

What is one to decide here? Does one decide that the problem of closure, defined as the double movement of belonging and non-belonging, as the play of transgression and restoration, is specifically constituted as a subversion of the Heideggerian conception of metaphysics? Or should one decide that the problem of metaphysical closure shows the massive scale of Derrida's repetition of Heidegger?

For essential reasons that will become clearer below, it is not a question of deciding or choosing between these two alternatives. The way of reading that I call *clôtural* consists in the detection of the flaw in the well-rounded (*eukukleos*) epoch of metaphysics, the pursuit of the break in the circularity of the *logos* (*ED*398/*WD* 271). The problem of closure does not enclose the space of a unitary history and foreclose the possibility of transgression, but rather traces the double necessity and double impossibility of both belonging to a history whose closure can be delimited and not belonging to a history whose closure we are unable to leave. There is no exit within a repetition of the tradition, and there is no exit without that repetition. It is only through a ceaseless and massive repetition of Heidegger's thought that an ellipsis arises from which the other to Heidegger's thinking may be approached. The relations between Derrida and Heidegger need to be situated in the space between repetition and ellipsis, where the textual exigencies of a repetitive exegesis approach the necessity of thinking something wholly other. To adapt one of Levinas's remarks, one might say that Derrida's work is to a great extent inspired by Heidegger's philosophy, but is governed both by a profound need to leave the climate of that philosophy and the conviction that one cannot leave it for a philosophy that would be pre-Heideggerian *DEE* 19/*EE* 19). My claim is that it is precisely in the suspension of choice or decision between two alternatives, a suspension provoked in and through an act of reading, that the ethical dimension of deconstruction is opened and maintained.

2.6   *Clôtural* Reading

I should like to reformulate the notion of *clôtural* reading in the light of the analysis carried out in this chapter. The notion of *clôtural* reading has already been introduced and defined as the production of a dislocation within a text, dividing the latter along the inseparable yet irreconcilable axes of belonging and not belonging to the metaphysical or logocentric tradition. The *clôtural* structure of textuality is indicated by the transgression and restoration of closure, where both the transgression and the restoration are maintained in a non-symmetrical and non-totalizable relation, a relation in which the *relata* remain absolute. This *clôtural* structure is provoked by an act of *reading* whereby two irreconcilable lines of thought open up within a text. The *clôtural* reading has two moments which, because they are produced only within a particular reading, vary according to the text that is being read. However, without wishing to reduce the specificity of *clôtural* reading, the following general pattern can be delineated. First, the text is engaged in a repetition of its internal exigencies through an act of 'commentary'. Second, within and through this repetition, an ellipsis, or moment of alterity, opens up within the text which allows it to deliver itself up to a wholly other reading. It is of vital importance to emphasize that the moment of alterity, the ellipsis within the text, is glimpsed only by giving oneself up to textual repetition. The ellipsis is the space within repetition.

Clôtural reading is in-*fin*-ite – that is, without end, apocalypse, or *eschaton*. It is situated in relation to an epoch that is closed, whose conceptuality is suspended or exhausted, but whose duration is possibly infinite. The epoch of metaphysics, like a dying star, is at its point of exhaustion, a point from which, paradoxically, it swells like a red giant to extend its domination and comprehend all resistance, ethical, political, or otherwise. *Clôtural* reading is the interruption of this epoch, the infinite deferral of its enclosing power through the alternation of repetition and alterity. The reference to epochality is of crucial importance here, because I employ the neologism *clôtural* in order to circumvent any formalistic understanding of the notions of closure and deconstruction.[57] Deconstructive reading is not a game or a formal 'strategy'[58] of engaging a text in a play of *différance* and presence, of reversal and displacement, a play that goes on *sub specie aeternitatis*. To describe deconstructive reading in these terms is to say as little about Derrida's thought as when Hegelian or Marxist dialectic is explained in terms of thesis, antithesis, and synthesis. The word *clôtural* attempts to re-situate deconstructive reading in relation to the closure of the history of metaphysics. As Levinas points out, the historical moment when philosophy becomes suspect and the history of Western philosophy enters its closure is not just any moment.[59] The possibility of *clôtural* reading arises only in relation to a specific and completed historical configuration which it ceaselessly seeks to repeat and interrupt.

Before going on, in the next two chapters, to give two extended examples of *clôtural* readings in commentaries upon Derrida's 'At this very Moment in this Work here I am' and Levinas's texts on Derrida,

I shall conclude this chapter by giving a more schematic account
of the way in which such a reading works, by briefly considering
Derrida's *Voice and Phenomenon* and 'Violence and Metaphysics'.

In the first chapter of *Voice and Phenomenon*, after introducing
Husserl's 'essential distinction' between the expressive sign (*Ausdruck*)
and the indicative sign (*Anzeichen*) and before explaining how Husserl
has the right (*droit*) to make this distinction by retreating into 'the
solitary life of the soul' (*VP* 22/*SP* 22), Derrida marks a pause in his
analysis (*Marquons une pause*) (*VP* 23/*SP* 23). The time of this pause
is to be filled with the hypothesis of a double or *clôtural* reading:
'Indeed, the movement that we are going to comment upon gives
itself to two possible readings' (*VP* 23/*SP* 23). There are two possible
readings of the problem of the sign in Husserl: 'on the one hand'
(*D'une part*) (*VP* 23/*SP* 23), Husserl seems to repress the question
'What is a sign in general?' He does not speak of a generalized *Zeichen*,
but rather, with a simple movement of the finger (*doigt*, *Zeigefinger*)
(*VP* 24/*SP* 23), he feels that he has the right (*droit*) to ignore the
question of the general sign and divide its essence into expression
and indication. Derrida's claim is that the problem of the sign –
which forms the subtitle to *Voice and Phenomenon* – will be the place or
root (*lieu*, *racine*) (*VP* 24–5/*SP* 24) where the oppositions employed
in Husserlian phenomenology will show their appartenance to traditional metaphysics.

'On the other hand' (*D'autre part*) (*VP* 25/*SP* 24), Derrida asks, by
what right do we have access to a unified, generalized concept of
the sign? By asking 'What is a sign in general?', is one not making the
ontological presupposition that there is *an* essence and *a* truth to the
concept of the sign? If the latter could be shown, then this would
represent a classical philosophical step which would return the concept of the sign to the degenerate metaphysics of classical ontology,
the Parmenidean *ti esti* (*VP* 26/*SP* 25) which Husserl sought to overcome. Husserl's intention is rather to show how the pure linguistic
expression is itself the possibility of truth and Being; his finger points
to the distinction between expression and indication, and avoids a
generalized notion of the sign.

Derrida thus sketches the possibility of 'two readings' of Husserl,
which together seem to comprise 'the historical destiny of phenomenology' (*VP* 26/*SP* 25). (1) *Second reading*: this would view phenomenology as the reduction applied to naïve ontology and the critique of

degenerate metaphysics. After sketching this second reading, or 'movement', Derrida opens a provocative and difficult footnote:

> Movement of which one can diversely interpret the relation to classical metaphysics or ontology. A critique that would have determinate, limited, but certain affinities with that of Nietzsche or that of Bergson. In any case, the critique belongs to the unity of an historical configuration. (*VP* 27/*SP* 25)

The second movement of the Husserlian text, as a critique of degenerate metaphysics, belongs to a historical configuration whose other representatives are Bergson and Nietzsche. This configuration engages in the strategy of reversal by which degenerate metaphysics – the Platonic-Christian epoch – is overturned. If the strategy of reversal marks the second movement of the *clôtural* reading, then the transition to the first movement can be seen in the continuation of the footnote: namely, 'that which, in the historical configuration of these reversals, continues metaphysics, such is one of the most permanent themes of Heidegger's meditation' (*VP* 27/*SP* 25). Derrida invokes Heidegger[60] here to point out that the strategy of reversal, the critical inversion of degenerate metaphysics, is a continuation of the metaphysical project. If one moves from the footnote back to the sentence which the footnote interrupts, the transition to the first moment of reading is complete: 'an other necessity also confirms the classical metaphysics of presence and marks the belonging of phenomenology to classical ontology' (*VP* 27/*SP* 25–6).

(2) *First reading*: Husserlian phenomenology is shown to belong to the metaphysics that it sought to criticize. The strategy of the first moment of reading is one where Derrida employs Heideggerian resources in order to show Husserl's appartenance to the metaphysics of presence. Derrida then explicitly states that it is this first moment, this first reading, that he has *chosen* to follow in *Voice and Phenomenon*: 'It is with this belonging (*appartenance*) that we have *chosen* to interest ourselves' (*VP* 27/*SP* 26; my emphasis). Derrida raises the possibility of a *clôtural* reading of Husserl, which would show how phenomenology both transgresses and restores metaphysics, only to deny that possibility and pursue one half of a double reading. Although this position is in accord with the express intention of *Voice and Phenomenon* – namely, to find out whether phenomenological necessity

dissimulates a metaphysical presupposition (*VP* 2–3/*SP* 4) – the *clôtural* reading is left in suspension at the end of the first chapter by a *decision* or act of choice, in accordance with which Derrida feels he has the right (*droit*) only to point the finger (*doigt*) at Husserl the metaphysician.

Is *Voice and Phenomenon* not therefore a *clôtural* reading? To a great extent this is true; by making a choice, Derrida gives himself the right to engage in a one-sided critical reading of Husserl. Indeed, might this not explain Derrida's remarks on *Voice and Phenomenon* in *Positions*, where he states that 'in a classical philosophical architecture, *Voice and Phenomenon* would come in first place' (*P* 13/*POS* 5)? Might not *Voice and Phenomenon* fit into a classical, philosophical architecture precisely because it is a failed *clôtural* reading – in other words, a critique?

However, if the above suggestion is well founded, why should Derrida say, as he does in the same passage in *Positions*, that *Voice and Phenomenon* is 'perhaps the essay which I hold to the most' (*P* 13/*POS* 4)? Is Derrida simply trying to deceive his readers at this point; or, more interestingly, might there not be a more nuanced, *clôtural* pattern of reading than Derrida's act of choice would lead one to believe? Although it is not my direct concern in this context, I believe that it could be argued, in much the same way as Gasché argues for Derrida's '*complex* continuation'[61] of Husserl's project of a pure logical grammar, that *Voice and Phenomenon* performs a *clôtural* reading of Husserl. Two of the domains in which this double movement can be detected arise in the discussions of subjectivity[62] and temporality.[63]

In order to move on to a text where it is the act of choice that is suspended and not the *clôtural* reading, I shall briefly examine 'Violence and Metaphysics'. Derrida's pattern of reading here is similar to that adopted in his reading of Husserl. Levinas's text is inserted into the *space between a double metaphysics*. In *Totality and Infinity*, Levinas defines metaphysics as the desire for the absolutely other (*TeI* 3/*TI* 33). Derrida sees Levinas as inaugurating something 'new, quite new, a metaphysics of radical separation and exteriority' (*nouveau, si nouveau, une métaphysique de la séparation et de l'extériorité radicales*) (*ED* 132/*WD* 88). This new ethical metaphysics constitutes a transgression, or 'dislocation' (*ED* 122/*WD* 82) of classical ontology and of the Greek thinking of Being which Husserlian phenomenology and Heideggerian 'ontology' are ceaselessly doomed to repeat. On Derrida's reading, this new metaphysics seeks to found itself upon the datum, or evidence, of an experience that has been dissimulated by the Graeco-German tradition: namely, the encounter with the other person (*Autrui*), the buried nudity of experience that continually denies the attempts of the Greek *logos* to comprehend and reduce its radical alterity. On Derrida's reading, Levinas's ethical metaphysics is an empiricism whose primal datum is the face of the other person. Understood in this way, Levinasian metaphysics is a 'return to the things themselves' (*aux choses mêmes*) (*ED* 159/*WD* 107–8), a new *philosophia protē* which seeks to undermine phenomenology and ontology.

However – and here we approach the dominant gesture of 'Violence and Metaphysics' – the transgression of phenomenology and ontology that is effected by Levinas's empirical metaphysics in fact presupposes the very things that it seeks to transgress. As has been shown, for Derrida, Husserlian phenomenology is both a new *philosophia protē* which returns to the things themselves and a philosophy that remains dominated, in its principle of principles, by an ancient metaphysics of presence. Conceived as such, the Husserlian text is suspended between the authentic metaphysics it sought to promote and the degenerate metaphysics it sought to reject. Adopting a similar argument, Derrida claims that Levinas's metaphysical overcoming of transcendental phenomenology presupposes that which it seeks to overcome ('It is difficult to see how...Levinas can separate himself from Husserl' (*ED* 177–8/*WD* 121; cf. *ED* 195–6/*WD* 133)), which does not negate the legitimacy of the attempt, although it leaves the Levinasian text suspended and hesitant in the space between two metaphysics.

Derrida adopts a similar gesture with respect to Levinas's relation to Heidegger. Although Derrida is explicitly in accord with Levinas's profound need to leave the climate of Heidegger's thinking ('In question here is a need whose natural legitimacy we would be the last to contest' (*ED* 215/*WD* 145)), he claims that Levinasian ethico-metaphysical transcendence presupposes fundamental ontological transcendence, and that 'Levinas confirms Heidegger in his purpose' (*ED* 209/*WD* 142). *A propos* Heidegger, then, Levinas's text is suspended between ontology and its ethical transgression, hence *within* the ontico-ontological difference.

There are several objections which, I believe, can be justifiably raised and maintained against certain elements of 'Violence and Metaphysics'. Indeed, many of the questions that Derrida asks seem to take the form of objections against Levinas.[64] However, my direct concern in this context is to delineate the *clôtural* pattern of Derrida's essay. A clue to the latter might be found in the distinction between 'two origins' (*ED* 124/*WD* 82) and two historical configurations that Derrida establishes in the opening pages of the essay: (1) the Greek *logos*, whose conceptual totality encloses the field within which philosophy is possible, a field within which Hegel, Husserl, and Heidegger tirelessly labour; (2) non-philosophy, as the attempt to escape the nets of the Greek *logos*. On Derrida's reading, Levinas attempts to escape Greek logocentrism through recourse to a Hebraic origin and a messianic eschatology which are opened from within an experience of alterity which the Greek philosophical tradition can neither reduce nor comprehend.

Although Derrida is respectful of the autonomy of each origin, his claim in 'Violence and Metaphysics' is that the only conceptual language available is that of the Greek *logos*. The attempt to articulate conceptually an experience that has been forgotten or exiled from philosophy can only be stated within philosophical conceptuality, which entails that the experience succumbs to and is destroyed by philosophy. This is the *necessity* that echoes throughout Derrida's essay (cf. *ED* 226/*WD* 152): the necessity of lodging oneself within philosophical conceptuality in order to destroy it (*ED* 165/*WD* 112), the necessity of being destroyed by philosophical conceptuality – a double necessity. 'Violence and Metaphysics' is suspended between these two origins in such a way as to maintain the dialogue between the Jew and the Greek and which postpones the *decision* of choosing between them.[65]

It is into the 'hollow space' (*creux*) (*ED* 124 and 152/*WD* 83 and 103) between the two origins that Derrida wishes to insert his reading, a reading that is *clôtural* to the extent that it seeks to locate Levinasian ethics between these two points of tension, by showing how the opening beyond the totality of the Greek *logos* in fact restores and repeats its internal exigencies ('It is this space of interrogation that we have *chosen* for a very partial reading of Levinas's work' (*ED* 124/*WD* 84; my emphasis)). This space of interrogation contains two gestures: first, the fidelity of commentary ('First of all, in the style of commentary, we would like to be faithful to the themes and audacities of a thinking' (*ED* 124–5/*WD* 84)). This fidelity, which encloses a perplexity (*ED* 125/*WD* 84), seeks to repeat the text. This task is carried out in the first two sections of the essay: 'Violence de la lumière' and 'Phénoménologie, ontologie, métaphysique'. Through the repetition of a 'commentary', the second gesture opens up, and Derrida's perplexity is disclosed ('Then we will attempt to pose some questions' (*ED* 125/*WD* 84)). These questions will be raised in the three sections of 'Différence et eschatologie', where Derrida stresses Levinas's appartenance to the Greek *logos* through a discussion of Hegel, Kierkegaard, Heidegger, and Husserl.

In contradistinction to *Voice and Phenomenon*, the 'two possible readings' that comprise the double gesture are both schematized and performed in 'Violence and Metaphysics', rendering it a 'successful' *clôtural* reading. Such 'success' is conditional upon the suspension of choice; Derrida insists 'We will not choose' (*Nous ne choisirons pas*) (*ED* 125/*WD* 84), and again, 'We will not choose between the opening and the totality' (*Nous ne choisirons pas entre l'ouverture et la totalité*) (*ED* 125/*WD* 84). *Clôtural* reading must not choose between the ethical opening and the logocentric totality; it must be undecided; it must be hesitant; it must become 'the philosophy of this hesitation' (*la philosophie de cette hésitation*) (*ED* 125/*WD* 84).

Can one choose not to choose? Does not a choice secretly announce itself within the suspension of choice? Derrida does not wish to explore the space of messianic eschatology that opens within experience; he merely wishes to indicate it (*ED* 124/*WD* 84), to point it out, like Cortez before the Pacific Ocean. At the limit of philosophical language, Derrida points towards a non-philosophical space which he has *decided not to decide* to explore. Consequently, his work is poised at the limit of logocentric language, looking across into the silence that exceeds metaphysical closure.

Or does a decision silently announce itself within Derrida's indecision? In the dialogue between philosophy and non-philosophy, does an unheard-of space silently announce itself within the *clôtural* reading as the common root of Hellenism and Hebraism? Such questions open up the ultimate horizon of 'Violence and metaphysics', a horizon upon which the status of the question must itself be decided. The space of interrogation becomes a space in which interrogation itself is interrogated. The question that introduces Derrida's essay is the question of the possibility of the question, (*ED* 118/*WD* 80)[66] a possibility that would be prior to questioning, a space that is indicated through interrogation but in which something other than interrogation is announced. What is silently announced in this space, as its possibility? Derrida responds: 'A dignity and an unbreachable (*inentamable*) duty of decision. An unbreachable responsibility' (*ED* 118/*WD* 80). Within this space, as this possibility, a decision is made about a duty, a dignity and a responsibility that cannot be breached, broken, or interrupted, but which breaches, breaks, and interrupts the totality and the ontology of the question ('What is x?'). Within the indecision and hesitancy of the *clôtural* reading, the unbreachable priority of a decision announces itself. Within the passivity of repetition and ellipsis, traversing the space that separates commentary from interpretation, an 'injunction' (*ED* 119/*WD* 80) is opened and a responsibility is maintained.

An ethical responsibility? An ethical injunction? An ethical decision? Of course, the question of the possibility of the question does not belong to the domain of the ethical, traditionally understood. Derrida points out that the ethical domain, with its laws and commandments, dissimulates the question of the possibility of the question (*ED* 119/*WD* 80). Such a possibility would be precisely 'ultra-ethical' in the manner discussed in chapter 1. For Derrida, this decision, which is 'almost nothing' (*presque rien*) (*ED* 118/*WD* 80) is the only possibility which is capable of founding a *community*, a community of decision, a dignified and responsible community:

> A community of the question, therefore, within that fragile moment when the question is not yet determined enough for the hypocrisy of an answer to have already initiated itself beneath the mask of the question, and not yet determined enough for its voice to have been already and fraudulently articulated within the very syntax of the question. A community of decision, of initiative, of absolute initiality, but also a threatened community, in which the question has not yet found the language it has decided to seek, is not yet sure of its own possibility within the community. A community of the question of the possibility of the question. This is very little – almost nothing. (*ED* 118/*WD* 80)

What is this community? A community of the question of the possibility of the question would not be a philosophical community, a Hellenistic *polis* of light like Athens, Sparta, Rome, Florence, or

Geneva. What, then? Perhaps only the promise of a community, a promise which speaks silently within philosophical discourse as its muted other. A promise of community prior to the question which opens philosophy, a promise of community and of a land promised for that community.

Is this all that the discussion of the ethics of deconstruction promises? The glimpse of a land promised for a community of responsibility? I cannot promise to answer these questions definitively, save to say that the question of the possibility of the question and its relation to community and politics will be the central concern of the final chapter of the book. However, it should be noted how the shadow of this promise haunts the path of the *clôtural* reading like Banquo's ghost, the bloodless spectre who recalls us to death, to the death of philosophy, to death as the non-philosophical horizon towards whose meaning we wander. To see the promised land and die? Perhaps.

NOTES

1 I would like to thank Dominique Janicaud for providing the original idea of working on the concept of metaphysical closure and John Llewelyn for his extremely helpful remarks on the word *clôture* in Derrida.

2 For an extensive, thorough account of the risks involved in any philosophical writing on Derrida's work, with particular attention to the question of context, see Geoffrey Bennington, 'Deconstruction and the Philosophers (The Very Idea)', *Oxford Literary Review*, 10 (1988), pp. 73–130.

3 I owe the following formulations in part to David Hult's 'Editor's Preface' in *Concepts of Closure*, Yale French Studies, no. 67, ed. D. F. Hult (Yale University Press, New Haven and London, 1984).

4 Cf. Glossary to *The Works of Geoffrey Chaucer*, ed. F. N. Robinson (Oxford University Press, Oxford, 1957).

5 Cf. *A Concise Etymological Dictionary of Modern English*, ed. Ernest Weekly (Secker and Warburg, London, 1952).

6 Littré, *Dictionnaire de la langue française*, Tome 2 (Gallimard/Hachette, Paris, 1963), p. 406.

7 Ibid. p. 407.

8 *Dictionnaire du français contemporain* (Larousse, Paris, 1966), p. 251.

9   Littré, p. 406.

10 Ibid.

11 Etymologically, *clôture* derives from the vulgar Latin *clausitura* and *clausura*, which ultimately derive from the verbs *claudere* and *claudo* which mean to close, envelop, or conclude, and thus have a very similar sense to the French verbs *clore* and *clôturer*. The nearest equivalent to the substantive *clôture* in Latin is *claustrum*, which denotes a boundary or confining space (as in claustrophobia). The nearest German equivalent is *Schließung*, with the verb *schließen* broadly resembling the Latin *claudere* (cf. S. Grimm, *Deutsches-Wörterbuch* (Hirzel; Leipzig, 1899)), although, as I discuss below, this is not the only plausible German equivalent. The word *clôture* might be translated in Greek by *peras*, which means end, extremity, issue, or accomplishment. Indeed, Derrida's 1966 Introduction to Husserl, 'La phénoménologie et la clôture de la métaphysique', appeared in the Greek journal *Epochēs* under the title 'Phainomenologia kai to peras tēs metaphusikēs', the word *peras* translating *clôture*.

12 The paper was originally given on 31 July 1959. However, when the text appeared in *Entretiens sur les notions de Genèse et de Structure*, ed. M. de Gandillac, L. Goldmann, and J. Piaget (Mouton & Co., Paris and The Hague, 1965), pp. 243–60 (hereafter *GS*), the discussion which followed Derrida's paper was included (*GS* 261–8), and a note was added, which stated that 'M. Derrida, qui a revu et complété son texte, a ajouté un certain nombre de notes explicatives et de références' (*GS* 243). In fact, this is something of an understatement, for it is clear that the text was extensively revised between 1959 and 1965. In virtue of the many resonances and similarities with the idioms, turns of phrase, and arguments of the 1964 essay 'Violence et métaphysique', I would suggest that the revision of 'Genèse et structure' is either contemporaneous with or immediately subsequent to the 1964 essay. This would also explain why, when the essay appeared in *ED*, it was placed *after* 'Violence et métaphysique' as the fifth essay in the volume. If 'Genèse et structure' were Derrida's first essay, it would appear in the premier place in the chronological sequence of the book. When the text was reprinted in *ED* in 1967, Derrida made a number of additions and a deletion: '*différence*' (*GS* 251) was changed to '*différance*' (*ED* 239/*WD* 161), 'Présence' (*GS* 253) to 'l'étrange *présence*' (*ED* 242/*WD* 162), and long passages based on the advances which Derrida had made in his research on Husserl around the time of *VP* were added at *ED* 244/*WD* 164 (cf. *GS* 255), *ED* 248/*WD* 166 (cf. *GS* 258), and *ED* 249/*WD* 166 (cf. *GS* 258). Crucial to the understanding of Derrida's relation to Husserl is Derrida's thesis on Husserl of 1953–4, published in 1990 as *Le Problème*

de la genèse dans la philosophie de Husserl (Presses Universitaires de France, Paris, 1990), which appeared only after the writing of this chapter was completed.

13 This point is brought out by Peter Dews in his *Logics of Disintegration* (Verso, London and New York, 1987), p. 6.

14 Cf. *Husserliana*, Gesammelte Werke, vol. 6 (Martinus Nijhoff, The Hague, 1976), pp. 378–9.

15 Cf. 'Origin of Geometry', in The *Crisis of European Sciences and Transcendental Phenomenology*, tr. David Carr (Northwestern University Press, Evanston, 1970), p. 369.

16 Ibid., p. 370.

17 Cf. Kant, *Critique of Pure Reason*, tr. Norman Kemp Smith (Macmillan, London and Basingstoke, 1929), p. 19.

18 Suzanne Bachelard, *La Logique de Husserl: Etude sur logique formelle et logique transcendentale* (P.U.F., Paris, 1957); tr. Lester E. Embree as *A Study of Husserl's Formal and Transcendental Logic* (Northwestern University Press, Evanston, 1963). All page references are to the translation. Derrida refers in particular to Pt 1, ch. 3, 'Theory of Deductive Systems and Theory of Multiplicities', pp. 43–63.

19 From Hilbert 'Über den Zahlbegriff', cited in Bachelard, *A Study of Husserl's Formal and Transcendental Logic*, pp. 60–1.

20 Bachelard, *Study*, p. 51.

21 From Husserl, *Krisis*, cited in OG 141.

22 D 248–9; tr. Barbara Johnson as *Dissemination* (University of Chicago Press, Chicago and London, 1981), p. 219.

23 Kurt Gödel, 'Über formal-unentschiedbare Sätze des *Principia Mathematica* und verwandter Systeme', *Monatschr. Math. Phys.* 38 (1931), pp. 173–98. For an illuminating discussion of Gödel's theorem, see Douglas Hofstadter, *Gödel, Escher, Bach: An Eternal Golden Braid* (Penguin, Harmondsworth, 1979), pp. 16–19, 438–60.

24 Cf. 'The Double Session', D199–318. In *The Tain of the Mirror. Derrida and the Philosophy of Reflection* (Harvard University Press, Cambridge, Mass., and London, 1986), pp. 201–318, Gasché classifies the 'infrastructures' (archē-trace, *différance*, supplement, iteration, and re-mark) as undecidables, and writes: 'I shall continue to speak of the infrastructures as syntactically undecidable' (p. 244).

25 Cf. Husserl, 'Philosophy as a Rigorous Science', in *Phenomenology and the Crisis of Philosophy*, tr. Quentin Lauer (Harper and Row, New York, 1965), pp. 71–147.

26 For a discussion of conditions of possibility and impossibility in Derrida, see Gasché, 'Beyond Reflection: The Interlacings of Heterology', in *Tain of the Mirror*, pp. 79–105.

27 In the first version of 'Violence et métaphysique', Derrida also employs the verb 'déclôt' (*RMM* 462, *ED* 213/*WD* 144), which translates Heidegger's *erschließen*. One should note the reference to closure (*Schließung*) contained in Heidegger's *Erschlossenheit* ('disclosure') and *Entschlossenheit* ('resoluteness').

28 Viz. *ED* 249/*WD* 166; *VP* 4/*SP* 5; *M* 187/*MP* 157; and *PC* 2.

29 Husserl, *Cartesian Meditations*, tr. Dorion Cairns (Martinus Nijhoff, The Hague, 1969), p. 13.

30 Ibid., p. 144.

31 Ibid., p. 139.

32 Ibid., p. 6.

33 Certain of the formulations of this essay are repeated in the Introduction to *VP*. Cf. *PC* 1–3 and *VP* 3–4/*SP* 4–5.

34 Derrida, 'Le retrait de la métaphore', *Analecta Husserliana*, 14 (1985), pp. 273–300.

35 Ibid., p. 281. For similar remarks on the form of metaphysical closure, cf. *M* xx–xxi and 206/*MP* xxiv–xxv and 172; *P* 77/*POS* 56–7. See also *Entretiens avec 'Le Monde'*. *1. Philosophies* (Editions la Découverte, Paris, 1984), p. 81; and Richard Kearney, *Dialogues with Contemporary Continental Thinkers* (Manchester University Press, Manchester, 1984), p. 111.

36 Hegel, *Vorlesungen über die Asthetik 1, Werke*, vol. 13 (Suhrkamp Verlag, Frankfurt am Main, 1970), pp. 42–3; tr. T. M. Knox as *Aesthetics. Lectures on Fine Art* (Oxford University Press, London, 1975), vol. 1, p. 24. See also idem *Grundlinien der Philosophie des Rechts* (Ullstein Verlag, Frankfurt, 1972), p. 17; tr. T. M. Knox as *Philosophy of Right*, (Oxford University Press, Oxford, 1952), p. 225 and *Enzyklopädie der Philosophischen Wissenschaften im Grundrisse* (1827) (Meiner Verlag, Hamburg, 1989), p. 41; tr. W. Wallace as *Hegel's Logic* (Oxford University Press, Oxford, 1975), p. 20. On the circle metaphor in Hegel, see *TP* 23–9; and, for an interesting discussion of the metaphor of the circle in Hegel and Heidegger, Dennis J. Schmidt, 'Beginnings, Origins, Circles and Spirals' in *The Ubiquity of the Finite. Hegel, Heidegger and the Entitlements of Philosophy* (MIT Press, Cambridge, Mass., 1988), pp. 96–124.

37 For an example of *ikhnos* in Plotinus, see 'On the Beautiful' (*Peri toi kalon*), in *Enneades 1*, tr. Emile Bréhier (Société d'Edition 'Les Belles Lettres', Paris, 1924), p. 98. On Levinas's explicit use of the Plotinian *ikhnos* as a model for his concept of the trace and its relation to Derrida, see Robert Bernasconi 'The Trace of Levinas in Derrida', in *Derrida and Différance*, ed. D. Wood and R. Bernasconi (Parousia Press, Coventry, 1985), pp. 32–4. For a more general discussion of the relation of Neoplatonism to the overcoming of metaphysical language, see Reiner

Schürmann, 'Neoplatonic Henology as an Overcoming of Metaphysics', in *Research in Phenomenology*, 13 (1983), pp. 25–41.

38 Derrida employs this formulation in 'La différance', while relating the thought of the trace to the closure of Saussurian linguistics: 'I have attempted to indicate the way out of the closure of this schema through the trace' (*M* 12/*MP* 12).

39 Such a view is argued for by Eugenio Donato, in 'Ending/Closure: On Derrida's Edging of Heidegger', in *Concepts of Closure*, pp. 3–22. Donato writes: 'Clearly Derrida's project is to rewrite the "history" of philosophy as it is proposed by Heidegger' (p. 12). 'Derrida's *closure* is a reading and a displacement of the Heideggerian notion of end' (ibid.).

40 An extended analysis of Heidegger's reading of Nietzsche is given by Derrida in *EP* 59–102. See also 'Interpreting Signatures (Nietzsche/ Heidegger): Two Questions', in *Dialogue and Deconstruction. The Gadamer–Derrida Encounter*, ed. D. Michelfelder and R. Palmer (State University of New York Press, Albany, 1989), pp. 58–71.

41 Cf. Heidegger, 'Überwindung der Metaphysik', in *Vorträge und Aufsätze* (Neske, Pfullingen, 1952), hereafter *VA*, Pt 1, p. 63; tr. Joan Stambaugh in *The End of Philosophy* (Harper and Row, New York, 1973), hereafter EOP, p. 84.

42 Heidegger, *Zur Sache des Denkens* (Niemeyer, Tübingen, 1976), hereafter *SD*, p. 62; tr. in *Basic Writings*, ed. D. F. Krell (Routledge and Kegan Paul, London and Henley, 1978), hereafter *BW*, p. 374.

43 Michel Haar, 'Le tournant de la détresse', *Cahiers de l'Herne. Heidegger*, Livre de Poche edition (Editions de l'Herne, Paris, 1983), pp. 331–58.

44 One might perhaps even speak of completion as the *end of the end of* metaphysics (I shall return to this theme below). In an essay entitled 'La fin de la fin de la métaphysique', *Laval Théologique et Philosophique*, 42, no. 1 (February 1986), pp. 23–33, Jean-Luc Marion reassesses the concept of the end of philosophy at work in Heidegger in light of a discussion of the *Vollendung* of metaphysics in Heidegger's 'The End of Philosophy and the Task of Thinking'. Marion concludes that the end of philosophy understood as completion (*l'achèvement*) does not entail the death of philosophy, but can rather be said to give rise to the notion of the end of the end of metaphysics. The latter notion connotes the possibility of a continuation of the metaphysical project which is more faithful to Heidegger's analysis than the apocalyptic absence of continuation suggested by the end of philosophy.

Broadly speaking, Marion agrees with Heidegger in *Zeit und Sein* (*SD* 4–6 *On Time and Being*, pp. 4–6) that Being must be thought from the perspective of the gift, or donation, of the *es gibt*; but he goes on to develop the provocative thesis that the giving of this gift is the act of charity. For Marion, in addition to Being, there is a 'second impensé de la métaphysique' (p. 32) – namely, love or charity. He claims that it is *love* that is the unthought of the tradition. The end of the end of metaphysics, therefore, would be the movement from the love of wisdom to the wisdom of love. 'La ruine de la philo*sophie* dégage au contraire l'énigme en elle de la *philo*sophie' (pp. 32–3). Marion's thesis has a marked similarity to Levinas's redefinition of philosophy in *Otherwise than Being*: 'Philosophy – wisdom of love at the service of love' (*La philosophie – sagesse de l'amour au service de l'amour*) (*AE* 207/*OB* 162). I return to Levinas's redefinition of philosophy in chapter 5.

On Marion's proximity to Levinas (and *vice versa*), see the fascinating debate between Levinas, Marion, and Lyotard in *Autrement que Savoir* (Osiris, Paris, 1987), pp. 66–95, esp. pp. 74–6, 78–88. For a concise and more general account of Marion's thought, see 'De la "mort de Dieu" aux noms divins: l'itinéraire théologique de la métaphysique', *Laval Théologique et Philosophique*, 41, no. 1 (February 1985), pp. 25–41.

45   R. Bernasconi, 'Levinas and Derrida: The Question of the Closure of Metaphysics', in *FF* 183.

46   Ibid., p. 199.

47   Vincent Descombes, *Le Même et l'autre* (Minuit, Paris, 1979), p. 161.

48   Ibid.

49   Or, to quote the whole passage: 'But metaphysics is powerless to think difference in itself, and the importance of what separates as much as what unifies (the differentiating). There is neither synthesis, mediation nor reconciliation in difference, but on the contrary a destination in differentiation. Such is the turning beyond metaphysics' (Gilles Deleuze, *Différence et répétition* Presses Universitaires de France, Paris, 1968), p. 90.

I am indebted to Dominique Janicaud for this point, Cf. Janicaud, 'Dépasser la métaphysique' and 'Heideggeriana', in *La métaphysique à la limite* (Presses Universitaires de France, Paris, 1983), pp. 11–24, 25–47, esp. p. 25.

50   Cf. 'Der Spruch des Anaximander', in *Holzwege*, 6th edn (Klostermann, Frankfurt, 1980), p. 323; tr. D. F. Krell and F. A. Capuzzi as *Early Greek Thinking*, (Harper and Row, San Francisco, 1975), p. 18. See also *ED* 213/*WD* 144 *et passim*, where Derrida proposes an extraordinary *rapprochement* of Heideggerian and Levinasian eschatologies, which, of course, raises the question of whether Derrida's criticisms of eschatology and apocalypse would extend to and include Levinas: 'The proximity of two "eschatologies", which, by opposed routes, repeat and place in question the entire "philosophical" adventure that issued from Platonism' (*ED* 221/*WD* 149). Of course, on Derrida's interpretation

of Heidegger, it is a moot point to what extent and in what sense Heidegger's conception of metaphysics is unitary. I refer the reader to Robert Bernasconi, *The Question of Language in Heidegger's History of Being* (Humanities Press, Atlantic Highlands, N.J., 1985), where, while admitting a unity to the Heideggerian conception of metaphysics, he carefully defines this, in contradistinction to Hegel's conception of the history of philosophy, as 'the persistence of a concealed beginning' (p. 11), and not in terms of totality.

51 See respectively, 'L'être écrit' (*G* 31–41/*OG* 18–26); *EP*; 'Ousia et grammē', 'Les fins de l'homme' (*M* 31–78/*MP* 29–67); (*M* 129–64/*MP* 109–36); 'Geschlecht. Différence sexuelle, différence ontologique', in *Cahiers de l'Herne. Heidegger*, pp. 571–95; 'Geschlecht II: Heidegger's Hand', tr. John P. Leavey Jr., in *Deconstruction and Philosophy*, ed. J. Sallis (University of Chicago Press, Chicago and London, 1987), pp. 161–96; and *E*.

52 Heidegger, *Zeit und Sein*, p. 9: *On Time and Being*, p. 9.

53 In this critique of Heidegger, Derrida finds an unlikely ally in Gadamer, who, despite strong reservations about Derrida's work (see above, chapter 1, note 6), agrees with him on the question of the unilateralism implicit in Heidegger's reading of the history of metaphysics in terms of *Seinsvergessenheit*. In an interview with 'Le Monde' in 1981, Gadamer says:

> Nevertheless, there is a point on which I distance myself from Heidegger. It seems to me that his interpretation of the Greek heritage is too unilateral. It is certain that nobody has shown better than Heidegger up to what point our Western culture is enrooted in Greek thinking. But his conception of the forgottenness of Being (*Seinsvergessenheit*), beginning with Plato and leading to the epoch of planetary technology, appears too exclusive to me. In my view, Heidegger fails to recognize that the forgottenness of Being goes together with a constant effort at the remembrance of Being (*Seinserinnerung*) that traverses the entirety of Platonism; all mystical thinking is an illustration of this, even including that which is connected with the latter in modern thinking. (*Entretiens avec 'Le Monde'*, p. 238)

54 Cf. 'Point de folie – Maintenant l'architecture', *A. A. Files*, Annals of the Architectural Association School of Architecture, no. 12 (London, 1986), pp. 65–75.

55 The word *clôture* appears in *M* at xx, 12, 17, 24, 58, 73, 75 (twice), 76, 93, 147, 153, 162, 179, 184, 202, 206 (twice), 211 (twice) 324.

56 Derrida, 'Le retrait de la métaphore', pp. 281, 279.

57 An example of such a formalistic understanding of the concept of

closure can be seen in Robert Platt, 'Writing, *Différance* and Metaphysical Closure', *Journal of the British Society for Phenomenology*, 17, no. 3 (October 1986), pp. 234–51. For example, 'Closure, in this view, is the eternal recurrence of opening and closing…The eternal opening and closing of metaphysics may be recognized, in just one way, as the interpenetration, the mutual appropriation, of *différance* and presencing' (p. 250).

58   That Derrida recognizes the over-valorization of the word 'strategy' in discussions of deconstruction, something for which he is partly culpable, is made clear in his 1980 thesis defence, where he unites:

> You have heard too much talk of strategies. Strategy is a word that I have perhaps abused in the past, especially as it has been always only to specify *in the end*, in an apparently self-contradictory manner, and at the risk of cutting the ground from under my own feet – something I almost never fail to do – that this strategy is a strategy without any finality; for this is what I hold and what in turn holds me in its grip, the aleatory strategy of someone who admits that he does not know where he is going. (II 50)

59   'Le moment où, dans l'histoire spirituelle de l'Occident la philosophie devient suspect n'est pas quelconque' (*DQVI* 126).

60   Here, as elsewhere in *VP/SP* (cf. *VP* 68, 82–3n., 93/*SP* 61, 74n., 83), the proper name of Heidegger functions as the hinge around which the possibility of the double, or *clôtural*, reading articulates itself. Each mention of Heidegger is a pause or ellipsis in the analysis, from which the ultimate orientation of Derrida's reading can be discerned.

61   *Tain of the Mirror*, pp. 245–51.

62   I would claim that *VP/SP* is profoundly two-faced. In 'La voix qui garde le silence' (*VP* 78–97/*SP* 70–87), Derrida employs the concept of auto-affection – after Heidegger's *Kant and the Problem of Metaphysics* (*VP* 93/*SP* 83) – in order to produce a double effect. First, Husserl privileges an auto-affective and metaphysically determined notion of the voice which falls prey to 'the traditional phonologism of metaphysics' (*VP* 90/*SP* 88); for Derrida, such would be 'the traditional face or side (*face*) of Husserlian discourse' (*VP* 91/*SP* 81). Second, a different aspect of Husserl's face appears, one which was 'tormented and contested from within' (*VP* 92/*SP* 82) and which doubted the security of 'these traditional distinctions' (*VP* 92 *SP* 82). This recognition leads Derrida to focus on the other side of Husserl's face, the side on which auto-affection opens up onto the movement of *différance* as the ground for the constitution of transcendental subjectivity.

In an important and difficult footnote (which Derrida has recently referred back to in a note to ' "Il faut bien manger" ou le calcul du sujet. Entretien (avec J.-L. Nancy)', in *Après le sujet qui vient, Cahiers Confrontation*, 20 (winter 1989), p. 114, n. 2), Derrida alludes to para. 36 of Husserl's lectures, *Phenomenology of Internal Time-Consciousness* (Martinus Nijhoff, The Hague, 1964), p. 100 (cf. *VP* 94n./*SP* 84n.), where it is claimed that the 'absolute properties' of what is metaphorically named the 'temporally constitutive flux' do not produce 'absolute subjectivity'; rather, when time is considered from the perspective of *différance*, this subjectivity becomes deconstituted.

63 To what extent does Husserlian phenomenology transgress the 'vulgar' Aristotelian concept of time? In 'Le signe et le clin d'oeil' (*VP* 67–77/*SP* 60–9), Derrida approaches one of the governing intentions of *VP*: if philosophical discourse is predicated upon the privilege of presence, then the presence of the present is itself thought from the 'fold of return' (*pli du retour*) (*VP* 76/*SP* 68) of retention and representation, and ultimately from the viewpoint of the trace. The primordiality of presence is folded back into the trace of the movement of *différance*, which is 'older than presence and procures for it its opening' (*VP* 76/*SP* 68).

But who is naming 'trace' and '*différance*' here? The important issue, which can only be sketched in this context, is whether these concepts are derived from a radicalization of Husserlian textuality or whether they are of Derrida's invention. If the parasitism of Derrida's readings is to be at all seriously considered, then I believe that the first of these options must be fully explored. Derrida's novelty as a thinker does not consist in what 'he' thinks — which makes 'his' work so unnerving for philosophers who wish to summarize his thinking or reduce his readings to a set of claims that can then be refuted — but rather in the radicality of the readings undertaken and the transformation that occurs within the texts that he reads.

A possible avenue of exploration with respect to Derrida's reading of Husserl would be to see whether the latter's analysis of temporality is transgressive of the metaphysical (i.e. Aristotelian) concept of time and whether Husserl's analysis of time-consciousness (*Zeitbewußtsein*) prepares the way for the Heideggerian breakthrough in the thinking of temporality in *Sein und Zeit* — an avenue simultaneously opened and closed off by Derrida in a brief remark (*VP* 68/*SP* 61). Heidegger writes: 'So far as anything essential has been achieved in today's analyses which will take us beyond Aristotle and Kant, it pertains more to the way in which time is grasped and to our "consciousness of time" (*Zeitbewußtsein*)' (*Sein und Zeit*, p. 501). This passage appears in one of the final footnotes of *Sein und Zeit*, a footnote to which Derrida devotes his 1968 essay 'Ousia et grammē. Note sur une note de *Sein und Zeit*' (*M*

31–78/*MP* 29–67) and in which, to my knowledge, Husserl's name *does not appear.*

64   I do not wish to claim that 'Violence and Metaphysics' is directed *against* Levinas, or that the essay is a *critique* of Levinasian 'ethics'. What is required is a more nuanced and parasitic reading, such as has been outlined in a number of Bernasconi's essays (see above, chaper 1, note 7). However, as I shall argue in the next chapter, many of the propositions of 'Violence and Metaphysics' are advanced upon Derrida's avoidance of the notion of pluralism, to which he confesses himself 'totally deaf' (*totalement sourd*) (*ED* 186/*WD* 127) and which, I would suggest, along with the other analyses contained in 'Beyond the Face' (*TeI* 232–61/*TI* 251–85), hold the key to an understanding of Levinas's project in *TeI*/*TI*.

65   Interestingly, Derrida returns to this distinction between the Jew and the Greek in the conclusion to 'The Politics of Friendship', *Journal of Philosophy*, 85, no. 11 (January 1988), pp. 632–44, where he compares the 'Greco-Roman' (p. 644) and 'Judeo-Christian' (p. 644) concepts of friendship.

66   Derrida employs the same formulation in the concluding lines of ' "Genèse et structure" et la phénoménologie', with reference to the question of the possibility of the transcendental reduction in Husserl: 'Elle est la question de la possibilité de la question' (*ED* 251/*WD* 167). As discussed above (note 12), the two texts were probably written during the same period.

3

Clôtural Readings I: 'Bois' –
Derrida's Final Word on Levinas

10 And the servant took ten camels of the camels of his master, and departed; for all the goods of his master were in his hand: and he arose, and went to Mesopotamia, unto the city of Nahor.

11 And he made his camels to kneel down without the city by a well of water at the time of the evening, *even* the time that women go out to draw *water*.

12 And he said, O LORD God of my master Abraham, I pray thee, send me good speed this day, and shew kindness unto my master Abraham.

13 Behold, I stand *here* by the well of water; and the daughters of the men of the city come out to draw water:

14 And let it come to pass, that the damsel to whom I shall say, Let down thy pitcher, I pray thee, that I may drink; and she shall say, Drink, and I will give thy camels drink also: *let the same be* she *that* thou hast appointed for thy servant Isaac; and thereby shall I know that thou hast shewed kindness unto my master.

15 And it came to pass, before he had done speaking, that, behold, Rebekah came out, who was born to Bethuel, son of Milcah, the wife of Nahor, Abraham's brother, with her pitcher upon her shoulder.

16 And the damsel *was* very fair to look upon, a virgin, neither had any man known her: and she went down to the well, and filled her pitcher, and came up.

17 And the servant ran to meet her, and said, Let me, I pray thee, drink a little water of thy pitcher.

18 And she said, Drink, my lord: and she hasted, and let down her pitcher upon her hand, and gave him drink.

19 And when she had done giving him drink, she said, I will draw *water* for thy camels also, until they have done drinking.

20 And she hasted, and emptied her pitcher into the trough, and ran again unto the well to draw *water*, and drew for all his camels.

Genesis 24

3.1 How the Work Works

'Bois' – this is Derrida's final word on Levinas; the final word of his
text *for* Emmanuel Levinas (*ECM* 60).

'Bois' – 'drink'; understood verbally, Derrida's final word articulates an imperative, it places the reader under obligation. It is an
imperative written without a point of exclamation in the intimacy
of the second person singular. It is not directed from a position of
height to an anonymous multitude; it is not the impersonal 'Buvons!'
or 'Buvez!', which, in a spirit of exclamation and camaraderie,
commands others to join in a toast or partake in a symposium. The
imperative 'Bois' does not call us to take on board nourishment, an
operation that Levinas has already described (*TeI* 100–3 *TI* 127–30)
and which always remains within the circuit of the separated ego and
its *jouissance*. To utter the imperative 'Bois' is to give to the other, to
let down one's pitcher and offer drink to the other; it does not mean
'Eat, drink and be merry'. Such a giving is inadequately described
through the image of friends nourishing themselves and their individuation in a spirit of collectivity and *bonhomie*. To utter the final
word – 'Bois' – is to nourish the hunger of the other, and is akin to
the tearing of bread from my own mouth. I interrupt my ego through
fasting and breaking the other's fast (cf. *AE* 72 *OB* 56).

'Bois' – 'drink'. What is being given here? What is being offered to
drink? Derrida's final words on Levinas are the following:

I WEAVE MY VOICE SO AS TO BE EFFACED THIS TAKE IT HERE I AM EAT –
APPROACH – IN ORDER TO GIVE HIM/HER (*LUI*) – DRINK (*BOIS*). (*ECM* 60)

The textual voice here speaks of weaving itself in order to be effaced.
As such, the voice is not in the process of disappearing; rather, it
effaces itself before an other; the voice is addressed to an interlocutor.
In the act of effacement, whereby the self is possessed by the other,
the voice persists and says, 'HERE I AM…EAT…DRINK.' The
voice offers something to the other, its arms outstretched and its
hands full, asking the other to approach. Upon the other's approach,
the voice holds out its gift and says, 'Bois'. The gift of drink is being
offered here. Derrida's final word on Levinas offers the gift of drink
to the other, a giving which, as I shall show, describes the generous

movement of the ethical work. Derrida's final word on Levinas describes that ethical work, where Derrida's text is given to Levinas.

'Bois' – 'drink'. The ethical work must be given in radical generosity. The work must be sent out from the Same to the Other without ever returning to the same. Levinas writes in 'The Trace of the Other':

> The Work (*L'Œuvre*) thought radically is indeed a movement from the Same towards the other which never returns to the Same. To the myth of Ulysses returning to Ithaca, we would like to oppose the story of Abraham leaving his homeland forever for a still unknown land and even forbidding his son to be brought back to its point of departure. (*EDE* 191)

Levinas thus opposes the nomadic wanderings of Abraham to the well-rounded narrative of the *Odyssey*.[1] The ethical work must possess a movement which exceeds the circle of the self and goes unto the other without ever turning back. Consequently, the work of the word 'Bois', the final word in Derrida's work *for* Levinas, describes the generous giving of the work to the other, the letting down of one's pitcher in order to let the other drink. The woman who will marry Abraham's son Isaac must fulfil the duty (*mitsva*; cf. *ND* 156[2]) of hospitality. Abraham's servant recognizes the woman when she lets down her pitcher and offers drink to him and his camels; her name is Rebecca. Thus it is in her response of responsibility to the stranger, by offering drink, that Rebecca fulfils the duty of hospitality and performs the ethical work. 'Bois' is the very event of the ethical work, the giving to the stranger without hope of return or remuneration. Derrida's final word on Levinas is the first word of responsibility, the establishment of the ethical relation.

However, this ethical and textual structure must begin to be complicated in order to describe adequately what is at work in 'En ce moment même'. I continue the quotation from 'The Trace of the Other':

> The Work (*L'Œuvre*), thought as far as possible, demands a radical generosity of the Same who, in the Work, goes towards the other. In consequence the Work demands an *ingratitude* of the other. Gratitude would be precisely the return of the movement to its origin. (*EDE* 191)

In order to stop the ethical work returning to the Same, the Other must receive the work *ungratefully*, because the movement of gratitude returns to the Same, as is the case in philanthropy. Therefore, one should not be grateful for ethical works; Eliezer should be ungrateful to Rebecca, and the addressee of Derrida's final word should show ingratitude. Should one then be grateful to Emmanuel Levinas?

To approach this question, it is helpful to consider the status and function of 'En ce moment même'. The essay appeared originally in *Textes pour Emmanuel Levinas*, a collection of essays, where each text is, in a very obvious sense, *for* Emmanuel Levinas, is destined *for* him, to pay him homage, forming part of a *Festschrift*, a commemorative work in which friends praise the author like guests seated at a symposium. Derrida's text forms part of an act of commemoration, in which the author's life and work are collectively recalled. Thus, 'En ce moment même' is a text that is addressed to an interlocutor or other who is known, addressed, and recalled in the work. Such is the conventional structure of homage.

The situation becomes more complex when one begins to consider the ethics of this textual structure. What ties the authors of *Textes pour Emmanuel Levinas* together in this act of commemoration is the fact that they can all recall Levinas's work. Levinas has worked for them, and they would like to pay him homage. But what work does Levinas's work perform? How does his work *work*? As we saw above, Levinas opposes Abraham to Ulysses, claiming that the ethical structure of the work is one which goes generously from the Same to the Other without ever returning to the same. Thus, on Derrida's reading, Levinas's work *works* by going out generously from the proper name and signature of Emmanuel Levinas towards the Other. Levinas's work is not circumscribed by the proper name of Emmanuel Levinas; it is a work that continually exceeds itself and opens itself to that which comes before and after nominalization. To employ a word favoured by Derrida, Levinas's work is possessed of a *dehiscence* (*ECM* 43[3]), where the work bursts open and goes unto the other without return, allowing it to perform the ethical.

Levinas's work has worked for Derrida and the other contributors to *Textes pour Emmanuel Levinas* precisely to the extent that it has let the work go unto the Other, allowing the Other to drink without the self quenching his or her thirst in the Other's grateful eyes. The logical and ethical necessity that haunts Derrida's essay is that by writing a text *for* Emmanuel Levinas, by paying homage to his work and recalling how his work works, one would return the work to its author, thereby betraying the ethical structure that Levinas's work tries to set to work. How, then, does one write a text for Emmanuel Levinas?

> Suppose that in giving to you – it little matters what – I wanted to give to him, him Emmanuel Levinas. Not render him anything, a homage for example, not even render myself to him, but to give him something which escapes from the circle of restitution or of the 'rendez-vous'. (*ECM* 24)

Derrida cannot pay homage to Levinas by giving his own text back to him. He must be cautious to avoid rendering to Levinas what is Levinas's, for in so doing, he would make the ethical relation correspond to the time of the 'rendez-vous' (' "that common time of clocks" ' ibid.), where the Other would render itself up and return to the Same.

> I would like to do it faultlessly (*sans faute*), with a faultlessness (*sans-faute*) that no longer belongs to the time or logic of the rendez-vous. Beyond any possible restitution, there would be need for my gesture to operate without debt, in absolute ingratitude. (Ibid.)

Returning to the quotation from 'The Trace of the Other' and the question of ingratitude, Derrida would like to sew a seamless, flawless work and then give it to Levinas with a flawlessness that would escape the temporality and speculative logic of the *rendez-vous*. However, the only way in which a text *for* Emmanuel Levinas can be written which would return Levinas's act of radical generosity is by being *ungrateful* and by writing a *faulty* text. Ingratitude is the only mode in which one can write a text *for* Levinas if that text is going to maintain the ethical structure that Levinas's work sets to work.

> If I must conform my gesture to what makes the Work (L'Œuvre) in his Work, which is older than his work, and whose Saying according to his own terms is not reducible to the Said, there we are, engaged before all engagement, in an incredible logic, formal and non-formal. If I restitute, if I restitute without fault, I am at fault. And if I do not restitute, by *giving* beyond acknowledgement, I risk the fault. (*ECM* 24)

This is indeed an incredible logic, a faulty logic, or logic of the fault. Yet it is a logic whose 'necessity' (*ECM* 58) or 'fatality' (*ECM* 56) is irreducibly ethical. In order to write a text for Emmánuel Levinas, I must not give it to him; I must make the text faulty in such a way that it does not return to the same but goes unto the Other.

'Bois' – 'drink'. I let down my pitcher, and the Other drinks from out of my own thirst. Levinas's work *works* in so far as it is given to someone other than Emmanuel Levinas. To write a text for Emmanuel Levinas, to create a work that maintains the Other in its otherness, entails, therefore, that the text or the work must not be given back to Levinas's name. To write a text *for* Emmanuel Levinas is to write a text that is not *for* him but for the Other. Consequently, it is ethically necessary for 'En ce moment même' to be ungrateful, faulty, and, to recall a word from Derrida's first essay on Levinas, *violent* (*ECM* 56).

Yet, it is important to point out that ingratitude, faultiness, and violence are not directed *against* Levinas; they are not moments of an external critique which would naïvely oppose itself to the supposed generosity, flawlessness, and peace of Levinasian ethics. Ingratitude, faultiness, and violence are the necessary conditions of a fidelity to Levinas's work, a work which works precisely to the extent that it cannot be returned to the proper name of Emmanuel Levinas. To schematize this, one might say that it is only in ingratitude, faultiness, and violence that the ethical Saying is maintained. To write a text *for* Emmanuel Levinas is to create a work that is neither *for* him nor *against* him, but one in which the modalities of for and against become inseparable yet inassemblable conditions for the possibility of ethical Saying.

'Bois' – 'drink', an imperative directed at a singular second person, the singular other who is my interlocutor. But who is the Other? If Derrida does not let his pitcher down so that Levinas may drink, but in order for the Other to quench his or her thirst, then who is this Other? If Levinas remains thirsty, then is 'Bois' Derrida's final word on *Levinas?* Indeed, is 'Bois' *Derrida's* final word? Is the textual voice in 'En ce moment même' that of Derrida or that of an other? Can one still speak of proper names here?

I here approach a major theme of 'En ce moment même': the question of the name. And if I am obliged to continue employing the proper names of Derrida and Levinas, for clarity's sake but also because of the grammar of propriety embedded in language, then it is with a provisionality that will become increasingly apparent. The pattern of reading in 'En ce moment même' can be said to articulate itself around the difference between the '*Pro-nom*' (Pro-noun or Fore-name) and the *nom propre* (the proper name). Recall that Derrida's *first* word on Levinas in 'En ce moment même' is the pronoun 'Il', which is the subject of the phrase 'Il aura obligé', a phrase which resounds throughout the early pages of 'En ce moment même' and which, to the knowledge of the textual voice (*ECM* 23) and my own, has never appeared in Levinas's work. Who is 'He'? A clue can be found in the final paragraph of *Otherwise than Being*, a passage itself cited in 'En ce moment même' (*ECM* 44):

> In this work which does not seek to restore any ruined concept, the destitution and de-situation of the subject are not without signification: after the death of a certain god, dwelling in the hinter-worlds (*les arrières-mondes*), the substitution of the hostage discovers the trace – unpronounceable writing – of that which, always already past – always 'he' ('*il*') – does not enter into any present and to whom neither the names designating beings nor the verbs where their *essence* resounds are suitable – but who, Pro-name (*Pro-nom*), marks with his seal everything that can bear a name. (*AE* 233/*OB* 185)

In a work which attempts to describe and enact the ethical work, subjectivity is ultimately described as a 'hostage' (*ôtage*) to the Other (*AE* 142/*OB* 112); that is, the subject is taken captive to the point of substituting itself for another (*AE* 16/*OB* 13). Substitution is the very subjectivity of the ethical subject, which means that the subject is structured as responsibility to the Other prior to preoccupation with oneself. Responsibility, Levinas writes, is the very religiosity of the subject (*AE* 150/*OB* 117). The religious claim being made here is that after the death of a certain god, subjectivity qua substitution and hostage discovers the trace of that which does not enter into any present and which is designated by the pronoun 'he'.

Pause for a moment to consider the implications of this phrase. Levinas is not opposing Nietzsche's account of the death of God by reintroducing some ruined concept; he accepts that God – the god of metaphysics, the god of onto-theo-logy, the god that reifies, or 'congeals', transcendence into a 'world behind the scenes' (*AE* 6/*OB* 5) – is dead. *After* the death of that god, the ethical subject is able to discover the sense (*sens*: both direction and signification) of transcendence that was lost or reified in metaphysics: the transcendence of the Other. Levinas's claim is that the subject as substitution, as being-for-another, discovers a trace in the Other's face which is that of the 'Il', the *Pro-nom*, the 'Fore-name' of that which comes before all named beings but which marks each being with its seal. Thus Levinas does not dismiss the death of God and the critique of metaphysical transcendence, but rather introduces them as preconditions for the possibility of religiosity and morality. In the important 1965 essay 'Enigma and Phenomenon' (*EDE* 207–9/*CPP* 64–6), Levinas opposes an order of presence and phenomenality (from the Greek *phaino*, to bring to light), in which entities are cleared and comprehended in their Being, to an order of the enigma (from *ainigma*, a dark saying or riddle), which attempts to set forth that which escapes comprehension or thematization: 'the otherwise than Being'. For Levinas, the enigmatic 'referent' of 'the otherwise than Being' is expressed by the third person singular (masculine) pronoun (*EDE* 199), an enigma he seeks to describe by the term 'Illeity':

> This way of leaving the alternatives of Being – we understand it with the personal pronoun of the third person, with the word *He*. The enigma comes to us from Illeity. (*EDE* 214/*CPP* 71)

The signifyingness (*signifiance*) of 'the otherwise than Being' in a work entitled *Autrement qu'être ou au-delà de l'essence* is ultimately borne by the 'Il' of Illeity. Although Levinas is not afraid to use the word 'God' – 'the overwhelming semantic event' (*AE* 193/*OB* 151), 'the apex of vocabulary' (*AE* 199/*OB* 156) – he employs the term 'Illeity' in order to avoid the inevitable onto-theo-logical thematization (i.e. God is a being) that the word 'God' entails. Illeity describes my non-thematizable relation with the Infinite, the direction of transcendence; it does not buttress any positive theology (*AE* 188/*OB* 147). Levinas's work *works* by giving the work to the 'Il'.

Recalling the schema that was sketched above, the work of Emmanuel Levinas is possessed of a certain dehiscence to the extent that it is a work that goes unto the Other without returning to the Same. One can now see that the Other to whom the work is ultimately addressed is 'Il', the trace of Illeity, who does not sign Levinas's work but who marks it with his seal. For Levinas, it is the trace of Illeity signalled in the 'Il' that constitutes the first act of obligation, that in a sense 'founds' the ethical relation. When I am faced with the other person, I enter into relation with the enigma of the trace of Illeity, and, in that 'intrigue' which binds me to the 'Il' from across the 'toi' (*EDE* 215–16/*CPP* 72–3), I am bound in an ethical obligation. Ethics is religion, but not theology.

It is now possible to understand the first of the 'one, two, three words' (*ECM* 22) which form the leitmotif of 'En ce moment même': 'Il aura obligé'. The 'Il' is the *Pro-nom* of the trace of Illeity. From the first word of Derrida's essay, 'Il', the textual voice alludes to the way in which Levinas's work *works* in so far as it is addressed to the trace that is otherwise than Being. Derrida's first word on Levinas, like his final word, is an enactment, or performance, of the ethical objectives of the latter's work.

Before pursuing the question of the name, what can one make of the second and third words of the phrase 'Il aura obligé'? The first thing one notices is that the tense, or temporality, of these words is the future anterior (or future perfect), which habitually describes an action that will have been performed by a certain time and which is formed in French (and in English) by compounding the future tense of one of the two auxiliaries *avoir* and *être* with the past participle of the main verb. The temporality of the future anterior is something that Derrida has exploited throughout his work, and its logic pervades 'En ce moment même'. Thus he writes: 'There is the future anterior, which I *shall have* frequently *used* nonetheless, having no other possible recourse. For example in the little phrase: "He will have obliged"' (*ECM* 48, my emphasis; cf. *ECM* 38, 39). The importance of the future anterior is that it is a tense that escapes the time of the present. It simultaneously points towards a future – 'aura' – and a past – 'obligé'. Consequently, the subject of the phrase, 'Il', cannot be said to be a subject present to itself; rather He/It is a subject that will have obliged in a time that is irreducible to the present. At several points in 'En ce moment même', Derrida refers to 'the dominant interpretation of language' (*ECM* 36, 49, 50) employed by 'philosophical intelligence' (*ECM* 48), which would seek to display all entities in the light of the determination of Being as presence. The significance of the future anterior is that it is a temporality irreducible to what Derrida would call 'the metaphysics of presence' or what Levinas would call 'ontology', and one which envisages a language that would escape the dominant interpretation. The future anterior is the temporality of the trace of Illeity: it is perhaps the time of ethics.

One begins to see how much is already presupposed in the first words of Derrida's essay 'Il aura obligé'. The subject of the phrase is the *Pro-nom*, or trace of Illeity, which provides the condition of possibility for all ethical obligation and which takes place in a temporality that escapes the metaphysics of presence or ontology. Derrida's first and final words on Levinas, 'Il aura obligé' and 'Bois', are ethical *performatives*.[4]

It has perhaps become clear by now that it would be misleading to interpret the Pro-nominal 'Il' as a pronoun that could be substituted for the proper name Emmanuel Levinas. 'He' is not Levinas; 'What I thus call – this work – is not, especially not, dominated by the name of Emmanuel Levinas' (*ECM* 23). Levinas's work *works* in so far as it resonates with the (masculine) third person singular pronoun. Thus, that work should not be dominated by his proper name, and he should exercise neither authorial nor signatorial (*ECM* 47) rights over it. Rather, Levinas's work sets the 'Il' to work, the 'He' who will have obliged.

However – and here we return to the theme of the play between the pronoun and the proper name and to the question of ethical violence – it would also be a mistake to distinguish radically Levinas's proper name and the pro-nominal 'Il'. A few lines below the above quotation, one reads that 'the subject of the phrase "he will have obliged" might be (*soit*) Emmanuel Levinas' (*ECM* 23). Thus, although the 'Il' is not dominated by the name of Emmanuel Levinas, the latter might be the subject designated by the pronoun. Continuing this thought in a slightly different formulation, the textual voice writes that it must renounce the supposed neutrality or anonymity of a discourse that employs the impersonal third person pronoun (*ECM* 23–4). Although the name of Emmanuel Levinas is rarely employed in 'En ce moment même', the textual voice makes it clear that the essay is not addressed to an anonymous addressee; 'I will not pronounce your name nor inscribe it, but you are not anonymous at the moment when here I am telling you this' (*ECM* 23–4).

Surprisingly, perhaps, what is at stake here is nothing less than the success or failure of Levinasian ethics. As has already been pointed out, for Levinas's work to work, it must be directed towards the wholly other, the trace of Illeity signalled in the phrase 'Il aura and must not be allowed to return to the Same. To return to the Same is to return to the name, the proper name of Emmanuel Levinas. Conversely, if Levinas's work *does not* work, then it will return to, or at least be indistinguishable from, the name of Levinas. Derrida's strategy here is complex, and is governed by a certain necessity which needs to be schematized. If Derrida simply showed how Levinas's work works by going unto the 'Il', then he would be merely repeating Levinas's generous ethical gesture and thereby returning Levinas's work to its author. As has already been established, the necessary response to Levinas's work is one of radical ingratitude. Thus, to reciprocate the generosity of the ethical gesture is to return the Other to the Same, and consequently to deny ethics. Therefore, in order to maintain the ethical moment, Derrida must commit an ungrateful violence against Levinas's work: he must show how the work *does not work*.

One way of showing how Levinas's work does not work would be to argue that it ultimately returns to his proper name and to the logic of the Same. Yet this begs the question: does not the necessary violence of ingratitude which was intended to preserve the ethical precisely deny the latter by returning the Pro-nominal 'Il' to the proper name of Levinas? In order to circumvent this objection, the structure of Derrida's reading must be deepened once again. It must be asked: To whom should Levinas's work be returned in order to maintain ethical alterity? Might not the answer be 'Elle', not E.L., the theme of the feminine that is developed in the final pages of 'En ce moment même' (*ECM* 51–60)? Is 'She' the Other to the wholly other, to whom the text is ultimately given?

'Bois' – 'drink'. The order of the Genesis narrative must be inverted and the roles reversed; Eliezer must let down his pitcher for her, Rebecca.

The shift from Levinas's name to the theme of the feminine is, once again, articulated around the difference between the proper name and the pronoun. Throughout 'En ce moment même', the textual voice replaces Emmanuel Levinas's proper name by the initials E.L. (cf. *ECM* 24, for the first occurrence of this). At certain strategic points in the essay, E.L. is substituted for 'Il', and the leitmotif of the essay reads: 'E.L. aura obligé' (*ECM* 45, 46). Now, if one elides the pronunciation of the two letters 'E' and 'L' in order to produce one phoneme, two things occur: first, the word 'El' is formed, which, as

Levinas points out in 'Le nom de Dieu d'après quelques textes
Talmudiques' (*ND* 158, a text which is referred to extensively in 'En
ce moment même'; cf. *ECM* 34–5, 38, 41, 56–8), is one of the proper
names for God in the Talmudic tradition. Second, one produces a
homonym for the third person singular feminine pronoun 'Elle'. It is
the second of these things which opens up the ultimate horizon of
'En ce moment même'. On the penultimate page of the essay (*ECM*
59), the pronoun 'Il' is replaced by 'Elle', and the leitmotif of the
essay is transformed into 'Elle aura obligé' ('She will have obliged').

'En ce moment même' can be said to move between three
formulations of an ethical imperative or performative: 'Il aura obligé',
'E.L. aura obligé' and 'Elle aura obligé'. The transition from the
pronoun 'Il' to the pronoun 'Elle' is mediated by the initialled proper
name of Levinas, E.L. On three occasions in 'En ce moment même'
Derrida employs the neologism 'entre(el)lacement' (*ECM* 49, 50, 51),
where the parenthetical (el) – the name of God, the name of Levinas –
stands between the 'inter' and 'lacing', on the threshold between the
interlacing of two opposed terms, in this case the pronouns 'Il' and
'Elle'. The *clôtural* fabric of Derrida's reading of Levinas is stretched
across these two pronouns, where the threshold that divides both the
masculine *Pro-nom* from the feminine *Pro-nom* and the pronominal
from the proper name is continually transgressed.

To sketch briefly this *clôtural* structure, there are two moments of
reading at work in 'En ce moment même'. First, Derrida tries to find
out how Levinas's work *works*; second, 'he' tries to show how
Levinas's work *does not work*. The first moment of reading shows how
Levinas's text resists the economy of the Same, or logocentrism, and
goes generously unto the Other: 'Il aura obligé'. Conversely, the
second moment of reading is the ingratitude and violence required
to maintain the alterity of the first moment. The second moment is
performed by showing how Levinas subordinates sexual difference to
ethical difference and thereby encloses both the 'Il' and the 'Elle' in
the economy of the Same. The work is not returned to E.L. but to the
Other of the wholly other: 'Elle aura obligé'.

'Bois' – 'drink'. Is this how Derrida's work works? Is this the final
word on Derrida's reading of Levinas? It has been shown above that
Levinas's work must be possessed of a dehiscence which maintains
the Saying of the pronominal 'Il' or trace of Illeity. Levinas's work
works in so far as it is interrupted by an alterity which refuses to

return the Saying of the work to the proper name of Emmanuel Levinas. The claim of my reading of 'En ce moment même' is that Derrida's work is governed by a similar necessity: the work of Derrida's work is one that must not be returned to and circumscribed by Derrida's proper name. 'En ce moment même' is possessed of a dehiscence which allows it to resonate with an alterity that must not be reduced to ontology and propriety. Derrida's work works in so far as it returns the text to 'Elle' and lets the voice of feminine alterity interrupt Levinas's work. To reduce the textuality of 'En ce moment même' to the proper name of Jacques Derrida (by saying, for example, 'In this essay, Derrida says…', 'Derrida's final word is…', and so on), as I have often been obliged to do, is to foreclose the opening announced by ethical alterity and to cover over the ethical interruption the the text seeks to maintain.

This point can be reinforced by an examination of the narrative structure of 'En ce moment même'. The text is not a monologue spoken by the signatory, Jacques Derrida; it is at the very least a dialogue for two voices, and one might even call it a 'polylogue' (cf. *FC* 8). The horizontal dash that precedes the first word of the essay indicates that somebody is speaking; the quotation marks denote a voice that is not necessarily that of the text's signatory. Turning the pages of the essay, one finds nine more of these dashes (*ECM* 27 (twice), 29, 30, 44, 45, 51, 59 (twice)), each denoting a change in the persona of the textual voice. Furthermore, 'En ce moment même' is spoken, or written, by a number of voices that are sexually differentiated into masculine, neutral (*sic*), or feminine. Now the interruption of Levinas's work occurs when the textual voice becomes that of a woman. This interruption can first be seen when the textual voice that begins the essay – 'il aura obligé' – calls across to an other, 'Where should you and I, we, let it be?' (*ECM* 26) and is interrupted by a new voice, that of the feminine Other – 'No, not let it be. Soon, we shall have to give it to him to eat and drink and you will listen to me' (*ECM* 27). The voice of the Other responds to its interlocutor (one might call the latter the voice of the Same), and promises that it will speak soon. This pattern of interruption is repeated on two further occasions: first during a discussion of the sexuality of the textual voice in the *Song of Songs* (– 'He or she, if the interruption of the discourse is required?' (*ECM* 29)) and secondly during a discussion of the work of 'Il' and its relation to the proper name of

Emmanuel Levinas (– 'Will it be said of "this work (*ouvrage*)" that it makes a work?' (*ECM* 44)). As I show below, the lengthiest interruption, beginning, – 'I knew' (*ECM* 51), which constitutes the second moment of reading, is the response of feminine alterity, the interruption of the woman reader in Levinas's work.

'En ce moment même' is not a monological text with one textual voice and one possible reading; rather, the text is structured as a double, or *clôtural*, reading. The first moment of reading, performed by the voice of the Same (a masculine reader), engages in a repetition of the Levinasian text, whereby the reader produces a commentary which tries to say the same as Levinas and shows how his work works. The second moment of reading, performed by the voice of the Other (a woman reader), is an interruption of the meaning (*vouloir-dire*) of the Levinasian text, which says something other to Levinas and shows how his work does not work. The deconstructive pattern of 'En ce moment même' is divided between the two moments of *clôtural* reading – repetition and alterity, Sameness and Otherness – which are performed by two sexually differentiated readers. But these two readings and readers do not constitute an opposition, or antinomy; rather, they maintain a relation of what was called above 'entre(el)lacement' – that is, an ethical relation that is respectful of the irreducibility of sexual difference.

'Bois' – 'drink'. This is not *Derrida's* final word on Levinas; it is not governed by *him* and his proper name. The final word of ethical obligation is always uttered by the Other, in this instance 'She', who interrupts Levinasian ethics and sets Derrida's work to work. Any consideration of the ethics of deconstructive reading must begin from this datum. But how should *I* read the work of Derrida's work in order to maintain the interruption? Does not the repetition implicit in *my* commentary foreclose any opening onto an ethics of sexual difference? How should I show gratitude to Derrida? As I argued above, commentary is never neutral, and my commentary upon Derrida's commentary upon Levinas undoubtedly conceals the opening that is so carefully prepared by a double, or *clôtural*, reading. However, and precisely through the double passivity of a commentary upon a commentary, such a reading, no doubt only in its interstices and hiatuses, may reflect some of the oblique rays of the deconstructive opening where the injunction is announced and the interruption is maintained.

3.2 How Levinas Writes his Work

I shall continue, then, in the manner of a commentary, by repeating the repetition of the first moment of reading. I will begin with an illuminating misquotation. While endeavouring to understand and explain the workings of Levinas's text, the textual voice stumbles across one of Derrida's early texts:

> His [i.e. Levinas's] 'text' (and I would even say *the* text, without wishing to efface an irreplaceable idiom) is always that heterogeneous tissue that interlaces both texture and atexture without uniting them. And whoever (as was written elsewhere of an other, very close and very distant) 'ventures to plot the absolute tear, absolutely tears his own tissue, once again become solid and servile in once more giving itself to be read'. (*ECM* 38)[5]

Two points need to be emphasized in relation to this passage. First, Levinas's text is a heterogeneous tissue[6] – that is, a substance composed of differing parts which maintain themselves in a relation of alterity. Levinasian textuality is composed of a certain texture and atexture, and it allows these opposing composite elements to maintain their absolute alterity while at the same time interlacing them and bringing them into relation. Returning to the first parenthetical remark in the above quotation, one notices that the word 'text' is given an italicized definite article (*the* text). Although the textual voice is hesitant here, as the use of the conditional tense would suggest, it is clear that when the textual voice speaks about Levinas's text, he is referring to *the* text. The structure of Levinasian textuality is a heterogeneous tissue similar to that which constitutes the structure of *the* text, of textuality in general. Second, and this confirms the first point, the textual voice proceeds to cite, strangely and as if from memory, one of Derrida's early texts while giving no indication of where the citation might come from. In fact, the quotation is drawn from the final three lines of Derrida's 1967 essay on Bataille and Hegel, 'From Restricted to General Economy' (cf. *ED* 407/*WD* 277). In the final pages of the latter, Derrida discusses Bataille's reading of Hegel (or, more precisely, Bataille's reaction to Kojève's reading of Hegel), and concludes that it is one that can be read from the left or the right, as a revolution or a reaction. Hegel's text itself contains and maintains both these heterogeneous possibilities; it is a text whose tissue can be absolutely rended through an act of Bataillesque *souveraineté* only to be mended once more into what, for Bataille, is the servility and laboriousness of Hegel's and Kojève's discourse.[7] This play of rending and mending, where differing elements enter into a relation in which they remain absolute in that relation, here defines the heterogeneous structure of textuality. As I shall show, the structure of Levinasian textuality serves as an *exemplum* for textuality in general, and a reading of the former gives some insight into the latter.

How, then, does Levinas produce this heterogeneous textuality? How does his work work? How does Levinas's work (*ouvrage*) allow the Work (*Œuvre*) to be produced? What sort of writing does this require? The Work (*Œuvre*) that Levinas's work (*ouvrage*) performs is the setting forth of the 'Il', the wholly other. Thus the question becomes:

> How does he manage to inscribe or let the wholly other be inscribed within the language of Being, of the present, of essence, of the Same, of economy, etc. (?). (*ECM* 27)

If the linguistic resources of logocentrism or ontology are the only ones available to us, and if the trace of Illeity is wholly other to the language of Being, what was called above the 'dominant interpretation of language', then how does that which is entirely foreign to logocentric or ontological discourse enter into it? In order to explain this enigma (which is the enigmatic possibility of ethics), should one not *reverse* the question and ask oneself:

> if that language is not *of itself unbound* (*d'elle-même déliée*) and hence open to the wholly other, to its own beyond, in such a way that it is less a matter of exceeding that language than of treating it otherwise with its own possibilities (*ECM* 27).

Although the dominant interpretation would claim that language is exclusively bound to Being and the Same, *perhaps* – and the modality of the *peut-être* in Levinas is something that intrigues the textual voice in 'En ce moment même' (cf. *ECM* 34–5 and *AE* 199/*OB* 156) – language is from the start *unbound* and therefore capable of being bound to the otherwise than Being, the wholly other. It is not a question of replacing the present language of ontology with an ethical language (as if there were two different languages!), but rather of writing in such a way that the Said of language is reduced to its Saying in a reduction that maintains a residue of the unsaid Said within the Saying. Levinas's writing enacts what was called above a 'spiralling movement' (*AE* 57/*OB* 44), in which language oscillates enigmatically, or undecidedly, between the Saying and the Said. As is made clear later on in 'En ce moment même', for Levinas it is not a question of simply overcoming language in the name of some irreducibly ontic 'beyond'. Language (*langue*) is as indispensable to ethics as the tongue (*langue*) in the mouth of the one who tears off bread in order to give it to the other (*ECM* 31). For Levinas, an ethics of silence would be irreducibly violent.

In the first moment of reading, and in order to provide insight into how Levinas's work works, the textual voice seeks out those places where unboundness, or dehiscence, are at work in Levinas's work. The textual voice selects three examples of unboundness, which, taken together, form the 'cryptic' (*ECM* 23) title to the essay. They are the phrases 'en ce moment même', 'dans cet ouvrage', and 'me voici'. These phrases are quotations from Levinas, and occur in his work precisely at those moments when he is considering how his work works. In the following pages, I shall pass over the examples of *ouvrage* and *Œuvre*, which have already been discussed, and also pass over in silence the 'me voici' (cf. *ECM* 28–9). The privileged example, which will permit the ultimate structure of Levinasian textuality to be discerned, will be the phrase 'En ce moment même'.

In order to elucidate the theme of unboundness, the textual voice quotes extensive passages from *Otherwise than Being*, in which Levinas employs the phrase 'en ce moment même' at the very moment when he is explaining how his work works. I shall begin by citing two passages as they appear in Derrida's essay:

> Every contesting and interruption of this power of discourse is at once related by discourse. It therefore recommences as soon as one interrupts it… This discourse will affirm itself as coherent and one. In relating the interruption of discourse or my being ravished by it, I retie the thread… and are we not, *at this very moment* (my italics, J.D.) in the process of barring up the exit which our whole essay is attempting, and encircling our position from all sides? (*ECM* 32, in *AE* 215/*OB* 169)

> The discourse which suppresses the interruptions of discourse in relat-
> ing them together, does it not maintain the discontinuity behind the
> knots where the thread is retied? The interruptions of discourse,
> recovered and related within the immanence of the said, are conserved
> as the knots in a retied thread (...). But the ultimate discourse, where
> all the discourses are uttered, I still interrupt it in telling it to the one
> who listens and is situated outside the Said that discourse says, outside
> all that it embraces. Which is true of the discourse that I am in the
> process of holding *at this very moment* (my italics, J.D.). (*ECM* 33, in
> *AE* 216–17/*OB* 170)

One should first note and underline the repetition of the phrase 'en
ce moment même' in these quotations. For it is a repetition which
involves a dislocation, or displacement, where the same phrase, when
repeated in two different but related contexts, interrupts itself and
says something wholly other. In the first passage, Levinas raises the
theme of interruption which also occurs in *Otherwise than Being* (*AE*
24, 214–16/*OB* 20, 169–71; cf. *ECM* 38). For Levinas, the interruption of essence or Being occurs in the reduction of the ontological
Said to the ethical Saying. Such an interruption of the Said by the
Saying denies the closure (*fermeture*) (*AE* 24/*OB* 20) of the Said and,
for Levinas, represents the only end (*fin*) (ibid.) that can be envisaged
for philosophical discourse. There is no simple and radical overcoming
of ontological or logocentric language through the ethical Saying of
the otherwise than Being; rather, the ethical is the momentary interruption of the *logos*. As such, any attempt to thematize ethical interruption will always retie the thread of philosophical discourse. Hence,
Levinas asks himself whether, in thematizing the ethical Saying within
the ontological Said of a book, he is, *at this very moment*, denying the
ethical breakthrough that *Otherwise than Being* attempts.

However, another picture of interruption emerges from the second
quotation. Levinas appears to be saying, first, that although the ethical interruptions of essence are retied in the thread of the ontological
Said, they are preserved as knots in such a thread; and second, that
the ultimate, or final, discourse, where all discourse is uttered, is still
interrupted by a Saying that is addressed to the one who listens, the
Other, or interlocutor, who is situated outside the Said, with whom I
have an ethical relation. Levinas's claim is that this ultimate interruption occurs in the discourse that he is holding *at this very moment*.[8]

Thus, in the interval that separates the repetition of the 'en ce
moment même', a certain dislocation has occurred. The repetition of

the same phrase has wholly other consequences.[9] In the first instance, at this very moment, I enclose the ethical interruption of essence within the ontological Said; while, in the second instance, at this very moment, I ultimately interrupt the Said. At the very moment when Levinas is explaining how his work works, one is confronted by an absolute heterogeneity, in which Levinas, through a repetition of the Same, says something wholly other. Indeed, one might say that it is precisely through the enactment of such a heterogeneity that Levinas's work works.

But how are these two instances of the 'en ce moment même' related? To approach this question, it is necessary to examine the metaphor of the retied thread (*le fil renoué*) that is employed in both these passages and which so intrigues the textual voice. In the first passage, the interruption of discourse is akin to the breaking of a thread which is itself retied in the ontological thematization of the Saying within the Said. In the second passage, the interruptions of discourse, although retied into the thread, are preserved as knots in the thread, and indeed, at this very moment, in addressing myself to the one who listens, I break the thread. Thus the two heterogeneous instances of the 'en ce moment même' linked together by a dislocating act of repetition, are related and tied together through the metaphor of the retied thread. The picture that is beginning to form is that of a single thread with a series of knots running along its length. These knots represent the moments of the ethical interruption of essence, each of which could in turn be interrupted, at this very moment, by addressing myself to an interlocutor.

Recalling the metaphor of the tissue, or fabric, that occurred in the passage from the essay on Bataille, one might say that Levinasian textuality is a fabric that is continually being rended and mended, and one in which the rending that takes place in ethical interruption is retied back into the body of the text as a fault or a flaw. As I shall show, the fabric of textuality is explained and deepened in 'En ce moment même', through the image of a *series* (*série*) of rends and mends, an unbound seriality of discourse.

But is the seriality which binds together these two instances of 'en ce moment même' one of reciprocity and strict equality? Does the play of rending and mending take place without priority? To address these questions, it is necessary to turn to a second example of the 'en ce moment même' in 'Le nom de Dieu d'après quelques textes Talmudiques' that is also cited at length by the textual voice:

Responsibility which, before the discourse bearing on the *said*, is probably the essence of language...

   It will of course be objected that if any other relation than
thematization may exist between the Soul and the Absolute, then
wouldn't the act of talking and thinking about it *at this very moment* (my
italics, J.D.), the fact of enveloping it in our dialectic, mean that
language and dialectic are superior with respect to that relation?

   But the language of thematization, which we are using *at this moment*
(my italics, J.D.), has perhaps only been made possible by means of
that Relation and is only ancillary to it. (*ECM* 34–5; *ND* 167)

One immediately notices the same unboundness that was in evidence
in the previous examples. After tentatively establishing that responsibility – *for* one's fellow humans *before* the self-effacement of the
transcendent God (*ND* 164) – is the essence of language, Levinas
raises the objection as to whether this essence is enveloped within the
thematizing language that is being employed *at this very moment*. But
he immediately goes on to claim that the language of thematization
that is being used *at this very moment* is only made possible by the
essence of language revealed in the relation to the Other. One thus
rediscovers the same heterogeneous fabric that was discussed above,
with the subtle but important difference that one instance of the 'en ce
moment même' is given priority over the other. In the passages cited,
the second instance takes precedence over the first: although the
language that is being used *at this very moment* is that of thematization
(in which the ethical rending of the fabric is continually being
mended by the hand of Being), this language is, *at this very moment*,
only made possible by the ethical relation which constitutes the
essence of language (in which the fabric is torn from the hands of
Being).

   In the repetition of the 'en ce moment même', a subtle, almost
inapparent, yet crucial dimension of alterity opens up, unbinding the
language of the tradition. The heterogeneous structure of textuality
gives an absolute priority to alterity, to the otherness in which the
conditions of possibility for ontology and logocentrism are located.
With specific reference to the two instances of 'en ce moment même'
from 'Le nom de Dieu', the textual voice writes:

   The second 'moment' will have forced the first toward its own
   condition of possibility, toward its 'essence' beyond the Said and

the Theme. It will have, in advance – but after the fact in the serial
rhetoric – torn the envelope. (*ECM* 37)

The ethical interruption of essence which must, of necessity, envelop
itself in the language of thematization, will always, of necessity, tear
that envelope. The double necessity that is at work here obliges one
to employ the language of the tradition; but at the very same
moment, one *will have been* obliged to interrupt this language and bear
it towards its own condition of possibility. The fabric of discourse is
not simply the play of rending and mending that was discussed above,
because Levinas finds a way of retying the knot which does not mend
the thread, one which produces an irreducible *supplement* to ontology:
ethical Saying. The structure of textuality becomes yet more complex:
'But there is in his text, perhaps, a supplementary nodal complication,
another way of retying without retying. How is this supplement of
the knot to be figured?' (*ECM* 40).

How indeed? As is remarked a few pages further on (*ECM* 44), the
singularity of the Levinasian text is due to the way in which it binds
itself together at the very moment at which its discursive structure is
unbound. The fabric of the text is both bound and unbound. The
bound language of thematization, which is employed in order to
thematize the non-thematizable, must not be allowed to envelop
the non-thematizable 'essence' of language. An irreducible non-
thematizability must – and one must be always be vigilant regarding
the ethical modality of the *must* (*il faut*) – stand apart from the thread
of the ontological Said where the moments of ethical interruption are
preserved as knots. There must be an 'interruption between interruptions' (*ECM* 40), a threadless supplement to the knot which
cannot be retied back into the ontological thread of the Said. The
picture that now emerges is one in which, within the knot of each
ethical interruption that has been tied back into the ontological
thread, there persists an irreducible supplement to the knot which is
the very interruption of interruption.

The fabric of the text, a texture of threads and knots, contains what
the textual voice calls a 'hiatus' (*ECM* 40) within each knot, which
constitutes what I called above 'atexture', a threadless moment in
the fabric. This moment of atexture, whether it be called 'the hiatus',
'the interruption of interruption', or 'the supplement of the knot',
is the point of ethical priority within the text, the Saying that is

the condition for the possibility of the Said. As the textual voice points out, this supplement to the knot is not unique; 'a sole interruption does not suffice' (*ECM* 40). There must be a multiplicity, or plurality, of knots, what is called a 'series' ('I have chosen to name this structure by the word *series*' (*ECM* 40)). One imagines a series of knots connected by a continuous thread, upon or within each of which is a nodal point of supplementarity. This image of the text as a play of binding and unbinding, where the mended interruption of essence is itself interrupted by a moment of irreducible ethical priority, is the way in which Levinas's work works. It is that which Levinas's writing enacts. The textual voice introduces the neologism *sériature* (*ECM* 42, 48, 49, 50, 51, 55) in order to explain the complex textual structure of obligation.

> An interrupted series, a *series* of interlaced interruptions, a series of *hiatuses* (...) that I shall henceforth call, in order to formalize in economical fashion and so as not to dissociate what is no longer dissociable within this fabric, *sériature*. (*ECM* 48)

With the word *sériature*, defined as the movement of binding and unbinding, the play of texture and atexture, a formal designation of the workings of Levinas's work has been attained. Formally and thematically, Levinas's work works as an interrupted series, or a series of interrupted interruptions, where the continuity and repetition of the series are continually placed under erasure (*série* + *rature* = *sériature*) by the energy of an ethical interruption.

The concept of *sériature* describes the relations between binding and unbinding, between being bound to ontological or logocentric language while at the same moment being unbound to that language. The fabric of Levinasian textuality is a *sériature* in so far as it maintains a tension between the thread (the ontological Said), the knot (the ethical Saying or interruption), and the hiatus (the interruption of interruption). What is unbound, non-thematizable, and wholly other to ontology and logocentrism can be articulated only through a certain repetition of ontological or logocentric language, a repetition that interrupts that language. Levinasian textuality (and perhaps textuality in general, *the* text) obeys a *sériatural* or *clôtural* rhythm of binding and unbinding which preserves the absolute priority of ethical obligation.

With such an understanding of the structure of Levinas's work, one can begin to take proper account of Levinas's language, and in particular the writing style of *Otherwise than Being*: the endless repetitions, the ellipses, ambiguities and contradictions, the unexplained and often tangential footnotes, the strange and austere beauty of the prose, the rhapsodic effect of the clause structure in Levinas's extended sentences, the simultaneous didacticism and uncertainty of many of his propositions. These phenomena are not, I would claim, simply of secondary importance, due to Levinas's relentless obscurity, circumlocution, and inability to say what he means clearly and distinctly. Rather, they are of primary importance, for it is precisely in the play of binding and unbinding, the oscillation or ambiguity of the Saying and the Said, that the ethical Saying of Levinas's work is maintained. In an eagerness to extract an ethics from Levinas, one may overlook the very writing that makes the formulation of that ethics possible. We are only just beginning to learn how to read Levinas.

3.3 How Levinas's Work does not Work

The first moment of reading has shown how Levinas's work works, and, as such, does not leave the order of commentary, where the dominant interpretation of the text is repeated and left intact. Commentary always belongs to the text that is being commented on, and derives from a decision not to disturb or dislocate the order of the text (a principle which extends, of course, to the commentary upon a commentary that I am writing at this very moment: 'Bois'). To repeat or comment on a text is ultimately to return that text to its author. Now, for reasons discussed above, to return Levinasian textuality to the proper name of Emmanuel Levinas is to deny the structure of ethical obligation and reduce the Saying to the Said. It is therefore ethically and, I would claim, deconstructively necessary for the repetition and commentary of the first moment of reading to be violated and transgressed in the second moment, a reading that leaves the order of commentary. As I argued in chapter 1, deconstructive reading is characterized by its double structure, its traversal of the space between commentary and interpretation.

The form of this violation and transgression is the ungrateful response which maintains the responsibility of ethical interruption by returning the text to 'Elle' and not to E. L. The transition from the first to the second moment of reading is marked by a shift in the grammatical gender of the textual voice. It is the woman reader who leaves the order of commentary and makes 'En ce moment même' a double reading.[10] The textual voice concludes its commentary by writing that it is 'impossible to approach his work without first of all passing, already, by the re-treat of its inside, namely, the remarkable saying of the work' (*ECM* 51). The voice of commentary faithfully traces the inside of Levinas's work and detects its ethical Saying. Yet, at the very moment when the ultimate sense of ethical Saying becomes manifest, when we finally understand how Levinas's work works, the voice of commentary addresses itself to an Other and asks for a response: 'You (come), obligated woman reader (*lectrice obligée*). You can still refuse to grant him that sense' (*ECM* 51). The textual voice calls to the feminine Other, the woman reader, asking her to come (*viens*)[11], to approach and refuse the sense of the ethical Saying.

'Bois' – 'drink'. From across the wide line space that divides two paragraphs and two voices, the feminine Other responds in responsibility:

> I knew. In listening I was nonetheless wondering whether I was comprehended (*comprise*), myself, and how to stop that word: comprehended (*comprise*). (*ECM* 51)

In virtue of the gendered status of French grammar, the additional '*e*' on the neutral (that is, masculine) past participle *compris* indicates that the gender of the textual voice is female. One finds further confirmations of the femininity of the textual voice in the subsequent pages of the essay, where the textual voice repeatedly refers to herself as a woman: 'Why should the son be more or better than the daughter, than *me*' (*ECM* 52, my emphasis); or again, 'The other as feminine (*me*)' (*ECM* 54, my emphasis), 'their common link to *me*, to the other as woman' (ibid., my emphasis), 'I speak from *my* place as a woman' (*ECM* 56, my emphasis).

If the transition from the first to the second moment of reading is effected by the shift from a neutral (masculine) reader, a *lecteur*, to a woman reader, a *lectrice*, then how does the woman read in order to return the work of Levinas's work to 'Elle'? she begins with an apparently innocent example of Levinas's *sériature*, an example of the work.

I shall give or take an example of it. More or perhaps another thing than an example, that of the 'son' in *Totality and Infinity*, of the 'unique' son or sons: 'The son is not my work (*œuvre*), like a poem or an object.' (*ECM* 51 and *TeI* 254/*TI* 277)

The example of *sériature* is the son, 'he' who is my 'work'. Of course, such an example is not at all innocent, because, by choosing the question of the son, the woman reader opens up the problem of the relation between sexual difference and ethical difference in Levinas. It is precisely this theme that will be the subject of the second moment of reading.

After giving the page reference to the quotation from *Totality and Infinity*, the woman reader casually throws in the following aside: 'I assume that the context is re-read' (*ECM* 51). But what is the context of this context? There are two contexts being referred to here: first, *Totality and Infinity* and second, 'Violence and Metaphysics'. In the fourth and final section of *Totality and Infinity*, entitled 'Beyond the Face', Levinas, as he does elsewhere in his work (*TA* 85–9/*TO* 91–4; *DEE* 157–65/*EE* 92–6), posits fecundity as the access to an account of existence that breaks with the Parmenidean unity of Being. The implicit claim here is that the Western philosophical tradition, from Parmenides to Heidegger, has always conceived of Being as a unitary 'concept', as the One. Levinas's thought of pluralism attempts to break with this monistic ontology by establishing 'a multiple existing' (*un exister multiple*) (*TeI* 195/*TI* 220), where I both am my son and am not my son, where my Being is split between myself and an other. For Levinas, fecundity is an 'ontological category' (*TeI* 254/*TI* 277), in which, through sexuality, Being becomes two, not one. My son is both the fruit of my loins and a being with a separate, independent existence. There is a *clôtural* or *sériatural* logic at work in fecundity, whereby I am both bound to my son and not bound to him. Although the personage of the son cannot be conflated with the 'He' of the trace of Illeity, one can see why the woman reader chooses fecundity as an example of Levinasian *sériature*. In fecundity my being is interrupted and doubled, and I attain an ontological condition of plurality, in which 'we thus leave the Parmenidean philosophy of Being' (*TeI* 247/*TI* 269). Thus, Levinasian ethics might be said to work only in so far as it sets the son to work.[12] It is because of fecundity that the 'dream of a happy eternity' (*TeI* 261/*TI* 284) or a 'victory over death' (*TA* 85/*TO* 90–1) cannot simply be discarded as aberrations.

In the second context, 'Violence and Metaphysics', a strange point of continuity relates it to 'En ce moment même'. As her reading gets under way, the woman reader parenthetically quotes Derrida's final words on Levinas in 'Violence and Metaphysics', from the final footnote:

> To himself, his text marks its signature by a masculine 'I-he', a rare thing, as was elsewhere noted 'in passing' a long time ago, by an other ('Let us note in passing on this subject that *Totality and Infinity* pushes the respect for dissymmetry up to the point where it seems to us impossible, essentially impossible, that it could have been written by a woman. The philosophical subject of it is man (vir)'). (*ECM* 52 and *ED* 220/*WD* 320–1)

The woman reader notes 'in passing' what Derrida footnoted 'in passing' some sixteen years earlier: namely, the masculine determination of ethical difference in Levinas's work. One might therefore read the second moment of reading in 'En ce moment même' as a continuation of this final footnote, as 'A Note to a Note in "Violence and Metaphysics"'. The woman reader takes up a position of alterity ('by an other') *not only* with respect to Levinas's work, but also with respect to 'Violence and Metaphysics'. Might one not consider the second moment of 'En ce moment même' as not only reflecting the necessary ingratitude towards Levinas's work, but also as a double reading of 'Violence and Metaphysics', as a re-reading of Derrida's early work in terms of the ethics of sexual difference?

Provisionally and schematically, in order to approach the second moment of 'En ce moment même' as a double reading of 'Violence and Metaphysics', it would be necessary to show how the latter is inhabited and dislocated by the former. To take an 'innocent' example of this, consider the fact that after the opening two expository sections of 'Violence and Metaphysics', 'The violence of light' and 'Phenomenology, ontology, metaphysics', the textual voice closes its commentary with the following footnote:

> We will not go beyond this schema. It would be useless to attempt, here, to enter into the descriptions devoted to interiority, economy,

enjoyment, habitation, femininity, Eros, to everything suggested under the title *Beyond the Face* and which the situation would doubtless merit many questions. These analyses are not only an indefatigable and interminable destruction of 'formal logic', they are so acute and so free as concerns traditional conceptuality, that a commentary running several pages would betray them immeasurably. (*ED* 161/*WD* 315)

Although 'Violence and Metaphysics' mentions some of the themes of 'Beyond the Face' – for example, those of pluralism (*ED* 132/*WD* 89) and fecundity (*ED* 127/*WD* 86) – one might say that the text *forecloses* a detailed discussion of them and erects a frontier, or limit, to its conceptual schema ('We will not go beyond this schema'), a frontier that is crossed by the phenomenological descriptions of 'Beyond the Face'. I suggest that the reason why these themes have to be excluded is not just because 'a commentary running several pages would betray them immeasurably' – a statement which, for the reasons discussed above, has more truth than might at first be imagined – but also because they would betray the conceptual schema of 'Violence and Metaphysics'. Now, if the governing intention of Levinas's work, that of the break with Parmenides, is achieved in those descriptions of eros, fecundity, and pluralism ('Existing itself becomes double. The Eleatic notion of Being is overcome' (*TA* 88/*TO* 92)), the very descriptions which the commentary of 'Violence and Metaphysics' cannot but betray – and which would betray the order of its commentary and of commentary itself – then does not their omission mark a serious flaw in the fabric of 'Violence and Metaphysics'? And is this a flaw which only the woman reader, both the betrayed and the betrayer, can discern? I suggest that it is plausible to read the second moment of 'En ce moment même' as a supplement to 'Violence and Metaphysics', whose supplementary logic would be to inhabit and dislocate the latter, betraying its conceptuality through a double reading and opening the text to an economy whose necessity would be ethical.

Returning to the context of the second moment of reading in 'En ce moment même', the woman reader is seeking to interrogate the link in Levinas's work between sexual difference – the other as another sex – and ethical difference – the other as Other (*Autrui*) and the other as 'He', the wholly other (*ECM* 52). It is important to stress from the outset that the woman reader will not simply claim that Levinas's work is anti-feminist, patriarchal, or sexist, but rather that by subordinating sexual difference to ethical difference and by trying to maintain the latter in a sexual *indifference* or *neutrality*, Levinas privileges the masculine. But how does this take place?

On the same page of *Totality and Infinity* on which Levinas speaks of the son as the work which attains a plurality within Being, he proceeds to substitute the word 'child' (*enfant*) for 'son' (*fils*); thus, 'I do not have my child, I am my child' (*TeI* 254/*TI* 277). Of this silent act of substitution, the woman reader asks: 'Is it that "son" is another word for "child", a child who could be of one or the other sex?' (*ECM* 52). If this is the case, if the work of the child is sexually indifferent, then 'Why couldn't the daughter play an analogous role?' (ibid.). If the neutral work can be as well described by the word 'child', then why should the word 'son' (*fils*) mark this indifference or neutrality more ably than the word 'daughter' (*fille*)? The work of the son in *Totality and Infinity* establishes an absolute ethical difference which is *sexually* indifferent. The sexual difference, the erotic life, that is so evocatively described in 'Phenomenology of Eros' is ultimately *aufgehoben* by the fecundity which establishes a meta-Parmenidean *ethical* difference.

The question now becomes: If ethical difference is sexually indifferent, then 'how can one mark as masculine the very thing that is said to be anterior or still foreign to sexual difference?' (*ECM* 52). It has already been established that if Levinas's work works, then it is precisely to the extent that it allows the trace of Illeity, the 'Il' of the wholly other, to glimmer in the face of the Other (*Autrui*). Now, if this 'Il' is sexually neutral, how can it be marked with a masculine pronoun? The silent slippage that occurs between 'child' and 'son' reveals that the supposed neutrality of ethical difference is marked, in Levinas's work, by a certain priority of the masculine. The sexual indifference of ethical difference treats masculinity and neutrality as synonyms. However, these are not the only pair of synonyms at work here, because by making sexual difference secondary to ethical difference and by marking the latter with a masculine pronoun, the secondary status of sexual difference becomes synonymous with the secondary status of the feminine. The problematic that ultimately guides the second moment of reading is given in the form of a question. The woman reader writes:

I come then to my question. Since the work is under-signed by the Pro-noun He (before he/she certainly, but He is not She), could it be that in making sexual alterity secondary, it becomes, far from letting itself be approached from the Work, his or the one that says itself there, the mastery, mastery of sexual difference, posed as origin of femininity? Hence mastery of femininity? (*ECM* 54–5)

Does not the supposed sexual neutrality of ethical difference lead ineluctably to a mastery of sexual difference and, synonymously, a mastery of the masculine over the feminine? If this is the case, then how can Levinasian ethics be considered ethical?

These questions take us right to the heart of the second moment of reading. The claim is that Levinas makes sexual difference secondary with respect to the sexually neutral wholly other. To mark the neutrality of the wholly other with a masculine pronoun is to make sexual difference secondary as femininity. Yet this state of affairs is about to undergo a reversal and be exposed to the supplementary logic of the double reading:

> The secondary status of sexual, and therefore, says He, of feminine difference, does it not thus come to stand for the wholly-other of this Saying of the wholly other, within its *sériature* here determined and within the idiom of this negotiation? (*ECM* 55)

By making sexual difference secondary to ethical difference and by equating sexuality with the feminine, does not the feminine, then, become wholly-other to the Saying of the wholly other? If 'She' is the other to 'He', and if 'He' is the wholly other, then 'She' is the other to the wholly other. The question then becomes: As the other to the wholly other, as a being that possesses greater alterity than the wholly other, does 'She' not demand greater ethical respect and priority than 'He'? 'The other as feminine (me), far from being derived or secondary, would become the other of the Saying of the wholly-other' (*ECM* 55).

The reversal that the woman reader is attempting here is one in which priority is given to that which was secondary. If 'He', the wholly other, 'will have obliged' us to an absolute obligation, then may not 'She', the other to the wholly other, have put us under an even greater, more primordial obligation? For the woman reader, the theme of the feminine constitutes 'a surfeit of un-said alterity' (*un surcroît d'altérité non-dite*) (*ECM* 55) within the *sériature* of Levinas's work. One might say that sexual difference is Levinas's 'blind spot'. But what economy governs this blind spot? How does Levinas remain blind to sexual difference? Two *enclosures* can be detected in Levinas's work: first, by making sexual difference secondary and by seeking to master the un-said alterity of the feminine, the 'Il' of the wholly other risks *enclosing* itself within the economy of the Same; second, by seeking to enclose sexual difference within ethical difference, Levinas *encloses* the feminine within the economy of the Same. The woman reader writes:

> Included within the same, it is by the same stroke excluded: enclosed within, foreclosed within the immanence of a crypt, incorporated in the Saying which says itself to the wholly other. (*ECM* 55)

Feminine alterity becomes enclosed within the Saying which says itself to the wholly other. The feminine is foreclosed within the immanence of a *crypt*.[13]

The economy of the blind spot is governed by these two enclosures: the enclosure of the trace of Illeity within the economy of the Same and the enclosure of the feminine within a crypt. Levinas remains blind to the priority of feminine alterity by circumscribing the feminine within the economy of the ethical and by inhuming her within the crypt of the Same. For the woman reader, the de-sexualization of the wholly other is a way of making the feminine secondary, and hence of failing to recognize 'Her' as the other to the wholly other. To recognize the absolute alterity of the feminine is to realize that 'She' replaces 'He' as the *Pro-nom* of Levinas's work: '*Elle aura obligé*'.

> Then the Work apparently signed by the Pro-noun He would be dictated, inspired and aspirated by the desire to make She secondary, therefore *by* She. (*ECM* 55)

The conclusion to the second moment of reading is that feminine alterity, as the other to the wholly other, 'pre-seals' (*ECM* 59) Levinas's work in such a way that it *does not* work for 'Him'. Levinas's work can only go unto the wholly other on the condition that feminine alterity is circumscribed and inhumed. The strange consequence of the latter is that Levinas's work is itself engaged in a denial of (feminine) alterity, and thus remains enclosed within the economy of the Same which it has continually striven to exceed.

If, during the first moment of reading, it was discovered that the way in which Levinas's work works was best described in terms of *sériature*, then the second moment has discovered a second *sériature* which shows how Levinas's work does not work for 'Il' but for 'Elle'. At the very moment when, with one hand, I weave the delicate fabric of the ethical text, another hand, a woman's hand, undoes my work. The question now becomes: How exactly does the repetition and commentary of the first moment of reading combine with the violence and interruption of the second moment in a text *for* Emmanuel Levinas? How do these two moments preserve the gift of the ethical? 'Bois'?

3.4   How the Work is Given to Levinas

The woman reader freely admits the violence of her reading: 'What I suggest here is not without violence' (*ECM* 56). It is a faulty violence, which leaves a flaw in *his* name and *his* work: 'violence faulty in regard to his name, his work' (*ECM* 56). Yet who is 'he' in this context? Against whom is the violence committed? Is it against 'him', Emmanuel Levinas? Or is it against 'Him', the wholly other?

As I noted above, the logic of the fault, of violence and ingratitude, is not accidental but essential to the ethical event of the text: 'Bois'. Ingratitude does not arise like an accidental evil; it is a necessity or fatality within ethical Saying (*ECM* 56). The necessity of Levinas's work is that its *work*, the 'Il', must be ungratefully received in order to maintain ethical alterity. In the second moment of reading, this alterity is maintained by returning the work to 'Elle' and not to E.L. Consequently, the violence that the woman reader commits is directed against 'Him', Levinas's work, and not against 'him', Emmanuel Levinas. Ingratitude and violence are perpetrated against the body of the wholly other and not against Levinas: 'It isn't him, but Him, that my fault comes to wound in his body' (*ECM* 56).

'Bois' – 'drink'. The fault has been committed. The violence has been done. The body of the 'Il' has been wounded. The text for Emmanuel Levinas has been written, and ethical alterity has been maintained. Yet how can this violent, wounding text be given to Emmanuel Levinas? What will become of this faulty text?

> If I wanted to destroy or annul my fault, I should have to know what becomes of the text that is writing itself at this very moment, where it can take place and what can remain of its remains. (*ECM* 56)

If (and the hypothetical character of this conjunction must be noted) the woman reader wanted to annul her fault and give her text to Levinas in a way that would still maintain the ethical, what would she be obliged to do? At this point, the text takes a further and final detour into 'Le nom de Dieu d'aprés quelques textes Talmudiques'. Levinas remarks that in the Talmudic tradition it is expressly forbidden to efface any of the names of God (*ND* 157). If one does, by some fault, efface one of His names, if one's hand slips on a page of the manuscript bearing His name, then, 'the entire page[14] upon which the error that motivates the erasure or effacement of the Name figures, must be placed in the earth like a dead body' (*ND* 157). The Torah is a body of writings which is given as much respect as the living body of a human being, and when that textual body is violated or fatally flawed, it must be buried in accordance with the same ceremonies that accompany human burial. The woman reader is intrigued here by the analogy between textuality, embodiment, and the act of burial. The body of the faulty text is not censorially burnt and reduced to a pile of ashes; rather, it is inhumed like a corpse and allowed slowly to decompose. The fault within the text disappears slowly as the text decomposes.

The woman reader finds a correspondence between this Talmudic anecdote and the status of her own text. To wound or violate the trace of Illeity by replacing the pronoun 'Il' with 'Elle' constitutes an act of effacement or erasure. The woman reader effaces the Pronoun or Forename of God and replaces it with 'Elle'. Now, in order to annul or destroy this fault, this text *for* Emmanuel Levinas must be placed in the earth and allowed to decompose. Thus, the faulty text is given to Levinas by burying it in the earth, where it is preserved in a process of slow decomposition. However, the burial of the text does not render it faultless and thereby deny ethical alterity by returning the text to its author. On the contrary, the fault is not erased; it is preserved in the process of decomposition. Ethical alterity is maintained because the fault, although inhumed, is still preserved, and hence the text is returned to 'Elle' and not to E.L. It is 'She', the feminine body, the body of feminine alterity, who is buried. It is she, the woman reader, who gives the dead body of the feminine to Levinas. 'His' work has been violated and given back to Him in the buried form of the feminine body, because this is the only way in which the ethical work can be maintained. After the burial, the text *for* Levinas becomes an absent work, what is called 'a work of mourning' (*un travail de deuil*) (*ECM* 57).[15] Consequently, the ethical work is a funeral work of mourning over the dead body of the feminine. The final scene of 'En ce moment même' takes place at a funeral.

The woman reader brings her reading to a close with the words 'Elle aura obligé'. However, the text does not end here, for another voice comes to interrupt the text:

– 'I no longer know if you are saying what his work says. Perhaps that comes back to the same. I no longer know if you are saying the contrary, or if you have already written something wholly other. I no longer hear your voice, I have difficulty distinguishing it from my own, from any other, your fault suddenly becomes illegible to me. Interrupt me.' (*ECM* 59)

Whose is the voice that interrupts and says 'I' here? It is clearly not that of the woman reader, for it is she who is interrupted. Returning to the hypothesis of the *clôtural*, or double, reading that I have argued for, I would claim that it is most plausible that the 'I' denotes the return of the masculine voice of the Same, the voice of commentary that showed how Levinas's work worked. On this reading, the second person singular pronoun 'you' would refer to the woman reader, and the possessive pronoun 'his' would refer to Levinas's work. Thus, the masculine textual voice no longer knows if the woman reader is saying what Levinas's work says. To say the same would doubtless return that work within the economy of the Same ('Perhaps that comes back to the same'). On the other hand, the textual voice also adds that it no longer knows if the woman reader is saying the contrary to Levinas's work or if she has written something wholly other. The masculine voice no longer knows if she is saying the same or something other to Levinas's work; the voice no longer knows how to read the reading. He no longer hears the woman's voice, and it becomes difficult to distinguish it from his own or from that of any other. It is at this point that the textual voice becomes plural, that the male voice becomes indistinguishable from that of the woman, that the two moments of reading become inter(el)laced, and that, at that very moment, the fault within the woman's reading becomes unreadable. The textual voice is unable to read Levinas's work in terms of one moment or the other. The two moments, or lines, of the *clôtural* reading suddenly cross and form the figure of a chiasmus. It is from within this unknowing, unreadable, undecidable position that the voice demands of the Other, 'Interrupt me'.

The response to this final call for interruption leads into the last scene of 'En ce moment même', the strange final paragraph of the essay. How is one to comment on it? Is it even capable of being read? In fact, despite its obscurity, the final paragraph resonates with many of the themes that have already been discussed. It can be approached as a liturgy – 'THE THING OF THIS LITURGY' (*ECM* 59) – in the Levinasian sense – that is, as a *leitourgia*, the Greek term which describes the movement of the work (*ergon*) from the Same to the Other (*EDE* 192). It is a liturgy spoken at a funeral, the funeral of the feminine Other: 'HERE AT THIS VERY MOMENT I ROLL UP THE BODY OF OUR INTERLACED VOICES CON-SONANTS VOWELS ACCENTS FAULTY IN THIS MANU-SCRIPT' (*ECM* 59). The 'I' that speaks here is the woman reader. It is she who rolls up the interlaced voices and moments of reading into the body of the text. It is she who gives the text to Levinas by bury-ing it in the earth: 'I MUST PLACE IT IN THE EARTH FOR YOU – COME LEAN DOWN' (ibid.). It is she who calls ('COME') to the Other to lean down over the place where the gift is buried. One imagines a man and a woman leaning over a grave at a funeral and looking down at the earth. The woman speaks: 'IT'S OUR MUTE INFANT A DAUGHTER PERHAPS OF AN INCEST STILLBORN' (ibid.).

The faulty text that wounds the jealous body of the 'Il' is 'Elle', the stillborn daughter whose fatally flawed body is buried and allowed slowly to decompose, thereby rendering the fault illegible. 'She' is the faulty body, the inhumed stillborn daughter. 'IN THE BOTTOM-LESS CRYPT THE INDECIPHERABLE STILL GIVES ITSELF TO BE READ' (*ECM* 60). The only way in which the daughter can be contained within ethical difference is by enclosing her within the bottomless crypt of the Same, within an economy that makes sexual difference secondary. The voice of feminine alterity speaks out from the closure of this crypt; the woman reader pleads, 'WE MUST HAVE A NEW BODY ANOTHER WITHOUT ANY MORE JEALOUSY THE MOST ANCIENT STILL TO COME' (ibid.).

The faulty text has been buried; the stillborn daughter decomposes within the crypt. Above, a woman's voice weaves (*TISSE*) and effaces itself (*M'Y EFFACER*). The gift has been given; the text for E.L. has been returned to 'Elle' and buried; ethical alterity has been maintained. The woman's voice calls to the Other, 'TAKE IT... APPROACH'; she beckons to the Other to come closer and receive the gift. Again, one imagines a woman and a man leaning over a grave; the man, the older of the two, plunges his hands into the earth and takes his stillborn daughter in his arms: 'BOIS'.

21 And the man wondering at her held his peace, to wit whether the LORD had made his journey prosperous or not.

22 And it came to pass, as the camels had done drinking, that the man took a golden earring of half a shekel weight, and two bracelets for her hands of ten *shekels* weight of gold;

23 And said, Whose daughter *art* thou? tell me, I pray thee: is there room *in* thy father's house for us to lodge in?

NOTES

1 On the theme of the 'cercle ulyséen' of philosophy, see Derrida's 'Ulysse Gramophone: l'ouï-dire de Joyce' in *Genèse de Babel*, Etudes présentés par Claude Jacquet (Centre National de Recherches Scientifiques, Paris, 1985), pp. 227–64; reprinted in *Ulysse Gramophone* (Galileé, Paris, 1987), pp. 57–143; page references to the original text. In this essay, through a reading of Joyce's *Ulysses*, Derrida tries to show that there is a pre-original *oui*, or 'yes', which breaches the circular movement of *The Odyssey*, the en*cyclo*paedic dialectic of philosophical appropriation. With a logic that should by now be familiar, this pre-logocentric, pre-ontological opening of the *oui* is, for Derrida, the *responsibility* which all discourse presupposes: 'The auto-position in the *yes*...is pre-ontological, if ontology says what-is or the Being of what-is. Discourse on Being presupposes the responsibility of the *yes*' (p. 257).

2 Cf. Cathérine Chalier, 'Ethics and the Feminine', in *RRL* 129.

3   For occurrences of this word in relation to Heidegger, cf. *EP* 95.

4   On the question of the performative, see *ECM* 46–7, and the reference
     to speech act theory, *ECM* 33–4. The relation of Levinasian ethics to
     speech act theory is discussed by Jan de Greef in 'Skepticism and
     Reason', tr. Dick White, in *FF* 181–202.

5   Strangely, when the textual voice copies the phrase from the essay on
     Bataille as part of *ECM*, it misquotes it. The quotation marks that
     surround the words 'absolute tear' and 'solid' suddenly rise like the
     curtain in a theatre, as Derrida is wont to say (*E* 53–4/*OS* 31). This fact
     is all the more ironical because Derrida makes so much of Heidegger's
     misquotation of quotation marks when the latter cites his 1933 Rectoral
     Address in his 1935 *Introduction to Metaphysics* (*E* 57/*OS* 57).

6   On the notion of the text as a tissue (*textus, texere, textile*), see the
     unoccasioned paragraph that is appended to the Bibliography of *ED*
     ('*texte* veut dire *tissu*') (*ED* 437). This note is discussed at length by
     Alan Bass in *WD* ix–xx.

7   For Bataille's reading of Hegel, see the few fascinating pages devoted to
     the subject in Bataille, *L'Expérience intérieure* (Gallimard, Paris, 1943),
     pp. 127–30.

8   Levinas employs formulations very similar to those from *OB* in *TI*. For
     example:

> And if I set forth, as in a final and absolute vision, the separation and
> transcendence which are the questioned *in this very work* (*dans cet ouvrage
> même*) these relations, which I claim form the fabric of Being itself, first
> come together in *my present discourse* (*mon discours présent*) addressed to my
> interlocutors: inevitably across my idea of the Infinite the other faces
> me – hostile, friend, my master, my student. (*TeI* 53/*TI* 81, my emphasis;
> cf. *TeI* 247, 271–2/*TI* 269, 295)

9   Is it through the act of repetition that one gains access to the wholly
     other? I would like to let this question suspend itself over the entirety
     of the present discussion. What interests Derrida in Levinas's use of
     language is precisely this repetition: 'The possibility of this repetition is
     the very thing that interests me' (*ECM* 23). In the repetition of phrases
     like 'en ce moment même' and also in the repetition that takes place
     within a Levinasian phrase like 'a passivity more passive than all pass-
     ivity' (*ECM* 47), a certain dimension of alterity opens up, whereby
     traditional terms like 'passivity' begin to signify something other than
     their traditional signification. The repetition of traditional language
     prepares the Saying of something wholly other to the tradition. In this
     regard, see Blanchot's remarks on repetition in *L'Ecriture du désastre*
     (Gallimard, Paris, 1980), pp. 14–5, 20, 72.

10　One might – and perhaps *should* – read the second moment of *ECM* in conjunction with Luce Irigaray's essays on Levinas: both the subtle and evocative reading of 'Phenomenology of Eros' (*TeI* 233–44/*TI* 256–66) undertaken in 'La fécondité' de la caresse', in *Ethique de la différence sexuelle* (Minuit, Paris, 1984), pp. 173–99, tr. Carolyn Burke as 'The Fecundity of the Caress' in *FF* 231–56, and the more directly critical reading given in 'Questions to Emmanuel Levinas. On the Divinity of Love', in *RRL* 109–18. In the latter, Irigaray articulates many of the themes raised in the second moment of reading: the function of the son (*fils*) in the relation of sexual pleasure (*volupté*) and the notion of the son as a work (*œuvre*); the subordination of the feminine to the *telos* of paternity, the question of the fault (*faute*) and the faultiness of (male) ethics; and the subordination of sexual difference and carnal love within monotheism, particularly Judaism. Indeed, Irigaray identifies a double gesture, or deconstructive tension, in Levinas's work, between two levels of discourse. On the one hand, the phenomenology of carnality and feminine alterity in 'Phenomenology of Eros' suggest that 'we are no longer in the order of metaphysics'. On the other hand, the institution of ethics through fecundity and paternity reinscribes Levinas within the metaphysics of patriarchy and male subjectivity. Although Levinas's phenomenology of feminine alterity interrupts metaphysics, Irigaray rightly claims that Levinas always privileges the second level of his discourse, at which he 'clings once more to this rock of patriarchy in the very place of carnal love' (p. 113). The difference between Irigaray (at least in her second essay) and Derrida is that she does not attempt to read Levinas deconstructively; rather, she engages in a powerful, necessary and compelling feminist *critique* of Levinas which speaks with a woman's voice. Derrida is a man, and, furthermore, in the second moment of reading, a man speaking with the voice of a woman. But is such a *mimēsis*, or mimicry, of the feminine by the masculine really plausible? Is it dangerous politically? Should it, too, become the subject of feminist critique?

　　For a more subtle and stratified discussion of the question of the feminine in Levinas, with reference to wider feminist issues, see Tina Chanter, 'Antigone's Dilemma', in *RRL* 130–46, and 'Feminism and the Other', in *the Provocation of Levinas*, ed. R. Bernasconi and D. Wood (Routledge, London and New York, 1986), pp. 32–56.

11　On the important theme of *viens* as the name for that which cannot be contained within philosophy, metaphysics, or discourse upon Being and which calls beyond Being and from the Other, see *AT* 31 where Derrida writes: 'For want of time, I shall limit myself to the word, if it is a word, and the motif "Come" ("*Viens*") that occupies other texts written in the meantime, in particular "Pas", "Living On" and "At this very moment in this work here I am", three texts dedicated, one could say, to Blanchot and to Levinas.'

12   Although the centrality of the paternalistic metaphor of fecundity is true of the works up to and including *TI*, one wonders whether this is also true of *OB*, in particular of what Levinas says of *maternity* – 'gestation of the other in the same' (*AE* 95/*OB* 75; cf. *AE* 130–9/*OB* 102–9) – as a metaphor for the substitution that characterizes ethical subjectivity. Although maternity is mentioned in *TI* (*TeI* 255/*TI* 278), the theme of fecundity (and the language of 'ontological categories') is absent from *OB*. Is one to conclude that Levinas's work has become less paternalistic to the extent that it has become less ontological? A careful, sensitive approach to these issues has been broached by Cathérine Chalier in *Figures du féminin* (La nuit surveillée, Paris, 1982); see esp. pp. 126–33 and 139–49. Of course, the real issue at stake in the use of the metaphors of fecundity, paternity, and maternity in the description of the ethical relation is precisely whether these terms are metaphors at all. If, as Levinas insists (*TeI* 257/*TI* 279), these terms are not to be interpreted biologically or taken literally, are they to be understood metaphorically? What is implied in the metaphorical use of the biological language of fecundity and maternity?

13   On the theme of the crypt in Derrida's work, see 'Fors: les mots anglés de Nicolas Abraham et Maria Torok', in *Cryptonymie: le verbier de l'homme aux loups* (Aubier-Flammarion, Paris, 1976); tr. Barbara Johnson, *The Georgia Review*, 31, no. 1 (1977), pp. 64–116. See also the discussion of Hegel's interpretation of *Antigone* in *Glas* (*GL* 198–263 *GLtr* 142–88), where Derrida focuses specifically on the theme of the crypt, or sepulchre.

14   In the transcription of this sentence that appears in *ECM*, the textual voice mistakenly substitutes 'manuscript' (*manuscrit*) for 'page' (*feuillet*), and writes: 'The whole manuscript then has to be buried' (*ECM* 57). Levinas writes that it is only the page that contains the fault that must be buried.

15   This reading should be closely shadowed by Derrida's *Mémoires pour Paul de Man*, and in particular the first lecture, 'Mnemosyne', which deals with the theme of an impossible mourning: 'Or is it that of the *impossible mourning* (*deuil impossible*), which, leaving the other his alterity, in respecting the other's infinite remove, refuses or finds itself incapable of taking the other within oneself, as in the tomb (*tombe*) or the vault (*caveau*) of some narcissism?' (*MPM* 27/*MPMtr* 6, my emphasis).

4

Clôtural Readings II:
Wholly Otherwise:
Levinas's Reading of Derrida

In this chapter, I follow the path of a dislocation. When Levinas reads Derrida, he renounces the 'ridiculous ambition of "improving"' (*NP* 89) a true philosopher. Levinas is content to cross Derrida's path in order to engage him in a philosophical encounter. I shall report this encounter by following the reading that Levinas gives of Derrida, a reading which, while continually transgressing the order of commentary, remains faithful, I believe, to the ultimate ethical orientation of the thinking under discussion. At stake here is the perverse fidelity of a dislocation in the act of reading.

Broadly, my claim is that Levinas gives a double-handed, or *clôtural*, reading of deconstruction. On the one hand, he sees Derrida's work as a continuation and completion of the Kantian critique of metaphysics, a continuation which somehow 'thinks through to the end' (*NP* 87) the epoch of critique. Deconstruction is distinguished by its critique of the determination of Being as presence, a critique which, Levinas claims, 'employs the present tense of the verb to be' and 'seems to offer an ultimate refuge to presence' (*NP* 85). On the other hand, if one side of Levinas's reading stresses the dependence of deconstruction upon the metaphysical tradition that it deconstructs – arguments that are hauntingly analogous to those raised by Derrida 'against' Levinas in 'Violence and Metaphysics' – this only tells half the story. For Levinas goes on to show that there is a moment of dislocation in deconstruction, where the latter's 'rigorous reflection' also 'lets us catch a glimpse of these interstices of Being where this very reflection unsays itself' (*NP* 86). Thus deconstruction remains located within the ontological tradition of critique, while, at the same time, dislocating that tradition and opening it to the ethical dimension in the Levinasian sense. In short, concealed within the Said of Derrida's texts – and Levinas is thinking in particular of *Voice and Phenomenon* – is an ethical Saying. Levinas does not divorce the ethical Saying of deconstruction from its location in the Said; rather, he shows how the Saying is maintained within the Said as the permanent possibility of the latter's interruption. I will pursue this dislocation by first establishing a schema of reading and then deepening and complicating it in discussions of scepticism and the function of the indicative sign in Husserl's concept of meaning. This study is an exposition and enactment of Levinasian hermeneutics.

4.1 It's Today Tomorrow

How does Levinas read and understand Derrida? Interestingly, this is one of the questions that the woman reader raises in Derrida's 'En ce moment même'. She writes: 'I always ask myself whether he understands me to be *against* a tradition that would have refused me that ontological dignity, or, better than ever, *within* that profoundly repeated tradition' (*ECM* 53). That is, the woman reader asks herself whether Levinas understands her to be against the ontological tradition or whether she represents a repetition of that tradition. In this first part, I want to explore an analogous question, namely: Given that Levinas understands the philosophical tradition *qua* ontology in terms of a forgetfulness or refusal of ethical alterity, does Derrida represent a continuation of that tradition, or do his works bring about the latter's overcoming?

Levinas opens this line of questioning in the first paragraph of 'Wholly Otherwise':

> May not Derrida's work cut into the development of Western thinking with a line of demarcation similar to that of Kantianism, which separated dogmatic philosophy from critical philosophy? Are we again at the end of a naïveté, of an unsuspected dogmatism which slumbered at the base of that which we took for critical spirit?[1] We may well ask ourselves. The Idea, as the completion of a series which begins in intuition without being able to end there; the Idea said to be 'in the Kantian sense of the term' would operate within intuition itself: a transcendental semblance itself generating metaphysics would create an illusion within presence itself, a presence that would ceaselessly be

found to be wanting. A new break in the history of philosophy? One that would also mark its continuity (*Nouvelle coupure dans l'histoire de la philosophie? Elle en marquerait aussi la continuité*). The history of philosophy is probably only a growing awareness of the difficulty of thinking. (*NP* 81)

Thus Levinas begins his reading of Derrida with a question that compares deconstruction to Kant's critical philosophy. The comparison with Kant is clearly of importance to Levinas, since he alludes to it in the only footnote to 'Wholly Otherwise' and repeats the formulation in a passage of the important essay 'La pensée de l'être et la question de l'autre' cited below. For Levinas, the first reaction to Derrida's thinking, its Kantian or, more properly, Humean moment, lies in its awakening of the critical spirit from the sleep of dogma. Derrida, like Kant, represents a critical watershed with respect to previous thinking. For Levinas, the epoch of critical philosophy is the period of philosophical crisis precipitated by Kant, continued by Husserl, and completed by Derrida.[2] In the second part of 'La pensée de l'être', after a broad discussion of the domination of philosophy by ontology, Levinas goes on to discuss the *crisis* of ontology. He claims that this crisis is rooted in the critique of metaphysics begun by Kant, a critique born out of the need for a philosophical 'vigilance' (*PEQA* 179) or tribunal of reason with an authority independent of that of traditional, dogmatic metaphysics. It is a critique of the 'transcendental illusion' – namely, the false dogma that the *a priori* forms of reason, valid for experience, constitute the nature of ultimate reality and hence that human understanding can have metaphysical knowledge of God and the soul as they are in themselves. For Levinas, the vigilance of Kantian critique is continued in Husserlian phenomenology in so far as the latter constitutes a critique of ontology in its denunciation of the 'transcendental illusion' and the degenerate speculation of *metaphysica specialis*. Henceforth, everything which is must be comprehended from within the horizon of its appearance to a constituting transcendental consciousness: 'All being must be understood in its genesis from the viewpoint of this privileged appearance in the "transcendental consciousness", from this phenomenon-being, from this presence or from this living present given to intuition' (*à partir de ce phénomène-être, de cette présence ou de ce présent vivant donné à l'intuition*)' (*PEQA* 181). The Husserlian comprehension of the Being of that which is in terms of its phenomenal appearance to intentional consciousness represents, for Levinas, 'the criticist end of metaphysics' (*la fin criticiste de la métaphysique*) (*PEQA* 180). By bringing Being back from its sojourn in a supersensible Platonic realm and giving it over to appearance, the advent of phenomenological critique marks an end to a certain metaphysics.

Returning to Derrida, Levinas claims that the Kantian and Husserlian tradition of ontological critique reaches its summation in the deconstruction of Husserlian phenomenology and of the 'Idea in the Kantian sense' carried out in Derrida's *Voice and Phenomenon*. In this sense, Derrida's work is a continuation of the tradition of metaphysical critique which consequently maintains a continuity with that tradition. Yet, if this were all that could be said about Derrida's work, then where, one might protest, is the novelty and radicality of the deconstructive approach? Might not the deconstruction of the concept of presence in Husserl constitute a critique of phenomenological critique and thus mark a break with the critical tradition? These questions are addressed in the following passage from 'La pensée de l'être', which repeats certain of the formulae from 'Wholly Otherwise' while engaging them in a subtle dislocation.

A privilege of presence that Derrida's *Voice and Phenomenon* specifically places in question. The very possibility of the plenitude of presence is challenged. Such a plenitude would always be postponed, always 'simply indicated' in the 'vouloir-dire' (in the *Meinen*), which, for Husserl, entirely referred itself to intuitive plenitude. A most radical critique of the philosophy of Being, for which the transcendental illusion commences at the level of the immediate. We may well ask ourselves, when faced with the importance and the intellectual rigour of *Voice and Phenomenon*, whether or not this text, in the same way as Kantianism, marks a line of demarcation with respect to traditional philosophy; whether or not we are, once again, at the end of a naïveté, awoken to the dogmatism which slumbered at the base of that which we took for critical spirit. To think through the end of metaphysics: it is not only the hinter-worlds which are meaningless, the world displayed before us also incessantly escapes us; lived experience postpones itself in lived experience. The *immediate* is not only a call to mediation, it is a transcendental illusion. (*Fin, pensée jusqu'au bout, de la métaphysique: ce ne sont pas seulement les arrières-mondes qui n'ont pas de sens, c'est le monde étalé devant nous qui se dérobe incessament, c'est le vécu qui s'ajourne dans le vécu. L'immédiat n'est pas seulement appel à la médiation, il est illusion transcendantale.*) (*PEQA* 181)

In this passage, Levinas's understanding of *Voice and Phenomenon* becomes more explicit. The most valuable insight of the latter work is its deconstruction of the concept of presence presupposed and privileged by Husserlian phenomenology. Husserl's 'principle of principles' – namely, that what *presents* itself to intuition in a primordial form is to be accepted as a source of evidence for knowledge[3], – is shown by Derrida to be, first, founded on a metaphysics of presence as ancient as Parmenides (*VP* 26/*SP* 25), and, second, subject to an infinite deferral whereby the *parousia* of presence is perpetually postponed (*VP* 111–14/*SP* 99–102). In this way, the phenomenon with which phenomenology works, which is founded on a plenitude of presence, is shown to steal itself away and conceal itself. The immediacy of experience is the new transcendental illusion. The intuitionistic data of lived experience, which are teleologically bound to the postulate of the 'Idea in the Kantian sense', are continually postponed in their presence, and opened to the deferring movement of *différance*.

For Levinas, the Kantian and Husserlian critique of ontology concerned itself with an attack on the transcendental illusion, on the Platonic distinction between Being and appearance, or the supersensuous and the sensuous, which, as Nietzsche remarked, constitutes the origin of metaphysics.[4] The consequence of this critique is the equivalence of Being and appearance: namely, that which *is* is what appears to consciousness, which is what Heidegger saw as Husserl's crucial insight into the phenomenality of Being.[5] Thus, the critique of ontology, in so far as it reveals the meaninglessness of all hinterworldly metaphysics, represents an end to metaphysics. Now Derrida, on Levinas's reading, by thinking through the end of metaphysics, deconstructs the concept of presence and shows how the phenomenon slips away from the phenomenologist *ad infinitum*. The immediacy of the phenomenon is shown to be derived not from presence but from *différance*, which is to say, 'The thing itself always escapes' (*La chose même se dérobe toujours*) (*VP* 117/*SP* 104). By thinking through the end of metaphysics, Derridian deconstruction thus represents both a continuation of the critical tradition and a break with that tradition; deconstruction is a *critique of critique, or a crisis of crisis* (*E* 94–7/*OS* 60–1). As both a continuation and a break, a summation and a demarcation, deconstruction occupies an essentially ambivalent position, standing both within the critical tradition and being critical of that tradition, employing the Said of critique while unsaying its Said. This is why, when Levinas asks in the first paragraph of 'Wholly Otherwise' whether Derrida represents 'a new break in the history of philosophy', he immediately adds, 'one that would also mark its continuity'. Might it not be that deconstruction itself is caught between the two stools of the break with the tradition and its continuity – that is to say, within the logic of closure?

Having established this question, I will now resume the reading of 'Wholly Otherwise'.

> In the meantime we walk in a 'no-man's land', in an in-between which is uncertain even of the uncertainties which flicker everywhere. Suspension of truths! Strange epoch! (*Nous marchons, en attendant, dans un no man's land, dans un entre-les-deux qui est incertain même des incertitudes qui, partout, clignotent. Suspension de vérités! Insolite époque!*) Perhaps in writing each of us feels this when we catch ourselves unawares using familiar notions with a surplus of precautions, while the new critique would challenge the sense of imprudence as the virtue of prudence. A new style of thinking is dawning on us in reading these exceptionally precise texts which are yet so strange. (*NP* 82)

Uncertain as to whether Derrida's work constitutes a break or a continuation of the tradition, Levinas considers the third option of the 'no man's land', a military metaphor first used to describe the area between the trenches of opposing armies in the First World War. In the meantime, while we are awaiting (*en attendant*), Levinas places Derrida's thinking *entre-les-deux*, between the two opposing forces of the break with tradition and its continuity. The immediate outcome of thinking in the 'no man's land' is that language becomes littered with uncertainty and precaution. The scare quotes that surround familiar words act as a shield that betrays a fear of being shot from both sides. Words are used in such a way that they are not used; that is to say, they are used under erasure. However, such uncertainty should not be viewed as a restriction on thinking, for a few lines further on Levinas sees it as a liberation from 'the alternative of truth and falsehood', an 'imperious alternative, thanks to which computers decide the fate of the universe' (*NP* 87).

In order to describe the effect that reading Derrida has upon him, Levinas offers two forceful, strange and complicated images, both of which are drawn from the period of the Nazi occupation of France. One might pause here to wonder why Levinas employs such overtly military metaphors to describe Derrida's work, particularly when one considers the determining place that war has had in the development of Levinas's thought. In both the Preface to *Totality and Infinity* and the second section of 'The Argument' in *Otherwise than Being*, a quasi-Hobbesian state of war is thematized as the ontological event *par excellence*: the domination of totality over individual subjects, the persistence of essence or the *esse* in the life and death struggle between egoisms, and the subordination of peace and its ethical imperatives to the mocking gaze of 'political man' (*TeI* ix–x/*TI* 21–2; *AE* 4–6/ *OB* 4–5). The phenomenological movement of Levinas's major texts begins from the experience of war and murder as that which is to be *reduced*. However, Levinas describes his reaction to reading Derrida in the following way:

> When I read him, I always recall the exodus of 1940. A retreating military unit arrives in an as yet unsuspecting locality, where the cafés are open, where the ladies visit the 'ladies' fashion store', where the hairdressers dress hair and bakers bake; where viscounts meet other viscounts and tell each other stories of viscounts, and where, an hour later, everything is deconstructed and devastated (*tout est déconstruit et désolé une heure après*); houses closed up or left with their doors open, emptied of their occupants who are swept along in a current of cars and pedestrians, through roads restored to their 'former glory' as roads when, in an immemorial past, they were traced by great migrations (*restituées à leur 'profond jadis' de routes, tracées dans un passé immémorial par les grandes migrations*). (*NP* 82–3)

Why should reading Derrida remind Levinas of the exodus of 1940? First, it would seem that the period of the Nazi occupation of France was an 'in-between' or interim period, between the third and fourth French republics. Second, the 'act' of deconstruction, like the arrival of an occupying force during wartime, destroys and devastates all that had hitherto existed, the nexus of social and commercial practices: the *café*, the *boulangerie*. The image then continues with a Dantesque vision of hordes of people fleeing their homes and heading westwards away from the advancing forces of occupation. To get some idea of the allusive depth of Levinas's writing here, look again at the final three lines and the words ' *"profond jadis"* ' and *'passé immémorial'* and the verb *'tracées'*. The phrase *'profond jadis, jadis jamais assez'* ('deep past, past never enough'), is a quotation from Valéry that Levinas alludes to in several places. In *Totality and Infinity,* it appears in 'The Dwelling', the chapter that enacts the movement from egoist separation to transcendence or ethics (*TeI* 145/*TI* 170). Levinas is seeking to demonstrate (and this has been a familiar theme since his doctoral dissertation in 1930) the primacy of representational or theoretical consciousness in Husserlian phenomenology. Against the latter, Levinas argues that consciousness is conditioned by *life*, by the 'I' of enjoyment that lives from the elements and nourishes itself. Thus, for Levinas, the subject of consciousness is traced, or haunted, by an anterior structure of subjectivity *qua* enjoyment, a structure inaccessible to consciousness – 'a deep past'. In the 1963 essay 'The Trace of the Other', the same allusion is recalled immediately after the first introduction of the thought of the trace in Levinas's work (*EDE* 198), as indeed it is in the 1964 essay 'La signification et le sens', where the trace is a sign for an absolute past which has never been present and which is beyond memory (*H* 64). A very similar formulation can be found in *Otherwise than Being,* where Levinas claims that the ethical self is older than the time of consciousness accessible to memory, in its "deep pastness, a pastness which is never enough" ' (*plus vieux que le temps de la conscience accessible au souvenir, dans son 'profond jadis, jadis jamais assez'*) (*AE* 134/*OB* 106). In *Otherwise than Being,* ethical subjectivity is described as a pattern of substitution whereby the Other is always already within the self or under my skin without the subject having exercised free or conscious choice. The self is sundered and hence responsible to the Other in a past that is irrecuperable to memory.

Returning to the image, one can see how the experience of wartime evacuation, the 'deconstruction' of the social and commercial practices of peacetime, both destroys normal everyday life while at the same time evoking the former glory, or deep past, of those roads when they were traced by great migrations. The roads down which the evacuees flee is compared to the trace of an immemorial past which evokes in the reader of Levinas, almost subliminally, a chain of concepts that describe the structure of ethical selfhood. This is a highly ambivalent image, for Levinas is intimating obliquely – and why so obliquely? What is the function of the obliqueness, or indirection, that one might call *literary* in this work? A vast question – that deconstruction both suspends the present in a no man's land, a time dominated by the synonymous concepts of Being and war, while at the same time allowing the trace of ethical peace to persist beneath the fact of war.

The allusiveness and ambivalence of Levinas's prose is continued in a second image:

> In these in-between days a symbolic episode: somewhere in between Paris and Alençon, a half-drunk barber used to invite soldiers who were passing on the road to come and have a free shave in his shop; the 'lads' he used to call them in a patriotic language which soared above the waters or floated up from chaos. With his two companions he shaved them free of charge – and it was today. The essential procrastination – the future *différance* – was reabsorbed into the present. Time came to its end with the end or the interim period of France. (*En ces jours d'entre-temps, un épisode symbolique: quelque part entre Paris et Alençon, un coiffeur à moitié ivre invitait les soldats qui passaient sur la route – les 'petits gars' comme il les appelait dans un langage patriotique planant au-dessus des eaux, surnageant dans le chaos – à venir se faire raser gratuitement dans son échoppe. Avec ses deux compagnons, il rasait gratis et ce fut aujourd'hui. La procrastination essentielle – la future différance – se résorbait dans le présent. Le temps arrivait à sa fin avec la fin ou avec l'intérim de la France.*) (*NP* 83)[6]

The anecdote is straightforward enough: a half-drunk barber and his two companions gave free shaves to soldiers passing on the road. How can this reminiscence possibly illuminate the work of deconstruction? To see the significance of this image, one must first understand the idiom of the 'free shave' (*rase gratis*). The idiomatic phrase '*Demain on rase gratis*' can best be translated by the English idioms 'That'll be the day' or 'It's jam tomorrow'. This implies that the matter under discussion is an impossibility, a pie in the sky idea that will never come to anything. In the light of this, the anecdote begins to assume greater significance, because the half-drunk barber is, *at this very moment*, shaving people free of charge: '*Il rasait gratis et ce fut aujourd'hui.*' It is happening not tomorrow but today. The impossible future is happening at this very moment – it's jam today! That Levinas should apply this image to Derrida shows that he considers that the *impossible* takes place in his work.

Yet, what is the impossible? Levinas writes, 'The essential procrastination – the future *différance* – was reabsorbed into the present.' Procrastination – that is, putting something off, or postponing it, until tomorrow – is drawn back into today. This procrastination, which, moreover, is essential and is etymologically embedded in the neologism *différance* through its derivation from the verb *différer*, to defer, is somehow reabsorbed into the present. What does this mean? Levinas is obliquely hinting that the futural movement of *différance*, its temporization, which always defers the fulfilment, or *parousia*, of presence, is reabsorbed into the present, thereby fissuring the latter and usurping its authority. 'Time came to its end,' writes Levinas, and by this he is alluding to the way in which what Heidegger calls 'the vulgar conception of time', as a linear, infinite series of now-points passing through and sustaining the primacy of the present – the time that was inhabited before the occupation, the time of the *café* and the *boulangerie* – is deconstructed by the invading force of Derrida's work. Derrida, like a half-drunk barber, performs the impossible through his deconstruction of the privilege of presence.

One would be correct in concluding that, thus far, Levinas has been intent on showing the disruptive power of deconstruction, its discontinuity with the tradition. However, this conclusion is instantly thrown into doubt by the qualifier that follows in 'Wholly Otherwise':

> Unless the barber was only as delirious as that fourth form of delirium described in the *Phaedrus*, in which, since Plato, the discourse of Western metaphysics has remained. (*A moins que le coiffeur ne fut aussi délirant que la quatrième forme du délire du Phèdre, où, depuis Platon, se tient le discours de la métaphysique occidentale*). (NP 83)

In the *Phaedrus*, love (*eros*) is judged to be akin to both delirium and drunkenness. The fourth form of delirium is that possessed by and possessing the lover. It is the most elevated form of madness, because the lover is possessed by the god, and each time he looks upon the face of the beautiful boy, the stumps of the wings of his soul start to itch, and he desires to take flight towards a knowledge of the true, supersensible realm. Beauty is the sole intelligible form which shows itself sensuously in the realm of appearance, and thus it is beauty that provides a bridge from the sensible to the intelligible, from the physical to the metaphysical. Philosophical *eros* is a desire for the metaphysical, a luxurious desire that has repeatedly nourished the metaphysical tradition.[7]

But what is Levinas suggesting by this allusion to the *Phaedrus*? His qualifier begins with the conjunction 'unless' – an adverbial phrase in French: 'a moins que'. Thus Levinas appears to be saying that *différance* would have performed the impossible deconstruction of presence *unless* the barber were only as mad and as drunk as the Platonic lover. 'Unless' therefore marks a caveat, or moment of hesitation, in Levinas's text. If the history of Western metaphysics has remained caught up in this Platonic *eros* – which may be true also of Levinas, the *Phaedrus* being the most frequently cited text in *Totality and Infinity* and being listed by Levinas as one of the five great books in the history of philosophy (*EeI* 27) – then the possibility of any deconstructive twisting free from metaphysics, the possibility of the impossible, remains at the very least aporetic.

For Levinas the figure of the half-drunk barber is a metaphor for both the transgression of metaphysics and its restoration, a double-handed movement enacted by Derrida's text. On the one hand, by giving a 'rase gratis', the barber performs the impossible feat of opening the Platonism of presence to the constitutive movement of *différance* and thereby breaking with the metaphysical determination of Being. On the other hand, the barber is the Platonic lover who, aroused by the beauty of the soldiers, calls to them as Socrates calls to the young Phaedrus at the beginning of their dialogue. The wings of the barber's soul begin to grow, and, intoxicated by the god, he ascends from the sensible to the intelligible, thereby restoring metaphysical desire. The word 'half' (*moitié*) must be stressed in the figure of the half-drunk barber; the deconstructive thinker, on Levinas's reading, is *half* Platonic lover, symbol for Western metaphysics, and *half* anti-Platonist voice, making possible the impossible other to the *logos*.

How is one to understand Levinas's understanding of Derrida? Returning to the guiding question raised above, it is clear by now that, for Levinas, Derrida's work represents *both* a break with the tradition *and* a continuity with that tradition, both the razing of the edifice of metaphysics to the ground and the restoration of that edifice. '*It's today tomorrow*': the double bind of Levinas's reading of Derrida is conveyed by the title of that portion of 'Wholly Otherwise' that has provided my focus. Levinas does not write 'Tomorrow is today', which would indicate that Derridian deconstruction had broken completely with Platonist metaphysics and its reversal in the critical tradition, and that the impossible had occurred. Nor does he write 'Today is tomorrow', which would suggest the continuity of Platonism even in its inverted form, in which the *parousia* of presence would be maintained through the teleological postulation of the 'Idea in the Kantian sense'. By writing 'It's today tomorrow', Levinas confounds and confuses both these possibilities: it is neither today nor tomorrow, and it is both today and tomorrow. Levinas understands Derrida's work in terms of the contradictory conjunction of the *neither* and the *both*, of continuation and rupture, of summation and demarcation. If the intentionality of the reading is momentarily reversed, it will be recalled that, in 'Violence and Metaphysics', Derrida reads Levinas precisely in terms of the problematic that Levinas has been shown to have found in Derrida. To belong to the tradition and to be against it, to be neither completely within the tradition nor completely free of it, such is the logic of closure. Levinas gives a *clôtural* reading of Derrida, which shows how deconstruction dislocates the limit that divides ethics from ontology. I would like to pursue this reading with a discussion of scepticism.[8]

4.2 Scepticism

How does deconstruction concern itself with the Other? To the extent that Derrida employs logocentric language in the deconstruction of logocentrism, might one not be a little sceptical about the possibility of deconstruction leaving the house of Being within whose architecture language shelters? Levinas writes:

> What remains constructed after the de-construction is certainly the stern architecture of the de-constructing discourse which employs the present tense of the verb to be in predicative propositions. (*Ce qui reste de construit après la dé-construction c'est, certes, l'architecture sévère du discours qui dé-construit et qui emploie au présent le verbe être dans les propositions prédicatives.*) Discourse in the course of which, amidst the shaking of the foundations of truth, against the self-evidence of present lived experience which seems to offer an ultimate refuge to presence, Derrida still has the strength to say 'Is it certain?' (*Est-ce sûr?*)[9], as if anything

could be secure at that moment and as if security and insecurity should still matter. One might well (*on pourrait*) be tempted to infer an argument from this use of logocentric language against that very language, in order to dispute the produced deconstruction; a path much followed by the refutation of scepticism, but where, although at first crushed and trampled underfoot, scepticism got back up on its feet to come back as the legitimate child of philosophy.[10] A path, perhaps, that Derrida himself has not always disdained from following in his polemic. (*Voie que peut-être Derrida lui-même n'a pas toujours dédaignée dans sa polémique.*) (*NP* 85)

The initial question raised by this passage is that of the relation between logocentric language and the language of deconstruction. For example, in so far as deconstructive discourse employs the copula in predicative propositions (S is P), Levinas wonders whether one might not be tempted to argue that deconstruction employs the very logocentric language that it seeks to deconstruct. That Derrida is himself acutely aware of such an objection to his work is evident from the first chapter of *Of Grammatology* (*G* 25/*OG* 14). It should be noted, however, that Levinas claims neither that he proposes such an argument nor that such an argument would be correct; rather, he employs the conditional tense (*on pourrait*) in order to emphasize the fact that such an argument is only a temptation. It is at this moment that Levinas introduces the important theme of scepticism. His claim is that if one were so tempted, and consequently decided to propose the above argument as a refutation of scepticism, then one would be following a path much trodden by the refutation of scepticism. Deconstruction could therefore be refuted as a modern form of scepticism.[11]

What is scepticism, and how is it refuted? The discussion of scepticism and its refutation, although mentioned in *Totality and Infinity* (*TeI* 175/*TI* 201), only becomes prominent in *Otherwise than Being* (*AE* 9, 198, 210–18/*OB* 7, 155, 165–71) and other later essays.[12] It is introduced in order to address a major objection to Levinasian ethics: namely, how can the unthematizable and non-ontological ethical relation to the Other be described in a language that is irreducibly ontological, a language that uses the verb 'to be' in predicative propositions? Is there not a logical contradiction here which would permit Levinasian ethics to be refuted? Levinas retorts, 'These are familiar objections', and claims that they are 'facile, like those that, since the beginning of philosophy, are thrown at scepticism' (*AE*

198/*OB* 155). It is important to note that Levinasian ethics is not a scepticism and that Levinas does not adopt a sceptical attitude; rather, he sees a homology between the classical refutation of scepticism and the objections thrown at his own work. As Bernasconi points out, Levinas gives no definition of scepticism and does not attempt to situate it historically, except to say that it is present 'at the dawn of philosophy' (*à l'aube de la philosophie*) (*AE* 9/*OB* 7).[13]

For Levinas, ontology is a discourse that refuses transcendence and alterity through a desire for comprehension and totality. In the philosophical tradition, the refusal of transcendence is often connected with the refutation of scepticism. From Plato's refutation of the Sophists onwards, one might consider the history of philosophy as a series of repeated refutations of scepticism. This can be illustrated by a couple of examples from the phenomenological tradition. Phenomenology, as the philosophical method *ne plus ultra*, is premised on the refutation of scepticism. In the *Prolegomena* to the *Logical Investigations* and in the context of Husserl's arguments against psychologism and relativism, scepticism is submitted to a classical refutation (*LU* i. 110–16/*LI* 135–9). For Husserl, the worst objection that can be made against a theory is that it denies the conditions of possibility for a theory in general – that is, that it denies its proper a *priori* grounds of justification in universal or objective validity. Such a theory would be nonsensical, because it would deny the possibility of stating itself as a theory. It would, in short, be self-refuting. If one defines scepticism as the theory that proposes such theses as 'There is no possible justification for knowledge' or 'All truth is subjective', then it is clear that scepticism is self-refuting and nonsensical. The thesis 'All truth is subjective' presupposes the very objectivity of truth that the thesis denies – that is, the claim of this thesis to convince others.[14] Similarly, scepticism is refuted – or, more precisely, shown not even to stand in need of refutation – in Heidegger's *Being and Time*. In Paragraph 44, after Heidegger has deconstructed the traditional concept of truth *qua* agreement or correspondence (*Übereinstimmung, adaequatio, homoiosis*) and has phenomenologically deduced a more primordial concept of truth, understood as discovery, being-uncovered, or unconcealment (*Entdecktheit, Entdeckend-sein, Unverborgenheit, alētheia*), Heidegger deepens the Husserlian refutation of scepticism (*SuZ* 228–9). Having demonstrated the necessary connection of Being and truth and of truth to the Being of *Dasein*, Heidegger goes on to claim that in so far as *Dasein is*, – that is, has *Existenz* as its Being – truth must be presupposed. In so far as *Dasein's* Being can be disclosed as care (*Sorge*) – that is, as an articulated structure of thrown projection – *Dasein* is 'in the truth' (*Dasein ist 'in der Wahrheit'*) – although it is simultaneously 'in untruth' (*Unwahrheit*) to the extent that falling, or ensnarement (*das Verfallen*), is also essential to it. The classical refutation of scepticism, repeated by Husserl, shows the nonsensicality of sceptical theses through formal argumentation. However, the latter presupposes that truth is located in the statement (*Aussage*), or is propositional. The radicality of Heidegger's thesis is that truth *must* be presupposed simply because *Dasein is*. Thus the sceptical denial of truth does not even need refuting, because in so far as the sceptic *is* – that is, exists with some understanding of Being – the sceptic is in the truth. Heidegger thus doubts that there has ever existed an 'actual' sceptic. Scepticism about the truth would demand an act of suicide.

Now Levinas does not deny the truth and force of such refutations of scepticism. Scepticism is the refutable par excellence; one might say that it exists only to be refuted. Levinas's point is simply that scepticism returns after each refutation; it is both 'le réfutable' and 'le revenant', that which returns like a ghost. Scepticism always returns to haunt the philosopher after its refutation, like Banquo's ghost returns to haunt Macbeth. Levinas's evidence for this claim is what he calls the 'periodic rebirth of scepticism' (*AE* 228/*OB* 171) in the history of philosophy, the fact that sceptical worries keep returning. What is of value in scepticism for Levinas – and here he finds an unusual ally in Hegel – is its opposition to dogmatism, understood in the Kantian sense as the holding of a definite, fixed doctrine. Scepticism negates the dogmatic position, just as ethical Saying reduces the ontological Said, and introduces movement into thinking. However, for Levinas, this movement is not dialectical. Although Hegel gives an extraordinary privilege to the ancient Pyrronic scepticism of Sextus Empiricus – which Hegel, in a gesture that Husserl repeats, carefully distinguishes from modern or Humean scepticism (Hume is carefully excluded from the true meaning of scepticism[15]) – he ultimately criticizes the sceptical negation of truth for remaining at the level of negation and not grasping itself as part of a positive speculative dialectic.[16] For Levinas, the binary opposition of dogmatism and its sceptical negation is not *aufgehoben* into a third level of speculative unity. Rather, scepticism and its philosophical refutation form a couple that can be neither married nor divorced; they are both inseparable and non-totalizable. Scepticism is indeed the legitimate child of philosophy, but it is a child that the parent cannot control. There is an irreducible difference – which, as will be shown, is also temporal; that is, *différance* – between scepticism and its philosophical refutation, a difference which inaugurates a movement of oscillation or alternation, what Levinas calls 'the enigma of philosophy' (*DQVI* 270). It is with this enigma that the heart of Levinas's interest in scepticism and in Derrida is reached.

Before exploring this enigma, I should like to look back at the passage from 'Wholly Otherwise' quoted above. Levinas states that if one were tempted to infer an argument against deconstruction on the basis of the claim that it employs the language of logocentrism, then one would be following a path much trodden by the refutation of scepticism. However – and here one now realizes why Levinas was hesitant about employing such an argument – scepticism is never refuted decisively; it always returns after each refutation as the legitimate child of philosophy. Therefore, if one were to try to refute deconstruction by arguing that it employs logocentric language, one would always leave the door open for the return of deconstruction. The Derridian sceptical ghost would always return to haunt a logocentric Macbeth.

However, look again at the final sentence of the passage: 'A path, perhaps, that Derrida himself has not always disdained from following in his polemic.' Suddenly the tables are turned; for Levinas is now claiming that the path of the refutation of scepticism has already been followed by Derrida himself in his *polemic*. The above remark announces a curious reversal: deconstruction switches from being the object of refutation to the subject that refutes. This claim has the corollary that if Derrida's polemics tread a path similar to that of the refutation of scepticism, then the objects of those polemics will, following Levinas's logic, return to haunt Derrida as legitimate children haunt the lawful father who has fled. The objects of deconstruction, be they Husserlian phenomenology or Rousseauist anthropology, will return to haunt and undermine the deconstructive polemic. Taking this line of thought a stage further, it could be asked: What implications does this argument have when the object of Derrida's polemic is Levinas himself? Is Levinas perhaps alluding to Derrida's 'polemic' against him in 'Violence and Metaphysics'? As was mentioned in chapter 1, Levinas seems reluctant to refer explicitly to 'Violence and Metaphysics'; thus there is no direct textual evidence to support or reject these questions. However, the *irony* of the situation should be noted, an irony highlighted by Blanchot in his discussion of Levinas's understanding of scepticism in *L'Écriture du désastre*.[17] The irony at work here is that the argument that Levinas claimed one might well be tempted to raise against deconstruction, which has the form of the refutation of scepticism and which Levinas then claims that Derrida has not always disdained to follow, closely repeats Levinas's own formulation of 'des objections bien connues' that could be made against his own project in *Otherwise than Being*. In a passage that would have merited discussion in Derrida's 'En ce moment même', Levinas writes:

> The very discourse that we are holding at this very moment (*en ce moment*) about signification, diachrony and the transcendence of the approach beyond Being – a discourse that means to be philosophy – is thematization, synchronization of terms, recourse to systematic language, constant use of the verb to be (*être*), bringing back into the bosom of Being all signification allegedly conceived beyond Being; but are we duped by this surreptition? The objections are facile, like those that since the birth of philosophy, are thrown at scepticism. (*AE* 198/*OB* 155)

Reading ironically, it is clear that the objections to Levinas which have the form of the classical refutation of scepticism represent Levinas's complicated assimilation of what he sees as the central argument of 'Violence and Metaphysics': namely, that the ethical Saying can be said only by way of an ontological thematization which consequently denies it. That Levinas views this as the dominant motif of 'Violence and Metaphysics' can be seen with reference to remarks given in interviews and discussions; for example, in an interview given in 1986, Levinas says: 'Derrida has reproached me for my critique of Hegelianism by saying that in order to criticize Hegel, one begins to speak Hegel's language. That is the basis for his critique.'[18] On the basis of such remarks, one might well be tempted to conclude that Levinas reads 'Violence and Metaphysics' as a polemic, or critique.

Following this line of thought, one might argue that Levinas's philosophical irony is possessed of a rare subtlety, because reducing 'Violence and Metaphysics' to an argument with the form of the classical refutation of scepticism would automatically entail that Derrida's 'deconstructive polemic' be subverted by that which it seeks to subvert. Refuted by ontology and exiled from reason, the ethical Saying would ceaselessly return to haunt deconstruction. Derrida's 'polemic' against Levinas would instantly backfire, and, in the guise of a discussion of scepticism, Levinas would succeed in replying to his critics.[19] But, is this all that can be said on the matter? Why is my discourse in the conditional tense?

I have insisted that deconstruction is not a form of critique, but is characterized by double, or *clôtural*, reading. Thus, for me, the phrase 'deconstructive polemic' is an oxymoron. It is of paramount importance to distinguish between a polemic, or critique, which, like the refutation of scepticism, declares war (*polemos*) on its opponent, and a *clôtural* critique *of* critique, which shows how scepticism returns after its refutation. At the end of chapter 2, I argued that 'Violence and Metaphysics' is a *clôtural* reading. Was I wrong in this? No; but that is not to say that Levinas's description of 'Violence and Metaphysics' is without any validity. Derrida's text is a *violent* reading, which both raises many critical objections to Levinas and, I would claim, ignores some of the paradoxes of thematization already present in his earlier works. There is a dominant critical strand in 'Violence and Metaphysics' (and some of Derrida's other work) which should not be reduced. I have shown in the previous chapter how Derrida's reading of Levinas in 'En ce moment même' becomes more nuanced in response to the problem of how the ethical Saying is said in the language of ontology. Thus, I would agree with Levinas in claiming that the path of the refutation of scepticism is one that Derrida 'has not always disdained from following'. However, I would add that such a path must be read as a single strand in a double reading. To anticipate the ultimate claim that Levinas will make for Derrida's work, it is not that deconstruction is assimilable to either scepticism or its refutation, but rather that deconstruction is *diachronic*; that is, it is sensitive to the distinction between the Saying and the Said. The enigma of deconstruction is the manner in which it signifies ethically.

Returning to 'Wholly Otherwise', it must be asked: Where is this second strand, or path, of reading? Levinas writes:

But, in following this path, one would risk missing one side of the signification which this very inconsequence bears. One would risk missing the incompressible non-simultaneity of the Said and the Saying, the *dislocation* [my emphasis] of their correlation – a dislocation which, although minimal, would be wide enough to swallow up sceptical discourse, but without stifling itself in the contradiction between what is signified by its *said* and what is signified by the very fact of articulating a *said*; as if simultaneity were lacking from the two significations, so that the contradiction broke the knot that tied them together; as if the correlation of the *Saying* and the *Said* was a diachrony of that which cannot be brought together; as if the situation of the *Saying* was already a 'memory retention' for the *Said*, but without the *lapse* of the instants of the Saying letting themselves be recuperated in this memory.

(*Mais en suivant cette voie on risquerait de passer à côté de la signification que comporte cette inconséquence même. On passerait à côté de la non-simultanéité incompressible du Dit et du Dire, à côté du déboîtement de leur corrélation; déboîtement minime, mais assez large pour que s'y engouffre le discours sceptique sans s'étrangler par la contradiction entre ce que signifie son **dit** et ce que signifie le fait même d'énoncer un **dit**. Comme si la simultanéité manquait aux deux significations pour que la contradiction brise le noeud où elles se nouent. Comme si la corrélation du **Dire** et du **Dit** était une diachronie de l'inassemblable; comme si la situation du **Dire** était déjà pour le **Dit** un 'souvenir de rétention', mais sans que le **laps** des instants du Dire se laissent récupérer dans ce souvenir.*) (NP 85–6)

To follow the path of the refutation of scepticism would be to miss out on one side of a two-sided signification, as well as the precise way in which those two sides cannot be brought together. The two sides of signification are those of the Saying and the Said. As was pointed out in chapter 1, the great innovation of *Otherwise than Being* is the model of the Saying and the Said as a way of explaining how the ethical signifies within ontological language. To recall this distinction, the Saying is my exposure – corporeal, sensible – to the Other, my inability to refuse the Other's approach. It is the performative stating, proposing, or expressive position of myself facing the Other. It is my body as an ethical performance, whose essence cannot be caught in propositions. On the other hand, the Said is a statement, an assertion, or a constative proposition (of the form S is P), about which the truth or falsity can be ascertained. In a psychoanalytic register, I claimed that the distinction between the Saying and the Said may correspond to Lacan's demarcation of the orders of *énonciation* (the subject's act of speaking) and *énoncé* (the formulation of this act of speech into a statement).[20] Given that philosophy speaks the language of the Said – that is, it consists of propositions and statements – the methodological problem that haunts every page of *Otherwise than Being* is the following: How is the Saying, my exposure to the Other, to be Said or given a philosophical exposition without utterly betraying this Saying? How does one write the otherwise than Being (*autrement qu'être*) in the language of Being without this simply becoming a being otherwise (*être autrement*)? (*AE* 9/*OB* 7). Or, in Kantian terms, how is the incomprehensibility of the moral law to be comprehended in its incomprehensibility?

Levinas's 'solution' to this problem is found in the method of reduction. He claims that the philosopher's effort consists in the reduction of the Said to the Saying, to show how my ethical exposure to the Other underlies any ontological exposition. But how is this reduction to be *shown*? Levinas insists that everything that shows itself takes place at the level of the Said (*AE* 57/*OB* 44). Recall that, for the early Heidegger, phenomenology is preliminarily defined as the letting be seen (*lassen sehen*) of that which shows itself (*was sich zeigt*) (*SuZ* 34). But, if this is the case, how does the Saying show itself? For Levinas, the Saying can be conveyed (*traduit*) only to the extent that it is betrayed (*trahit*) within the Said. This entails that the Saying has to show itself within a more complex discursive structure. The Saying is not the permanent Husserlian *epochē* of the Said; rather, the reduction is the exposure of the Saying by way of a continual contestation of the Said. The Saying shows itself within the Said by interrupting it. This logic of interruption is similar to the logic of scepticism, whereby the sceptic can expose the sceptical thesis only by presenting it in a language that refutes that thesis. But this is not an end to scepticism, for the sceptic will return to interrupt the language of philosophy through conveying and betraying his thesis. Levinas writes (in a formulation favoured by Blanchot): 'Language is already scepticism' (*AE* 216/*OB* 170); that is, the Said is always subverted by a Saying that speaks at the price of betrayal. The Saying is a performative disruption of the Said that is instantly refuted by the language in which it appears.

However, in following this method, has one left philosophy behind? After all, Levinas is a philosopher, and his Saying must be said by way of a rigorous philosophical method that cannot be evaded through poetic, oracular, edifying, or fragmentary discourse. His analyses remain, from first to last, faithful to the *spirit*, if not the letter of Husserlian phenomenology (*AE* 230/*OB* 183). As I mentioned in chapter 1, the philosopher's effort is to enact within language a spiralling movement between the Saying and the Said, an ethical writing that Levinas performs in *Otherwise than Being*. The reduction uses the unavoidable language of the Said, and attempts to avoid, or unsay, that Said by finding the Saying within it. Yet – and this is crucial – *this reduced Said retains a residue of the unsaid Said within the Saying. The reduction is never pure or complete.* This leaves philosophy in a spiralling movement between two orders of discourse, that of the Saying and that of the Said, whereby the ethical signifies through the oscillation, or alternation, of these orders. It is precisely this alternation that constitutes, for Levinas, the enigma of philosophy (*DQVI* 270).

Yet what is the time for philosophy? To get to the heart of Levinas's interest in scepticism, it is necessary to understand that the two orders of discourse that have been outlined, those of the Saying and the Said, do not occur in the same time. They are, as Levinas says, 'non-simultaneous' and 'incompressible'. In the reduction of the Said to the Saying, one moves from one order of temporality to another: from 'synchrony to diachrony'.[21] As its etymology suggests, 'synchrony' is the bringing together, or understanding of phenomena within a unified temporal order; for example, within the conception of time as a linear, infinite series of punctual moments spread along the axes of past, present, and future – what one might call the spatial representation of time as a line, the abstract time of physics, the time rendered immobile by Zeno's paradoxes. In short, synchrony reduces time to space. It is a conception of time that lets the past be recalled and the future predicted. 'Diachrony', on the other hand, refers etymologically to the coming apart of time, the inability to recall the succession of instants within memory or to predict the instants to come. Diachrony is an immemorial, dispersed temporality which escapes and passes by; it is 'le passe-temps' that Levinas speaks of in 'Wholly Otherwise' (*NP* 83), or the time of the ' "profond jadis" ' discussed above. It is time as the punctual present falling out of phase with itself (*le déphasage de l'instant*) (ibid.), the time of the lapse (*lapsus*) that will not let itself be synchronized. In a Bergsonian sense, diachrony is the *real* time of subjectivity: unique, unrepeatable, and mobile. It is the time of *la durée* as opposed to the simultaneous time of *res extensa*. Levinas's Bergsonian claim is that diachrony is the real time of Saying, whereas synchrony is the abstract time of the Said. Furthermore, he privileges diachrony over synchrony, arguing that the former is, in a strongly Heideggerian formulation, the temporalizing of time (*la temporalisation du temps; die Zeitigung der Zeitlichkeit*). Diachrony is the primordial, or authentic, time from which the vulgar, inauthentic conception of time as synchrony is derived.

Levinas's basic and extraordinary claim is that the concrete case in which time temporalizes itself as diachrony is in the everyday event of my responsibility for the Other (*AE* 12/*OB* 10). The Other's alterity is that which I cannot lay hold of, that which always exceeds my grasp or my free decision. This line of argument refers back to Levinas's earlier analyses of temporality in *Time and the Other* and *Totality and Infinity*. In his polemic against Heidegger, Levinas places the essence of time in postponement, essentially the postponement of death that occurs in and as the mortal will. Time is not grasped in Being-towards-death and the fateful assumption of *Dasein's* finitude; rather, time is realized in Being-against-death. To be a self is to have the time to be against death. To be a temporal being does not demand the heroic virility of *Dasein* grasping itself by shattering against death (*SuZ* 385); rather, the essence of temporality is temporization: postponement, procrastination, patience (*TeI* 195–225/ *TI* 220–47). Time is experienced in the passivity of an undergoing; in the temporality of Malone's waiting for death in Beckett's *Trilogy*. Time is undergone as senescence, the passivity of ageing (*AE* 65/*OB* 51). However, the 'marvel' (*TeI* 213/*TI* 237) of time for Levinas is futurition; that is, a relation to the future that is not achieved through laying hold of the future, as Heidegger does in his analyses of understanding (*Verstehen*) and projection (*Entwurf*). Rather, time is 'the lack of any hold upon the future' (*TA* 71/*TO* 80). The relation to the future is achieved not through the ontological grasp, but through the ethical caress. The caress anticipates the future without dominating it (*TA* 82/*TO* 89). Ultimately, for Levinas, my future is realized through fecundity; that is, through a relation with the child who is both the same as me and yet transcends me.

For Levinas, diachrony and alternation constitute the time of philosophy (*AE* 213/*OB* 167), and the philosopher's effort is to stay at the extreme situation of a diachronic thought (*AE* 9/*OB* 7). Returning to the passage from 'Wholly Otherwise', the Saying and the Said cannot be united in simultaneity because they do not belong to the same temporal order. Levinas insists that there persists a 'dislocation' (*déboîtement*), a medical term for the dislocation of a limb, whereby the Saying is wrenched from its locus in the Said without ever being able to return to it. The correlation of the Saying and the Said is diachronic; that is to say, it cannot be brought together into synchronic time. It is as if there is a delay, or a lapse of time, between my exposure to the Other, which is Saying, and the exposition of that Saying in a Said, or proposition. As Levinas puts it, it is as if 'language is grafted upon the most invisible difference of time' (*NP* 88). In Derridian terms, the relation between myself and the Other is one of *différance*. In Lacanian terms, the *énonciation* and the *énoncé* are not simultaneous. If the Saying and the Said occurred at the same time, then the affirmation of the Saying could be refuted by its negation in the Said. And it is here, finally, that the heart of Levinas's interest in scepticism is reached. Scepticism is premised on the refusal to synchronize the implicit affirmation of its Saying (for example, the belief that all truth is subjective) with the negation of this Saying in the Said (the thesis 'All truth is subjective' is self-refuting because it presupposes the very objectivity of truth which it denies). The veracity of the refutation of scepticism is conditional upon there being a contradiction between what the sceptic says and the semantic or logical conditions of possibility for this Saying when it is articulated in the language of the Said. The philosopher simply points out this contradiction ('a path, perhaps, that Derrida has not always disdained from following'), and proceeds with the refutation. However, such a contradiction is possible only if it is assumed that the Saying and the Said occupy the same synchronic temporality. What intrigues Levinas about scepticism is that it is insensitive to its own contradiction and proceeds 'as if (*comme si*) the affirmation and negation did not resound in the same time' (*AE* 213/*OB* 168). Scepticism proceeds as if it were sensitive to the distinction between the diachronic and the synchronic, the Saying and the Said. It is as if scepticism were sensitive to the difference between my unthematizable ethical relation to the Other and the ontological thematization of this relation. Note the recurrence of 'as if' in these sentences. It is not as if Levinas denies the refutation of scepticism in order to rebut the Derridian 'objections' raised against his own work; he simply sees the coupling of scepticism and its refutation as a model for the way in which his philosophical writing signifies ethically. *Ethics signifies enigmatically*, as a determinate pattern of oscillation, or alternation. One might say that ethics signifies *undecidably*. As Levinas puts it:

> The truth of truths would not therefore be capable of being gathered into an instant, nor into a synthesis where the supposed movement of the dialectic comes to a standstill. *The truth of truths lies in the Said, in the Unsaid and in the Otherwise Said – return, resumption, reduction*: the history of philosophy or its preliminary. (*NP* 86; my emphasis)

Having established the second path of reading that opens up in diachronic Saying, does Derrida follow it? How does deconstruction concern itself with the Other? Levinas continues:

> It is not therefore absurd that a rigorous reflection lets us catch a glimpse of these interstices of Being where this very reflection unsays itself. One can see nothing without thematization, or without the oblique rays which it reflects back, even when it is a question of the non-thematizable. (*NP* 86)

Two paths are being delineated in this passage: first, that of thematization which proceeds through rigorous reflection, and second, that of the non-thematizable interstices of Being. On the one hand, as can be seen from the first paragraph of the Introduction to *Being and Time*, ontological discourse is always thematic (*thematisch*) – that is, it is a comprehensive discourse in which the Saying is petrified in the Said and in which rigorous investigation wants to produce (albeit often without success) the seamless totality of the Book (*AE* 217/*OB* 171). On the other hand stands the Other, that which resists ontological comprehension and always slips away behind the theme which tries to define it. The non-thematizable Saying to the Other would occur in the interstices of Being, the minute openings in the fabric of thematization which would allow one to stand between (*intersistere*) the ontological domain and that which it excludes.[22] The two paths do not constitute an opposition, dividing the domains of ethics and ontology; nor is one required to judge critically between them, as with the paths the goddess displays to Parmenides. Rather, they are seen to intersect and cross one another in a relation of interdependence. What is of interest here is that Levinas claims that it is precisely the rigorous reflection of the ontological Said that unsays itself and reduces itself to its Saying. Furthermore, ontological thematization is the necessary condition for any consideration of the non-thematizable. One can see nothing without thematization, and all talk of an ethics without ontology is blind. Once again, the relation of the Saying to the Said is not one of absolute independence, but rather the interdependence of irreconcilable orders of discourse.

The 'rigorous reflection' alluded to by Levinas refers to Derrida's work, and in particular *Voice and Phenomenon*. The claim would appear to be that although Derridian deconstruction is a work of ontological reflection and thematization, it enacts the reduction of the Said to the Saying. There is thus a *dislocation* at work in Derrida's work, whereby the Saying of the deconstructive text unsays its Said and uproots itself from its ontological locus. Two incompressible, yet inseparable, paths are breached by deconstruction: first, the path of ontological thematization, the order of the Said and synchrony, and second, the path of ethical non-thematization, whereby the Said is reduced to its diachronic Saying. The 'structure' of the deconstructive text is one of absolute dislocation, where two incommensurable orders are placed in a relation in which they remain absolute. Such is the *clôtural* pattern of Derrida's text.

I have now arrived at a formal designation of the way in which Derridian deconstruction signifies ethically. I shall proceed by giving a concrete example in order to demonstrate this claim: that of the treatment of the Husserlian indicative sign, which Derrida discusses in *Voice and Phenomenon* and which Levinas takes up in 'La pensée de l'être et la question de l'autre'.

4.3 Indication

In the second part of 'La pensée de l'être et la question de l'autre', after a brief assessment and eulogy of Derrida's work, Levinas makes the following apparently critical remarks about deconstruction:

> A critique [that is, Derrida's] which, however, remains in some way faithful to the gnoseological [*gnoséologique*] signification of meaning, to the specific extent that the deconstruction of intuition and the perpetual postponement of presence that it shows, are exclusively thought

from the perspective of presence treated as a norm and where Husserlian indication – the *Anzeige* – which does not comprise or call for [*comporte*] any intrinsic signifier, but which joins together two terms without any prefiguration, albeit in the hollow space of the indicated in the indicator [*fût-ce en 'creux' de l'indiqué dans l'indiquant*], does not let itself be expelled from any signification and make a scandal of it (even if this scandal should not frighten us) [*ne se laisse expulser d'aucune signification et y fait scandale (même si ce scandale ne devait pas faire peur)*]. (*PEQA* 182)

This is an extremely condensed and exasperating passage. To begin to unpack it, a point of philosophical translation is required. Levinas claims that Derrida is faithful in some way to the gnoseological signification of meaning. In French, *gnoséologie* has the same range of philosophical application as *Erkenntnistheorie* in German, or 'theory of knowledge' in English. It designates the *a priori* analysis of the faculty of knowing, such as that performed by Kant in the First Critique. *Gnoséologie* should therefore be distinguished from *épistémologie*, which means the study or philosophy of science, a term employed to describe, for example, the work of Gaston Bachelard.[23] If, as can be shown by comparison with other passages,[24] Levinas is using the term in its habitual sense, then his claim is that Derrida remains in some way faithful to the determination of meaning given in the theory of knowledge. But which theory of knowledge? Judging from the context, it would appear to be Husserl's account of meaning in the *Logical Investigations*, subtitled *Untersuchungen zur Phänomenologie und Theorie der Erkenntnis*. This general claim can be divided into two more specific claims.

First, the deconstruction of the privilege of presence is considered exclusively from the perspective of presence treated as a norm. Levinas makes a similar point in 'Wholly Otherwise', where he asks, 'But is not the attempt at a positive utterance of the failure of presence to itself still a way of returning to the presence with which this positivity merges?' (*NP* 87). Levinas appears to be objecting here to Derrida's general characterization of philosophy as a metaphysics of presence, where the deconstruction of that metaphysics prohibits any attempt at a statement of non-metaphysical positivity except as an inevitable return to presence, and where each attempt to think the other of philosophy is merely 'one more blow for philosophical knowledge' (*un coup de plus au savoir philosophique*) (*M* i/*MP* xi). In brief, Levinas claims – as so many others have done – that Derrida travels a philosophical *via negativa* that overstates the domination of presence and thus remains poised on the margins of an ontology that can be deconstructed but never definitively exceeded. Or – and this is crucial – is this just how Levinas reads Derrida's philosophical *intentions*? My intention has been to show how Levinas reads Derrida's *text* by locating within it a non-ontological Saying. Regardless of its intentions, Derrida's text signifies ethically. In the fourth section of 'La pensée de l'être', Levinas shows how these moments of ethical Saying are said in the history of philosophy, citing examples from Plato, Aristotle, Descartes, Kant, Hegel, Bergson, and Heidegger. The history of philosophy says more than it wants to say (*veut dire*), and in saying this it names the ethical. For the moment, Derrida stands at the end of this history.

Second, the Husserlian indicative sign that Derrida discusses in *Voice and Phenomenon* cannot be expelled from signification or meaning, thereby scandalizing it, in quite the way Derrida describes. It is specifically this claim that Levinas develops in the third part of 'La pensée de l'être', where he argues that Derrida failed to radicalize sufficiently the concept of indication and that, furthermore, a radicalized concept of indication would open up a dimension of ethical transcendence perhaps unintended by Derrida but nonetheless enacted by his text. Indication is the unintended Saying of the ethical in Derrida's deconstruction of Husserl. It is this claim that I will now explore.

It is first necessary to recall some 'Essential Distinctions'. In the first Logical Investigation, Husserl seeks to clarify the relation between linguistic expression (*Ausdruck*) and the meaning (*Bedeutung*) conveyed by that expression. It is evident to rough reflection that there is a certain 'parallelism' between thinking and speaking – that is, between words employed in verbal expressions and what is signified by those words, the meaning that those words hit upon. However, although 'we all know that words mean something' (*LU* ii. 13/*LI* 257), it is necessary, Husserl claims, for a rigorous reflection to determine and analytically clarify the relation between expression and meaning. This is the task of the First Investigation: *Ausdruck und Bedeutung*. Husserl addresses an ambiguity in the term 'sign' (*Zeichen*), arguing that every sign is a sign for something, but that not every sign has meaning. Only signs whereby a sense is expressed (*ausgedrückt*) have meaning; for example, the expression 'The three perpendiculars of a triangle intersect in a point' expresses an ideal meaning that can be demonstrated geometrically. It should be noted that Husserl's habitual examples for the ideality of meaning are logical, mathematical, or geometrical expressions – that is, expressions that can be demonstrated objectively. He distinguishes expressive, meaningful signs from meaningless signs in the sense of indications (*Anzeichen*). It is the latter that are of interest in this context. Husserl goes on to give some examples of indicative signs: 'In this sense a brand is the sign of a slave, a flag the sign of a nation'; or again, 'We say the Martian canals are signs of the existence of intelligent beings on Mars' (*LU* ii. 24/*LI* 269–70). Indications refer to the whole field of notes and marks (*Kennzeichen, Merkzeichen*) and to the graphic and writing in general. A knot in a handkerchief is an indicative sign, as is the indicator on a car. Such indications function in the following way: an indicative sign A (the knot in my handkerchief) points out a state of affairs B (that I must remember to go to the dentist). The essential distinction between an expression and an indication is that whereas the terms of the former are logically and necessarily related (for example, the proposition 'The three perpendiculars of a triangle intersect in a point' and the unequivocal, objective geometrical meaning of this proposition), the terms of an indicative relation are contingent, and are formed along the lines of the association of ideas. I see the knot, and associate it with my anticipated visit to the dentist; the connection of terms is felt (*ein fühlbares Zusammenhang*) rather than necessarily inferred (*LU* ii. 29–30/*LI* 273–4). (In another register, one might say that indication introduces Saussure's thesis on the arbitrariness of the sign; indeed, this is how Husserl is read in 'Signature, Event, Context' (*M* 378–81/*MP* 318–21).) Husserl draws a distinction between the associative demonstration of an indicative relation (*Hinweis*) and the necessary, demonstrative proof (*Beweis*) of an expressive relation (*LU* ii. 25–8/*LI* 271–3). Of course, Husserl recognizes that there is an irreducible interlacing or entanglement (*Verflechtung*) (*LU* ii. 24/*LI* 269) of expressions and indications in living discourse and that all expressions function as indications in communicative speech (*LU* ii. 33/*LI* 277). However, despite this *de facto* interlacing, Husserl insists on the *de jure* distinction between indication and expression in order precisely to preserve the independence of meaning which he submits to further refinement in the remainder of the Investigation. Thus, in order to produce an account of linguistic meaning that will underpin both the logical theory outlined in the 'Prolegomena' to the *Investigations* and the entire epistemological adventure of his subsequent phenomenology, Husserl must reduce the indicative sign.[25]

In *Voice and Phenomenon*, it is precisely the threshold of the distinction between indication and expression that is deconstructed – that is to say, rendered rigorously undecidable – and that provides the starting point for Derrida's analysis of Husserlian phenomenology (*VP* 17–33/*SP* 17–31). The thrust of Derrida's argument is that Husserl's desire to maintain the uncontaminated ideality of meaning through the distinction of expression from indication undermines itself and that the purity of the expressive sign is always already, or 'originally', entangled (*enchevêtré; verflochten*) (*VP* 22/*SP* 21) with indication. Meaning is therefore inhabited, or contaminated, by the contingency, worldliness, and physicality – predicates that can be placed under the rubric of a generalized concept of textuality and writing – that Husserl wanted to expel into indication. However, Derrida is intent to show that such entanglement does not occur simply at a secondary level, where expressions are employed indicatively in communicative discourse, and where they impart their meaning through what Husserl calls 'intimation' (*Kundgabe*). Rather, the entanglement is originary (*VP* 97/*SP* 87); that is to say, at the origin, indication is always added to expression in a relation or logic of supplementarity (the verb *suppléer* means both to make up for a lack and to add to something that is already complete, thereby instigating a logic that breaks with the principle of non-contradiction). Derrida's reading bifurcates the origin, and shows the interdependence of that which was essentially meant to be distinct. The effects of this reading on Husserlian phenomenology are not merely local. Derrida writes:

> The entirety of Husserl's enterprise – well beyond the *Logical Investigations* – would be threatened if the *Verflechtung* coupling indication to expression was absolutely irreducible, in principle inextricable, if indication were not simply added to expression in a more or less dogged adherence, but inhabited the essential intimacy of its movement. (*VP* 28/*SP* 27)

The entanglement of expression and indication threatens by implication all the subsequent distinctions of Husserlian phenomenology –

for example, the transcendental and the worldly, the transcendental ego and the psychological ego – and the entire future problematic of the reduction (*epoché*). By showing how the entanglement of expression and indication is irreducible and how the threshold that divides them is a chiasmus that is perpetually 'double crossed',[26] Derrida indicates how the ideality of meaning always bears the trace of an exteriority that cannot be reduced, a trace that Levinas will see as the mark of ethical transcendence.[27]

Levinas's radicalization of indication is carried out in the full knowledge of both Husserl's and Derrida's analyses. This radicalization does not so much consist of a reading of Derrida as a series of rhapsodic shorthand notes, enchained together, that show how the notion of indication can be built into Levinas's conception of ethics. He begins by recalling that, from the ontological point of view, the indicative relation would possess 'the poorest signifyingness (*signifiance*)'; the associative relation that binds the knot in my handkerchief to my visit to the dentist is semantically inferior to that which joins a mathematical or logical expression to its meaning. The terms of an indicative relation are not identical in the way in which the statement $2 \times 2 = 4$ is identical with its meaning. In an indicative relation it is not the same to think and to be. There is, to use Levinas's word, an 'extrinsicality' between the indicator and the indicated; my handkerchief could signify a trip to the shops as easily as a visit to the dentist. Turning the hierarchy of expression and indication on its head, Levinas asks rhetorically: 'The extrinsicality (*extrinsécité*) of terms – the radical exteriority that shows itself in pure indication – difference (*la différence*) – does it not go back to a regime of meaning, to an intelligibility that does not reduce itself to the manifestation of a "content in Being" (*contenu en être*) or to thought?' (*PEQA* 182).

Mention of exteriority here provides the clue to Levinas's treatment of indication: he assimilates the indicative relation to the ethical relation of exteriority; that is to say, 'a relation in the exclusion of all relation' (*PEQA* 183). In *Totality and Infinity*, the ethical relation is described ultimately as the 'rapport sans rapport' (*TeI* 271/*TI* 295), or the absolute relation, in which the terms of the relation absolve themselves from it. For Levinas, such a relation is created and maintained by language (*TeI* 9/*TI* 39). It is only when the interhuman relation takes this form that it can escape from Heidegger's ontological comprehension of the other in *Mitsein*, Hegel's dialectic of recognition, or Husserl's phenomenological constitution of the Other as *alter ego*, and signify ethically. Thus, it is clear that Levinas views the indicative relation as an exemplum for the ethical. That which is indicated in indication cannot be reduced to being an object for self-consciousness, an adequate representation or the correlate of my intentionality. Rather, the indicative relation is one in which I am affected by the 'absolutely other' (*PEQA* 183).

Levinas continues: 'Indication, a relation of pure extrinsicality of the one to the other, without there being anything in common, nor any "correspondence" between them, a relation of absolute difference which is not the decrease (*le décroît*) of some intuition' (ibid.). The indicative relation is one of absolute difference, in which the Other enters into a relation with me in which he or she is absolved from the relation, one in which difference is maintained. My being affected by the Other establishes a relation to that which transcends me and which cannot be represented or thematized by self-consciousness. It is a relation of association in which the primary datum of sociality – the ethical relation – takes form. What Levinas finds in the indicative relation is a relation of non-identity, in which the Other is not a perceived, real or ideal object assimilable to self-consciousness but in which what is indicated refuses to give itself up to the self, maintaining its absolute difference – or what Derrida calls spacing (*espacement*) – and thereby placing the psyche in a relation of utter passivity, or patience. Relating this back to the analysis of scepticism, the indicative relation is diachronic. 'In the adjournment or the incessant *différance* [Levinas emphasizes the 'a' in *différance*] of this pure indication, we suspect time itself, but as an incessant diachrony' (ibid.). The temporality of indication is differantial: temporality as temporization. Indication institutes a relation in which there is an irreducible *différance* – both spatial and temporal – between the Same and the Other, in which interhuman relations are not governed by the *parousia* of presence. Time tempor(al)izes itself in the postponement, or patience, of an ethical *durée*, which, incidentally, for Levinas, is the time of the relation to God (*l'à-Dieu*). A meditation on the indicative sign leads back to a regime of meaning more ancient than the disclosure of Being in phenomenology and ontology: what Levinas calls 'the meaning of life purely lived without reason to be' (*sens de la vie purement vécue sans raison d'être*) (*PEQA* 184). Indication indicates how an ethics of *différance* is possible.

With this extraordinary discussion of indication in mind, one can begin to understand how Levinas's *clôtural* reading of Derrida works. Derrida's deconstruction of the threshold that distinguishes indication from expression permits Levinas to view indication as indicating the ethical moment within deconstruction. Such an insight is premised on both the success and the failure of *Voice and Phenomenon*. The latter's success consists in its recognition of how the exteriority of indication contaminates the ideality of meaning, while its failure consists in overlooking the ethical implications of the indicative sign. Derrida both fails to name and cannot fail to name the ethical. On a Levinasian account, Derrida's text shares the paradoxical signifying structure operative in other major philosophical texts, Descartes' *Meditations* being the best example;[28] it represents both a transgression of ontology, whereby the ethical moment is manifested in the privileging of the indicative sign, and a repetition of ontology, a rigorous critical reflection, which fails to radicalize the ethical moment. Derrida's text obeys a *clôtural* rhythm of dislocation in which two incommensurable orders of discourse intersect: the Saying and the Said. Just as Husserl, on Derrida's reading, failed to draw the consequences of his own text (*VP* 109/*SP* 97) by remaining faithful to the intuitionistic imperative of presence and consequently deriving difference from the *parousia* of the 'Idea in the Kantian sense' and not from *différance*, so too Derrida, on Levinas's reading, fails to draw the consequences of his own text by failing to emphasize the irreducible exteriority of indication in Husserl's account of meaning and the ethical consequences of his deconstruction of phenomenology. Levinas's *clôtural* reading of Derrida echoes Derrida's *clôtural* reading of Husserl.

What consequences can be drawn from what has been said?[29] I would like to pursue the thought of indication by taking a further step back into the *Logical Investigations*. In the fifth paragraph of Investigation 1 (a passage scrupulously commented on in Chapter 3 of *Voice and Phenomenon*), Husserl sets aside a sense of expression not necessary for his purpose (*LU* ii. 30–1/*LI* 275). Expressions as meaningful signs have a more limited range of application than the word *Ausdruck* might suggest to a German speaker. Husserl provisionally limits expressions to every discourse or every part of discourse (*jede Rede und jeder Redeteil*). For Husserl, it does not matter 'whether or not such discourse is actually uttered (*ob die Rede wirklich geredet*), or addressed with communicative intent to any persons or not'. As will be shown in the eighth paragraph of the same Investigation, an expression is only present to its meaning, without contamination by indication, when it is spoken in silent internal soliloquy. The phenomenological voice is, in Derrida's formulation, 'the voice that keeps or guards silence' (*la voix qui garde le silence*) (*VP* 78/*SP* 70), a voice which maintains its self-presence and presence to meaning by cutting off all relations with the outside, the exterior and the worldly – that is, with textuality in general. If the highest moment of philosophical dialectic is the dialogue of the soul with itself, then this dialogue takes place in silence. Such a definition of expression excludes a broader sense of the term: namely, that found in 'facial expressions and the various gestures (*das Mienenspiel und die Geste*) which involuntarily accompany discourse without communicative intent'. Such 'expressions' are not spoken, and do not therefore possess *Bedeutung* in the manner of verbal expressions. Husserl concludes: 'They only mean in the sense of indicating' (*im Sinne von Anzeichen*) (*Lu* ii. 31/*LI* 275). Consequently, the line of demarcation that divides expression from indication, and the meaningful from the meaningless, follows the distinction of the verbal from the non-verbal or the non-facial from the facial. It is this dimension of unspoken, non-verbal indication which I would briefly like to explore, because these non-verbal 'facial expressions and gestures' that Husserl excludes from *Bedeutung* are precisely, for Levinas, a vital locus of ethical signification.[30]

The influence of Husserl on Levinas would seem to be at its most evident when, in *Totality and Infinity*, he characterizes the ethical relation in terms of *expression*. Furthermore, if expression is the way in which the Other is manifested to the Same, then expression takes place in *discourse* ('discours' translates the German word *Rede*), and it is discourse which produces *signification* (*TeI* 35–42/*TI* 64–70). Indeed, pursuing this homology, it would be interesting to compare Levinas's account of ethical discourse with Husserl's analysis of essentially occasional expressions (*wesentlich okkasionelle Ausdrücke*) in the third chapter of Investigation 1 (*LU* ii. 77–96/*LI* 312–26), an analysis that Husserl still considered a *tour de force* (*ein Gewaltstreich*) in his 1913

Foreword to the second edition of the *Logical Investigations* (LU i. xiv/*LI* 48). It is here that Husserl analyses expressions whose meaning fluctuates or is ambiguous – that is to say, situations in which expressions are employed indicatively – such that meaning can be understood only with reference to the entire personal context of a speaker's utterances. For instance, the indexical phrase 'I wish you luck' can be used in countless different contexts with differing meanings; hence an understanding of the sense of the proposition would have to take account of the concrete particularity of who was being referred to in the personal pronouns. One might want to claim that in so far as Levinasian ethical discourse is verbal, it can be assimilated to Husserl's essentially occasional expressions.

However, such a *rapprochement*, although of interest, is limited, because Levinas claims that the expression of ethical discourse represents a 'veritable inversion' of what is characterized as Husserlian 'objectifying cognition' (*TeI* 39/*TI* 67). Levinas's account of the signification of expressive ethical discourse cannot be reduced to the Husserlian model for the production of meaning through verbal expressions. For Levinas, the line of demarcation between signification and non-signification does not correspond to the distinction between the verbal and the non-verbal. Levinas gives the name 'face' (*visage*) to that which is revealed in expression, and it is the face that is the condition of possibility for ethical signification. If the face does not reside at the bottom of discourse, then that discourse is ethically meaningless. Now, although the revelation of the face must take place in discourse and although it is to a large extent true that discourse means speech for Levinas – once again, the enduring influence of the *Phaedrus* on *Totality and Infinity* can be seen in Levinas's deeply Platonic exclusion of rhetoric (*TeI* 42–4/*TI* 70–2), and for this reason alone, Derrida is to some extent justified in classifying Levinas as a phonocentric thinker (*ED* 152/*WD* 102–3) – ethical discourse is not restricted to verbal acts. It is the thought of ethics as non-verbal communication that I would now like to pursue.

Despite Levinas's belief that speech (*la parole*) is an 'incomparable manifestation' (*TeI* 157/*TI* 182), he reserves a privileged place for non-verbal communication. In *Totality and Infinity*, Levinas writes of 'the language of the eyes' which it is 'impossible to dissemble' and which 'speaks' (*parle*) (*TeI* 38/*TI* 66). The ethical relation to the Other need not be expressed only through the *droiture* of speech; it can also be expressed 'in the sense that implements, clothing and gestures express' (*TeI* 157/*TI* 182). Non-verbal indicative signs can signify ethically. However, the privilege of non-verbal signification is most forcefully and eloquently expressed in 'Language and Proximity', an essay which first appeared in the 1967 edition of *En découvrant l'existence avec Husserl et Heidegger* (*EDE* 217–36/*CPP* 109–26). After once again setting his discussion in a Husserlian context, Levinas proceeds to define ethics as a relation between terms that cannot be united by a synthesis of the understanding or in terms of the subject/object opposition (*EDE* 225/*CPP* 116). From the standpoint of the self, the ethical relation is a relation with an absolutely singular other whom I can neither include nor exclude from my psyche. The Other defies ontological comprehension within intentional consciousness, and yet insinuates him or herself within the psyche in a way that cannot be ignored. Levinas claims that the event which establishes this relation is the primordial Saying, or 'original language' (*le langage originel*).[31] Now, this original Saying is not a verbal utterance: language does not begin with a message or proposition spoken by the Other: 'Aidez-moi'. It is, rather, the non-verbal manifestation of 'skin and human face' (*peau et visage humain*). The ethical essence of language, from which the experience of obligation derives, originates in the sensibility of the skin of the Other's face. The meaningful relation to the Other is maintained by a non-verbal language of skin. This line of thought is continued in *Otherwise than Being*, where Levinas begins his exposition by describing the movement from Husserlian intentionality to sensing or sentience (*be l'intentionalité au sentir*) – that is, a relation in which the conscious subject is reduced to a relation of subjection to the Other. *The subject is subject*, and the form that this subjection assumes is sensibility. Sensibility is my subjection, vulnerability, or passivity towards the Other, a sensibility that takes places 'on the surface of the skin, at the edge of the nerves' (*sensibilité à fleur de peau, à fleur de nerfs*) (*AE* 18/*OB* 15). The entire phenomenological thrust of *Otherwise than Being* is to 'ground' ethical subjectivity in sensibility and to describe sensibility as proximity to the Other, a proximity whose basis is found in substitution (*AE* 23/*OB* 19). The ethical self is an embodied being of flesh and blood, a being who is capable of hunger, who eats and enjoys eating. As Levinas writes, 'Only a being that eats can be for the Other' (*AE* 93/*OB* 74); that is, only such a being can know what it means to give its bread to the Other from out of its own mouth. Recall that, for Levinas, Heidegger's *Dasein* is never hungry (*TeI* 108/*TI* 134). Ethics is not an obligation towards the Other mediated through the formal and procedural universalization of maxims or some appeal to good conscience; rather – and this is what is truly provocative about Levinas – ethics is *lived* as a corporeal obligation to the Other, an obligation whose form is sensibility. It is because the self is sensible – that is, vulnerable, passive, open to wounding, pain, and the movement of the erotic – that it is worthy of ethics. Ethics, for Levinas, is enacted at the level of skin. Consequently, the privilege of the ethical is preserved not simply through the primacy of speech, but also through sensible tenderness, physical contact, and the movement of the caress (*EDE* 227/*CPP* 118). As Edith Wyschogrod has argued, the movement from ontology to ethics can be plausibly described in terms of a transfer from the privilege of sound, voice, and sight – which Derrida's work has done so much to deconstruct – to the primacy of touch and tactility.[32] The original language of proximity whereby the self is related to the Other is achieved in non-verbal sensibility. 'The relation of proximity...is the original language, language without words or propositions, pure communication' (*EDE* 228/*CPP* 119). Language is originally wordless approach and tactile contact. It is the nudity and aphonia of skin, the taciturn eloquence of the stammer.

The consequence to be drawn from this discussion of non-verbal discourse is that an objection can be raised against the accusations of humanism and anthropocentrism that are often directed against Levinasian ethics. Such accusations claim that the ethical relation in Levinas is founded upon discourse and that discourse simply means speech. Consequently, it is claimed, one only has ethical obligations towards beings that can speak – in other words, human beings. One might conclude from this argument, as indeed Derrida has recently done, that Levinasian ethics has no way of experiencing responsibility towards plants, animals, and living things in general (*le vivant en général*) and that despite the novelty and originality of Levinas's analyses of ethical subjectivity, he ends up buttressing and perpetuating a very traditional humanism, that of Judaeo-Christian morality.[33] This issue is very sensitively discussed by John Llewelyn when he explores the question 'Who is the Other (*Autrui*)?' by asking whether animals – dogs in particular – can obligate humans to the same degree as other human beings, Llewelyn argues:

In the metaphysical ethics of Levinas I can have direct responsibilities only towards beings that can speak, and this means beings that have a rationality that is presupposed by the universalizing reason fundamental in the metaphysics of ethics of Kant.[34]

Although Llewelyn and Derrida are to some extent justified in their suspicions regarding Levinas's humanism – it must be noted, however, that Levinas always speaks of a humanism of the other man (*humanisme de l'autre homme*) – I believe that the above discussion of non-verbal communication suggests that their objections are not based on a complete picture of Levinasian ethics. If they were, then the nature of those objections would have to change, and their content become more nuanced. To offer only one example that might provide the basis for a more complex reading of Levinas's humanism: in a striking passage in *Otherwise than Being*, Levinas writes thus of an ambiguity in ethical signification: 'The incarnate ego, the ego of flesh and blood, can lose its signification, affirming itself as an animal (*s'affirmer animalement*) in its conatus and its joy' (*AE* 100/*OB* 81). In its egoist *jouissance*, the self can affirm itself as an animal, and as one animal in particular, a dog. Levinas continues: 'It is a dog that recognizes as its own Ulysses coming to take possession of his goods.' It is a dog, Argus, who first recognizes Odysseus's true identity beneath his disguise upon his return to Ithaca. As Levinas writes in 'Nom d'un chien ou le droit naturel', it was a dog, Bobby, 'the last Kantian in Nazi Germany' (*DL* 216), who alone recognized Levinas and his fellow Jewish prisoners of war as human beings during their time in the camps in Germany. The ambiguity of ethical selfhood is that it is only as an animal, as a being that eats and is capable of giving its food to the Other, that I can be for the Other.

To conclude, the original *logos* of ethics from which the experience of obligation derives can be shown to be rooted in the non-verbal and consequently non-logocentric (recall that it is *verbum* that translates *logos* in the Latin Vulgate) sensible relation to the Other. If the condition of possibility for ethical obligation is sensibility towards the face of the Other, then the purview of the word *Autrui* can be extended to all sentient beings. To quote Llewelyn quoting Bentham, the question with regard to human obligations towards animals is not 'Can they reason? or Can they talk? but, *Can they suffer?*'[35] The ethical signification of discourse is conditioned by an indicative relation to the face of the Other, a dimension of signification – the Saying – that precedes and exceeds the meaning borne by the Said and is the condition of possibility for both verbal and non-verbal ethical discourse. I cannot evade the Other's demand by refusing to communicate or by mumbling to myself in soliloquy; the Other insinuates him or herself within me sensibly through a corporeal and voiceless approach. Ethics is a relation of sentient singularity prior to universalization and rationality. Neither I nor Bobby nor Argus need to universalize our maxims in order to be capable of giving and receiving respect. However, as I will show in the next chapter, this exclusion of universalizing reason from the ethical relation serves to found an acount of politics in which rationality and universalization are moments in the philosophical legitimation of political life.

NOTES

1   Of course, in the context of Kant's *Prolegomena zu einer jeden künftigen Metaphysik*, it is Hume who awakens Kant from his dogmatic slumber (*Werke*, vol. 4 (Cassirer, Berlin, 1913), p. 8; tr. P. Carus (Open Court, La Salle, Ill., 1902), p. 7). Interestingly, in the discussion which followed Derrida's paper 'La différance', included in *Derrida and Différance*, ed. D. Wood and R. Bernasconi (Parousia Press, Coventry, 1985), p. 145, Derrida was asked: 'Is your philosophy, which is in the process of being born, a form of scepticism or is it indeed a philosophy in the sense of a philosophy that bears a content? You are perhaps introducing us to a new Hume, and perhaps we need one.' Derrida, showing his Husserlian background, responded sharply: 'It is certainly not a scepticism.' However, he immediately went on to say: 'Hume, whom you cite, proposed a kind of philosophy of difference – that interests me greatly' (p. 146).

2   It is surprising and even mistaken, that Levinas does not consider Heidegger's work to be part of this critical tradition. At times it seems that much of what Levinas wants to ascribe to Derrida could also refer to Heidegger: the critique of the vulgar conception of time, the de (con)struction of the history of ontology, the increasingly ambivalent relation to phenomenology.

3   Cf. *Ideen, Husserliana*, vol. 3/1: (Martinus Nijhoff, The Hague, 1976), p. 51; tr. W. R. Boyce Gibson (Allen and Unwin, London, 1931), p. 92.

4   *Werke*, vol. 4/2: Nietzsche, *Menschliches Allzumenschliches* (Walter de Gruyter, Berlin 1967), p. 23.

5 Heidegger, 'Seminar in Zähringen', in *Seminare*, Gesamtausgabe, vol. 15 (Vittorio Klostermann, Frankfurt am Main, 1986), pp. 372–400.

6 In this connection, the following passage from Christa Wolf's *Accident. A Day's News* (Virago, London, 1989) testifies to the same historical events from the opposing perspective:

> Heinrich Plaack was the first man I met who still suffered when he told me about the war, about 'our boys'. No person could tell the worst things of all, he said. But just a small example: In France, where the people had all fled before us, the houses stood empty and the baggage packed. They had to leave everything behind. And so, with his gear all dirty and ragged, he had also gone into a house once and taken a fresh shirt his size and a pair of socks, he was the first to admit it. But he had still taken care not to disturb anything else, to leave everything in order. When he had come again the next day, however, it looked as if the place had been a stopover for vandals. His own brothers-in-arms had had a go at the trunks and suitcases. They had broken everything open, they had pulled the fresh, clean bed linen onto the floor and then they had stomped around on it, for nothing and no good reason, just feeling boisterous and looking for kicks. Then he had said to his lieutenant, who was an all right guy when you got him alone: Things ain't going right, sir, he had said, and the lieutenant had replied: Right you are, Heinrich. No respect for anything – there was no way things could go right. (p. 43)

7 Plato, *Phaedrus*, 250e–257b.

8 The definitive article on the theme of scepticism in Levinas, which traces it as a response to Derrida's 'Violence and Metaphysics', is Robert Bernasconi's 'Skepticism in the Face of Philosophy', in *RRL* 149–61. I have referred to this article throughout the following discussion.

9 For this phrase in Derrida, see *VP* 106/*SP* 95.

10 This phrase occurs at least three times in *Autrement qu'être* (*AE* 9, 108n., 231/*OB* 7, 192n., 183). On the English translation of this phrase, see Bernasconi, 'Skepticism in the Face of Philosophy', p. 160.

11 For some examples of refutations of deconstruction which echo the classical refutation of scepticism and share the same fate as the latter, see C. Butler, *Interpretation, Deconstruction and Ideology* (Oxford University Press, Oxford, 1984), esp. ch. 5, 'Deconstruction and Scepticism'. See also S. J. Wilmore; 'Scepticism and Deconstruction', *Man and World*, 20 (1987), pp. 437–55. Wilmore writes: 'What I will consider is the movement of deconstruction as a sceptical force in literary theory' (p. 438).

12 See esp. 'De la signifiance du sens', in *Heidegger et la question de Dieu*, ed. R. Kearney and J. S. O'Leary (Grasset, Paris, 1980), pp. 238–47; partially reprinted as 'Façon de Parler', in *DQVI* 266–70. The

remainder of the text was reprinted under its original title in *HS* 135–42.

13 For a thorough account of ancient scepticism, see J. Annas and J. Barnes, *The Modes of Scepticism* (Cambridge University Press, Cambridge, 1985). It is important to note that ancient scepticism is not, like modern scepticism, doubt about the possibility of certain forms of philosophical or theoretical cognition; it is not metaphysical doubt, but practical doubt about the entirety of one's beliefs. To use the later Foucault's terminology, scepticism is a practice of the self.

14 This belief in the non-sensicality of scepticism is shared by Wittgenstein in the *Tractatus*, where he writes: 'Scepticism is not irrefutable, but obviously nonsensical' (*Tractatus Logico-Philosophicus*, tr. D. F. Pears and B. F. McGuinness (Routledge and Kegan Paul, London, 1961), 6.51). For the early Wittgenstein, all that can be *said* are the propositions of natural science, whereas the ethical is transcendental and cannot be put into words. As Wittgenstein makes clear in an unpublished preface to the *Tractatus*, the point of the book is precisely the transcendental silence of the ethical (cf. *Prototractatus*, ed. B. F. McGuiness *et al.*, (Routledge and Kegan Paul, London, 1971), pp. 15–16). For Levinas, ethics is synonymous with *Saying* and distinct from silence. Silence is violence, and he even goes so far as to claim, for reasons precisely denied by Husserl (*LU*ii 35/*LI* 271), that silent discourse with oneself is not even possible (*AE* 217/*OB* 171). However, whether the belief in the refutability of scepticism and the claim about the silence of the ethical are enough to deny any possible *rapprochement* between Wittgenstein and Levinas will have to remain an unresolved if intriguing question. On this topic, see Jean Greisch, 'The Face and Reading: Immediacy and Mediation', in *RRL* 67–82, esp. 71–4.

15 Hegel, *Enzyklopädie der Philosophischen Wissenschaften im Grundrisse* (1827) (Meiner Verlag, Hamburg, 1989), p. 57; tr. as *Hegel's Logic*, by W. Wallace (Oxford University Press, Oxford, 1975), p. 64; and *LI* 137–8.

16 Hegel, *Enzyklopädie* pp. 53 and 91–2. *Hegel's Logic*, pp. 52 and 118–19.

17 'Scepticism, a name that strikes out its etymology and all etymology; is not indubitable doubt, nor is it any simple nihilistic negation; it is rather irony. Scepticism is in relation with the refutation of scepticism.' (*Le scepticisme, nom qui a rayé son étymologie et toute étymologie, n'est pas le doute indubitable, n'est la simple négation nihiliste: plûtot l'ironie. Le scepticisme est en rapport avec la réfutation du scepticisme.*) Blanchot, *L'Écriture du désastre* (Gallimard, Paris, 1980), p. 123. Blanchot also refers to Levinas's 'scepticisme invincible' in 'Notre compagne clandestine', *In Textes pour Emmanuel Levinas*, ed. F. Laruelle (Jean-Michel Place, Paris, 1980). pp. 80–81.

18 'The Paradox of Morality: An Interview with Emmanuel Levinas', *In The Provocation of Levinas*, ed. R. Bernasconi and D. Wood (Routledge, London and New York, 1988), p. 179. See also Levinas's remarks in *Autrement que savoir* (Osiris, Paris, 1987), p. 69: 'Can one reproach me, as Derrida amicably reproaches me, for speaking Hegelian language whilst at the same time challenging Hegel?'

19 For a discussion of Levinas's account of scepticism that sees it as Levinas's response to objections, see Jan de Greef, 'Scepticisme et raison', *Revue Philosophique de Louvain*, 82 (August 1984), pp. 365–384; tr. Dick White in *FF* 159–79. For a critical discussion of this essay, see Bernasconi, 'Skepticism in the Face of Philosophy', p. 161, and S. Critchley, 'Scepticism – a reply to the critics? A discussion of Jan de Greef's "Scepticism and Reason"', in 'The Chiasmus: Levinas, Derrida and the Ethics of Deconstructive Reading' (Ph. D. thesis, University of Essex, 1988), pp. 292–303.

20 Cf. Lacan, *The Four Fundamental Concepts of Psychoanalysis*, tr. A. Sheridan (Penguin, Harmondsworth, 1979), pp. 138–42. See also Lacan's fascinating remarks on scepticism (which once again seem to privilege ancient scepticism): 'Scepticism is an ethic. Scepticism is a mode of sustaining man in life, which implies a position so difficult, so heroic, that we can no longer even imagine it' (ibid., p. 224).

21 On this topic, see Jeanne Delhomme, 'Savoir Lire? Synchronie et Diachronie', in *Textes pour Emmanuel Levinas*, pp. 151–65, in which this distinction is traced back to Bergson's division between *la durée* and *la simultanéité* in the *Essai sur les données immédiates de la conscience*, which Levinas cites as one of the five great books in the history of philosophy (*EeI* 28). Far from alluding to Saussurian linguistics, the notion of diachrony represents Levinas's assimilation of *la durée*. In 'La pensée de l'être', Levinas grants Bergson a place in the history of philosophy equal to that of Plato and Descartes, because it was Bergson's insight into *la durée* that first seized 'the very diachrony of time' (*PEQA* 185). For a helpful account of Bergson, see Leszek Kolakowski, *Bergson* (Oxford University Press, Oxford, 1985).

22 The phrase 'interstices of Being' also occurs in *DEE* 171/*EE* 99 and *TeI* 128, 197, 208/*TI* 154, 221, 232.

23 Cf. André Lalande (ed.), *Vocabulaire technique et critique de la philosophie*, 15th edn (P. U. F., Paris, 1985), pp. 387–8; and Joachim Ritter (ed.), *Historisches Wörterbuch der Philosophie* (Schwabe Verlag, Basel and Stuttgart, 1974), vol. 3, p. 715.

24 'At the height of its gnoseological adventure, everything in sensibility means intuition, theoretical receptivity from a distance (which is that of the look)' (*AE* 94/*OB* 75). For a similar formulation, see *AE* 46/*OB* 36;

also *AE* 80/*OB* 64: 'Western philosophy has never doubted the gnoseological, and consequently ontological, structure of signification.'

25   In this connection, see Donn Welton's exemplary and innovative analysis of indication and essentially occasional expressions in *The Origins of Meaning* (Martinus Nijhoff, The Hague, 1983), esp. pp. 8–48. Welton's reading deepens and challenges Derrida's *VP* and extends discussion of indication and expression to an unpublished manuscript by Husserl from 1908.

26   Cf. John Llewelyn, *Derrida on the Threshold of Sense* (Macmillan, London and Basingstoke, 1986), p. 26.

27   As an aside, the function of the indicative sign in Heidegger's *Sein und Zeit* should be noted. Heidegger discusses the sign because it is that ready-to-hand, or handy (*zuhanden*), thing which manifests the referential structure of the totality of the ready-to-hand in a manner that is not present-at-hand, or objectively present (*vorhanden*). Heidegger writes: 'A sign is something ontically ready-to-hand (*ein ontisch Zuhandenes*), that functions both as this determinate thing (*Zeug*) and that which indicates (*anzeigt*) the ontological structure of readiness-to-hand, of referential totalities and worldhood' (*SuZ* 82). It is in such passages of *Sein und Zeit* that one witnesses a definite inversion of the primacy of expression and a restitution of indication (Heidegger even speaks of the knot in a handkerchief (*SuZ* 81)) in the explication of the categorial structure of the world.

28   For Levinas's reading of Descartes, see 'Philosophy and the Idea of Infinity' (*EDE* 165–78/*CPP* 47–59).

29   As far as I am aware, 'La pensée de l'être' is the only place in Levinas's work where one finds such a positive reading of the indicative sign in Husserl, which would suggest the extent to which the reading is dependent on the specific context of Derrida's *VP*. However, the word 'indication' does appear in other of Levinas's texts. In 'Façon de parler', the phrase 'the indicative proposition' appears in a discussion of the ambiguity of philosophical language (*DQVI* 268). In the important 1965 essay 'Enigma and Phenomenon', the indicative sign is introduced with reference to the trace. Levinas argues that if the significance of the face of the Other is to be maintained, a new order of indication is required ('It would need an indication revealing the withdrawal of the indicated, instead of a reference that rejoins it. Such is the trace in its emptiness and desolation' (*EDE* 207/*CPP* 65). However, this connection of the trace with indication must be tempered by a remark in *OB* in which Levinas argues that the trace cannot be reduced to the level of the sign, least of all the indicative sign: 'The signifyingness of the trace for comportment; a signifyingness of which one would be wrong to forget

the an-archical insinuation by confusing it with indication' (*AE* 155/*OB* 121). The theme of indication is also distinguished from the order of the trace in the 1963 essay 'The Trace of the Other' (cf. *EDE* 200–1).

30 The interhuman implications of indication are briefly recognized by Derrida in his commentary on this passage. Thus he writes: 'There is perhaps something in the relation to the Other (*dans le rapport à autrui*) which makes indication irreducible' (*VP* 39/*SP* 37).

31 It is clear that in light of Derrida's reading of Rousseau in *G*, any allusion to theses on the origin or essence of language is problematic. However, might it not be possible to give a non-verbal reading of the essence of language as it is established in *TI*? Is the first word – 'You shall not commit murder' (*Tu ne commettras pas de meutre*) (*TeI* 173/*TI* 199) – spoken? Might it not simply be expressed by the ethical resistance of the Other's face?

32 Edith Wyschogrod, 'Doing before Hearing: On the Primacy of Touch', in *Textes pour Emmanuel Levinas*, pp. 179–203. For example: 'By reversing the order of tactility and vision and by interpreting touch as "pure approach, pure proximity", Levinas's rich descriptions of touch point in this direction' (p. 198). And again: 'In freeing tactility from general theories of sensation, we are able to explore the bond between tactility and an ethic which depends upon such metaphors as proximity, non-allergy and obsession' (p. 199).

33 Cf. ' "Il faut bien manger" ou le calcul du sujet. Entretien (avec J.-L. Nancy)', in *Après le sujet qui vient, Cahiers*, 20 (Winter 1989), p. 108. In the same context Derrida makes a similar series of remarks about Heidegger's discussion of animality in *Die Grundbegriffe der Metaphysik*, ed. F.-W. von Herrmann, in *Gesamtausgabe*, vols 29–30 (Vittorio Klostermann, Frankfurt am Main, 1983).

34 John Llewelyn, 'Am I Obsessed by Bobby? (Humanism of the Other Animal)', *RRL* 241. This essay offers a subtle and profound analysis of the problems involved in extending Levinasian ethics to include obligations towards non-human beings.

35 Ibid., p. 234.

5

A Question of Politics:
The Future of Deconstruction

5.1 Introduction

If, as I have argued in this book, the pattern of reading that is found in deconstruction can be understood as an unconditional ethical demand in the Levinasian sense, then is this in itself an adequate response to the question of politics? If deconstruction can provide new resources for thinking about ethical responsibility, then does this also entail a satisfactory account of political responsibility? What is the political moment in deconstruction? Can deconstruction provide an account of justice and a just polity? More precisely, as I asked at the end of chapter 1, what is the relation between the rigorous undecidability of deconstructive reading and the need for political decisions and political critique? If politics is the moment of the decision – of judgement, of justice, of action, of antagonism, of beginning, of commitment, of conflict, of crisis – then how does one take a decision in an undecidable terrain?

In this concluding chapter, then, it will be a question of politics – which is perhaps the most *unsurprising* question to demand of deconstruction. Indeed, it is a question commonly enough asked: Does Derridian deconstruction avoid political responsibility? Moveover, the ever increasing chorus of (often hostile) politically motivated critiques of deconstruction risks dominating and distorting the entire reception of Derrida's work. It has perhaps become something of a banality to speak of Derrida's withdrawal from the political, of his silence and hesitation with regard to political issues, of his complex reticence on Marx and Marxism, of his alleged complicity in the supposedly unquestionable political guilt of Heidegger and Paul de Man. In brief, the political question can be asked irresponsibly and employed as a reason for avoiding, censoring, or simply refusing to read Derrida's work. Sadly, in the aftermath of the Heidegger and de Man affairs, there is abundant evidence – particularly in non-academic journals and newspapers – of how the opening of a political question can be crudely employed as an accusation or as a means to close down the space opened by original thinking.

Such is not my intention. On the contrary, I want to raise a question of politics in Derrida's work in a way that will ultimately deepen and extend the deconstructive opening for thinking that I have sought to describe in this book. It would not be inaccurate to say that political questions have come to dominate Derrida's thinking in recent years: one has only to look at his recent work on democracy and European identity, his responses to de Man's and Heidegger's political engagement, his work on friendship, on apartheid and Nelson Mandela, on law, on nationalism and philosophical nationality, on *Geschlecht*, on the university, on nuclear criticism, on the teaching of philosophy (and the list could be continued). Further, it would be absurd to look to Derrida's biography to confirm any thesis claiming political quietism; the facts are well known and do not need to be repeated here. Derrida's thinking, then, is to a large extent dominated by the question of politics, or, more precisely, by the question of 'that which has always linked the essence of the philosophical to the essence of the political' (*M* 131/*MP* 111). Anyone who doubts this need only read the opening pages of the 1968 paper 'The Ends of Man'.

So why join this chorus of complaint? Why raise the question of politics? I shall argue that it is not so much an avoidance of the question of politics that characterizes Derrida's work, but the way in which politics is discussed, which itself needs to be questioned. I shall claim that Derrida's work results in a certain *impasse* of the political (an impasse: a road, or way, having no exit or outlet, a blind alley or *cul-de-sac*). My argument throughout this book has been that, with some understanding of Levinas's work, it is possible – and indeed plausible – to understand deconstruction as an ethical demand which provides a compelling account of responsibility as an affirmation of alterity, of the otherness of the Other: 'Yes, to the stranger'. However, I shall argue that deconstruction fails to navigate the treacherous passage from ethics to politics, or, as I shall show presently, from responsibility to questioning. Deconstruction fails to thematize the question of politics *as* a question – that is, as a place of contestation, antagonism, struggle, conflict, and dissension on a factical or empirical terrain. The rigorous undecidability of deconstructive reading fails to account for the activity of political judgement, political critique, and the political decision. Far from taking an anti-Derridian stance, I shall attempt to write a political supplement (in the full sense of the word) to deconstruction, a supplement that will conclude by imagining the future of deconstruction.

The general direction of my investigation can be signposted by raising two questions that will return as leitmotifs in the following discussion: first, *is a politics that does not reduce transcendence still possible?* and second, to quote Levinas, '*What meaning can community take on in Difference without reducing Difference?*' (*AE* 197/*OB* 154). I shall pursue my argument in three main stages: I will begin with a reading of Derrida's 1987 text, *Of Spirit*, which will allow me to restate briefly what I see as the ethical moment in deconstructive reading and to build a bridge, using the context of *l'affaire Heidegger*, to the question of politics and political responsibility. This will enable me to articulate the impasse of Derridian deconstruction, an impasse that is confirmed by other writings of Derrida on political topics. As a consequence of these critical remarks (or rather question marks) regarding Derridian deconstruction and as an exploration of this impasse of the political, I will then discuss the work of Philippe Lacoue-Labarthe and Jean-Luc Nancy, who have extended and deepened the analysis of the political from a perspective inspired by Derrida. After showing how the impasse of the political is continued and complicated in Lacoue-Labarthe's and Nancy's retracing of the political, I will seek a way out of this impasse by examining Levinas's traversal of the passage from ethics to politics in *Totality and Infinity* and *Otherwise than Being*, a traversal that, on my reading, offers a markedly different conception of political and communal space, a space that permits a reformulation of the political function of philosophy within democracy.

5.2   The Question of the Question: An Ethico-Political Response to a Note in *Of Spirit*

In order to raise the question of ethical and political responsibility in Derrida's work with any plausibility, that work must first be approached on its own terms – that is to say, through the textual practice of deconstruction as it engages in the reading of a specific text. Such an *attention* to Derrida's work, what he recently described in another context as 'an "ethico-political duty"' (*un 'devoir ethico-politique'*) (*LI* 249/*LItr.* 135), must be carried out before any compelling *assertion* can be made about the ethical or political status of that work. In short, it is necessary to proceed obliquely. I shall therefore approach the question of deconstruction and politics through a brief reading of Derrida's 1987 text 'on Heidegger and Nazism' (*MPM* 161/*LSS* 600), *Of Spirit*; a profoundly self-referential text, I would claim, whose rigour is outmatched only by its obliqueness. I shall offer a reading of *Of Spirit* based on a long footnote (*E* 147–54/*OS* 129–36) which has already been the focus of some discussion[1] and which was written as a response to an intervention by Françoise Dastur at the Essex colloquium on 'Reading Heidegger' in 1986.[2] I will try to show how this footnote sets the agenda for a *re-reading* of Heidegger and – more obliquely and perhaps more importantly – of Derrida, a reading specifically in terms of the question of ethical and political responsibility.

Derrida's 'hypothesis' in *Of Spirit* is the following:

> Such at least is my hypothesis – to recognize in it [Heidegger's interpretation of the word Spirit, *Geist*] in its very equivocation or *indecision* [*indecision*; my emphasis], *the edging or dividing path* (*le chemin de bordure ou de partage*) which ought, according to Heidegger, pass between a Greek or Christian – even onto-theological – determination of *pneuma* or *spiritus*, and a thinking of *Geist* which would be other and more originary. (*E* 128/*OS* 81–2)

According to Derrida, Heidegger's thinking moves between two determinations of Spirit, one belonging to onto-theo-logy or metaphysics, that of the 1933 Rectoral Address and the 1935 *Introduction to Metaphysics*, which Heidegger said ought to be avoided early in *Sein und Zeit*, and the other pointing towards a more originary and non-metaphysical thinking that appears most forcefully in the 1953 essay on Trakl, 'Language in the Poem'.[3] The movement of Heidegger's thinking oscillates *indecisively* between these two possibilities, and it is this very indecision that fascinates Derrida: 'That's what I like about Heidegger. When I think about him, when I read him, I'm aware of both these vibrations at the same time' (*E* 109/*OS* 68). Heidegger's thinking moves relentlessly between two borders, the metaphysical and the non-metaphysical, alternately striking both and producing a dissonant resonance. However, the undecidability of such an experience of reading and Derrida's consequent refusal to choose one determination of Spirit rather than the other – what I have described as the pattern of *clôtural* reading – does not agnostically side-step a confrontation with the ethical and the political; rather, it provides a space wherein the latter can be addressed. My claim has been that it is precisely in the suspension of choice or decision between two alternatives, a suspension provoked in, as, and through a practice of *clôtural* reading, that the ethical dimension of deconstruction is opened and maintained. I have argued that an unconditional duty or affirmation is the source of the injunction that produces deconstruction and that the textual practice of *clôtural* reading keeps open a dimension of alterity or transcendence that has ethical significance.

In his reading of 'Language in the Poem', Derrida comes across the word *versprechender* ('more promising') (*US* 77/*OL* 194). This leads him to focus on the notion of the promise (*la promesse; das Versprechen*), and occasions a short digression regarding Paul de Man's reading of Rousseau's *Social Contract* in *Allegories of Reading*, in which, at the end of a discussion of the nature of the promise, de Man rewrites Heidegger's formula *die Sprache spricht* (language speaks) as *die Sprache verspricht* (*sich*) ('language promises [itself]') (*E* 146/*OS* 93).[4] With this minimal and seemingly contingent digression, Derrida notes that he has perhaps 'left the order of commentary, if something like that exists' (*E* 146–7/*OS* 94). However, as he leaves the order of commentary, the indispensable moment of repetition whereby the dominant interpretation of the text is reconstructed (*LI* 265/*LItr* 143), Derrida moves on to *the question of the question* which forms the subtitle of *Of Spirit: Heidegger and the Question*. What is the question of the question? Derrida writes:

> It remains to be known if this *Versprechen* is not the promise which, opening every speaking, makes possible the very question and therefore precedes it without belonging to it: the dissymmetry of an affirmation, of a *yes* before all opposition of *yes* and *no*. (*E* 147/*OS* 94)

The thought here concerns the possibility of a promise that would render questioning possible without, however, belonging to the order of interrogation. It is the question of a promise, a moment of affirmation that, as discussed in chapter 1, Derrida has elsewhere described in the language of Kant's ethics as an unconditional categorical imperative. As if to clearly signal this departure from the repetitive order of commentary, Derrida opens an eight-page footnote which deals at length with the question of the question and which, I would claim, opens both the ultimately *ethical* orientation of *Of Spirit* and provides the key to Derrida's reading of Heidegger.

Derrida's most general concern in this footnote, then, is to elucidate a form of language that would precede and render possible all questioning of the form: what is x? – that is to say, all *ontological* questioning, in so far as every question asks after the essence or Being of an entity. The centrality of the question (*die Frage*) to Heidegger's thinking is apparent from as early as the Introduction to *Sein und Zeit* (*SuZ* 5–8), where it is the question of the meaning of Being (*die Frage nach dem Sinn von Sein*), which has today been forgotten and which must be formulated (*gestellt*) and submitted to repetition or recapitulation (*Wiederholung*), and where the project of fundamental ontology is organized according to the tripartite schema of that which is asked about in any investigation (*das Gefragte*), namely, Being; that which is to be interrogated (*das Befragte*), namely, *Dasein*; and that which is to found out by the asking (*das Erfragte*), namely, the meaning of Being. The very possibility of fundamental ontology is conditional upon *Dasein's* distinctive relationship (*Bezug*) with the question of Being. If *Dasein* can raise the question of Being, or if Being is an issue for *Dasein*, albeit initially only in a vague and average manner, then this shows that *Dasein* has an understanding of Being (*Seinsverständnis*) and that *Sein und Zeit* can, literally and logically, begin. *Sein und Zeit* begins by showing the necessity (Section 1), the structure (Section 2), and the ontic and ontological priority (Sections 3 and 4) of the *Seinsfrage* and the way, or method (Sections 5–7), that will be followed in the elaboration or working out (*Ausarbeitung*) of this question. Heidegger's thought begins from the necessity of making the question of Being a question once again for us, as it was for the Stranger in Plato's *Sophist*. It is questioning that will take hold of the forgottenness of Being as forgotten.

Some 25 years after the publication of *Sein und Zeit*, in the 1953 lecture 'The Question Concerning Technology', Heidegger appears to maintain this priority of questioning, the latter being characterized as the piety of thinking (*Denn das Fragen ist die Frömmigkeit des Denkens*).[5] However, despite this undoubted priority, Derrida (at the prompting of Françoise Dastur) locates a moment in Heidegger where the question itself undergoes an inversion (*Umkehrung*) (*US* 176/*OL* 72), or reversal (*Bouleversement*) (*E* 150/*OS* 131). In the course of the three lectures that comprise 'The Nature of Language' (*Das Wesen der Sprache*) (*US* 158–238/*OL* 57–108), which originally date from 1957–8, Heidegger re-reads his statement that questioning is the piety of thought and adds:

> The lecture ending with that sentence was already in the ambiance of the realization that the true stance of thinking cannot be to put questions, but must be listening to the grant or pledge (*daß die eigentliche Gebärde des Denkens nicht das Fragen sein kann, sondern das Hören der Zusage dessen sein muß*). (*US* 176/*OL* 72)

It is with this notion of the *Zusage* (in French, *gage*: pledge or grant, as in *mortgage*, literally a death pledge) that Derrida locates the *Umkehrung* in Heidegger's thinking. Prior to the putting of questions to language (i.e. what is the essence of language?), it is clear that language has already been granted (*schon zugesprochen sein*) (*US* 175 *OL* 71). All questioning requires the prior pledge, or *Zusage*, of that which is put in question. Thus, for the later Heidegger, the primary datum of language is *das Hören der Zusage*, listening to the grant or pledge. As is clear from Derrida's 1987 text on Michel de Certeau, the *Zusage* is a moment of affirmation in Heidegger's text, 'in short, a *yes*' (*PSY* 646).

Derrida then proceeds to draw out the implications of this inversion, tracing it back across some dominant moments in Heidegger's work. What is significant about the *Zusage* is that all forms of questioning are always already pledged (*gagé*) to respond to a prior grant of language. The question and the questioning stance of philosophy are always a response to and a responsibility for that which is prior and over which the question has no priority.

> It [the question] responds in advance, whatever it does, to this pledge and of this pledge (*à ce gage et de ce gage*). It is engaged by it in a

responsibility it has not *chosen* (*qu'elle n'a pas choisie*) – and which assigns it even its liberty. (*E* 148–9/*OS* 130; my emphasis)

What is primary in language is that to which one is responsible, which has not been chosen. The liberty and choice of the questioning attitude are subordinated to a prior responsibility. The origin of language is responsibility (*E* 151/*OS* 132). My language begins as a response to the Other. In short, it is ethical.

In this footnote, then, Derrida is proposing nothing less than an agenda for the *re*-reading of Heidegger, which readers of the latter are now better prepared to recognize a need for and which arises as a response to the questions of politics and ethics, a response made all the more urgent by *l'affaire Heidegger*. Derrida continues:

This is useful not only for *reading* Heidegger [emphasized in the French – *lire* Heidegger – and is an allusion to the Essex colloquium of the same name] and serving some hermeneutical or philological piety. Beyond an always indispensable exegesis, this *re-reading* sketches out another topology for new tasks, for what remains to be situated of the relationships between Heidegger's thought and other places of thought – or of the engage (*de l'en gage*) – *places which one pictures as regions but which are not* (*ethics or politics*)...(*E* 151/OS 132–3; my emphasis)

After the inversion of Heidegger's thinking that the thought of the *Zusage* offers, the task of re-reading would not simply content itself with the hermeneutic piety of *reading* Heidegger, but would *re-read* Heidegger's corpus with a view to both excavating the thought of responsibility within it (Derrida himself lays down several markers for the itinerary of such a re-reading (*E* 151–2/*OS* 133)) and rethinking the relation between 'regional ontologies', like ethics and politics, and the truth of Being.

Of Spirit is an almost 'classical' example of a deconstructive reading – the strictest and most rigorous determination of figures of oscillation or undecidability in a text – which shows how the thought of responsibility emerges in such a reading. Derrida's text is a response, both to the highly critical readings of Heidegger's political involvement,[6] and also, more importantly and self-referentially, to the accusation that his own work (so often caricatured as 'l'Heideggerianisme français'[7] simply avoids discussions of ethical and political

responsibility and that deconstruction leads to either an amoral
anarchism or a de-politicized quietism. On a more sinister level,
another version of the same polemic might argue that Derrida's work
is indeed political, but that, because of its 'Heideggerianism' – and
Heidegger's thinking was, as everyone (*das Man*) now knows with
complete assurance, 'fascist right down to its most intimate compo-
nents'[8] – deconstruction necessarily entails a fascist politics. This sort
of argument, or rather assertion, is proposed, surprisingly, by Man-
fred Frank and quoted approvingly by Habermas in his Preface to
the German edition of Farias's *Heidegger and Nazism*. After lauding
Habermas's *The Philosophical Discourse of Modernity*, Frank writes:

> The new-French theories are taken up by many of our students like a
> gospel. (...) I think the phenomenon is frightening, because it seems
> to me that young Germans are sucking back in, under the pretence of
> an opening to what is French and international, their own irrationalist
> tradition, which had been broken off after the Third Reich.[9]

One might infer from this kind of statement that Derrida's avoidance
of politics is merely a dissimulation of the textual fascism implicit in
deconstructive reading. I noted above that *Of Spirit* begins with the
question of avoidance in Heidegger. In light of the above political
accusations, which crudely infer 'the politics of deconstruction' from
what is cursorily assumed to be the truth of Heidegger's political
engagement ('Heidegger is a Nazi; Derrida is Heideggerian; therefore
Derrida is a Nazi'), it should now be asked: Who or what is being
charged with avoidance in *Of Spirit*? Who or what is being defended?
Is *Of Spirit* a defence of Heidegger? Or is it Derrida's self-defence
before a political tribunal?

I would claim that *Of Spirit* is an elaborate act of ventriloquism,
whose subject is necessarily double, in which Derrida addresses the
question of ethical and political responsibility in his own work
through a reading of Heidegger. It is claimed, after all, that the
semantic ambivalence of the word *Geist* and its cognates in Heidegger's work 'perhaps decides the very meaning of the political as
such' (*E* 19/*OS* 6). However, the obliqueness of this remark – and
indeed of *Of Spirit* as a whole – is necessary to Derrida's response. I
would claim for Derrida what he claims about Heidegger in the short
1987 text 'Comment donner raison': namely, that the *immediate presen-*

tation of a question or a problem is a disaster for *thinking* and that all that Derrida is seeking to do in *Of Spirit* is to keep open the possibility of thinking in spite of the disaster, the disaster that would forbid the reading of Heidegger or Derrida in the name of some political purification process. For Derrida, 'the vigilant but open reading of Heidegger remains in my eyes one of the indispensable conditions, one of them but not the least, for trying to comprehend better and to tell better why, with so many others, I have always condemned Nazism.'[10] It is not by prohibiting the reading of Heidegger and Derrida that the threat of fascism is avoided. Indeed, quite the opposite might be true.

Of Spirit, then, deconstructively responds to both the reductive critique of Heidegger's politics and the supposed avoidance of politics or quasi-fascism of Derrida's own work. It is a response which has as its horizon the thought of responsibility, of language as a response to the Other. By posing the question of the question, Derrida asks if questioning is indeed at the origin of thinking and, consequently, if all thinking is, in a Levinasian sense, ontological. The question of the question challenges the priority of ontology, and finds in language an irreducible dimension of responsibility. To quote Levinas,

> If the question *what?* in its adherence to Being, is at the origin of all thinking...all research and all philosophy go back to ontology....But the question of the Question is more radical. Why does research take the form of a question? How is it that the *what?* already plunged in Being so as to open it up the more, becomes a demand (*demande*) and prayer (*prière*), a particular language inserting into the communication of the given (*donné*), a call for help, for aid, addressed to the Other (*autrui*)? (*AE* 30–1/*OB* 24)[11]

Prior to all questioning, deconstruction opens a dimension of responsibility – grant, pledge, prayer, demand, call, Saying – that precedes ontology and puts me into relation with the Other.

On my reading, such would indeed appear to be Derrida's response to the question of ethical and political responsibility in Heidegger's and his own work. Furthermore, this would seem to be the only deconstructive response that Derrida *could* make to this question. He responds to insinuation and polemic by producing a quite exemplary deconstructive reading of Heidegger – that is, an open, convincing, vigilant, thoughtful reading. What more could one expect from

Derrida? After all, could one reasonably expect Derrida's work not to be Derridian?

I would claim, further, that Derrida's response to Heidegger's politics typifies the deconstructive gesture with regard to the question of ethical and political responsibility: namely, '*there can be no moral or political responsibility without this trial and without this passage by way of the undecidable*" (*LI* 210/*LItr* 116; my emphasis)[12]. One finds this gesture repeated throughout Derrida's writings on political topics, and by way of two further examples, chosen almost at random, I will quickly look at Derrida's essay on Paul de Man's politics, 'Like the Sound of the Sea Deep within a Shell' and a recent text on the problem of European identity, 'L'autre cap'.[13] The former text turns entirely on the question of responsibility and of how one is to respond to the revelations of Paul de Man's wartime journalism. Derrida's reading of de Man is dominated by the *clôtural* rhythm of 'on the one hand' and 'on the other hand' (*MPM* 169–70/*LSS* 607). On the one hand, de Man's wartime journalism seems to correspond to the official rhetoric of the occupying German forces in Belgium. On the other hand, Derrida claims that a closer reading shows how that rhetoric is brought into question and contradicted. De Man's texts are thus enclosed within a double bind that does not allow a simple 'decision de justice' (*MPM* 215/*LSS* 643) to be taken with regard to any alleged complicity with National Socialism. This logic of the double bind is extended (and perhaps even stretched to breaking point) in a reading of de Man's most damning article, 'Les Juifs dans la littérature actuelle'.[14] On the one hand, de Man seems to give his consent to the plan to rid Europe of 'the Jewish problem' by 'the creation of a Jewish colony isolated from Europe', which 'would not entail, for the literary life of the West, deplorable consequences' (*MPM* 190/*LSS* 623). On the other hand, Derrida claims, audaciously, that this text itself proceeds towards a demystification or critique of 'vulgar anti-semitism' (*MPM* 191–2/*LSS* 624).

Similarly, in 'L'autre cap', Derrida claims that any responsible notion of European identity must obey a double and contradictory imperative.[15] To be European means obeying a duty to both recall what Europe is or was, while at the same time opening Europe to the non-European, welcoming the foreigner in his or her alterity. It is a double duty, to criticize both totalitarianism and the new religion of Capital that threatens to take its place. It is a duty to respect both difference and singularity, while at the same time maintaining the universality of law – for example, the necessity of international law.[16] Hence, to be responsibly European is to experience the undecidability of a double bind.

Thus deconstructive reading responds to political topics by giving a rigorous *clôtural* reading of a text (in the general sense) and by showing how the undecidability of reading has its horizon in the thought of irreducible responsibility, an affirmation of alterity. I have demonstrated the ethical significance of the latter. The question that remains – and it is precisely the way in which the question *remains* that I want to pursue – is whether Derrida's approach is an adequate response to politics. If, as has been shown in *Of Spirit*, the ethical moment in deconstruction asks the question of the question, the primacy of responsibility to the Other, then is there not also a necessary moment of questioning that would be directly related to politics? Is not politics precisely the domain of questioning – that is, of contestation, antagonism, struggle, conflict, and dissension? What is the relation, in Derrida's work, between the rigorous and responsible undecidability of deconstructive reading and the necessity for political decisions and political critique? To adapt a remark of Blanchot's – and I am thinking in particular of the essay on de Man – is there not a point at which the practice of an art becomes an insult to the victims?[17]

Deconstruction can certainly be employed as a powerful means of political analysis. For example, showing how a certain dominant political regime – apartheid, say – is based on a set of undecidable presuppositions is an important step in the subversion of that regime's claim to legitimacy.[18] Showing, as Ernesto Laclau has done, how the terrain of the social does not attain closure, but is an ever incomplete, undecidable structure, is a crucial step in the subversion of dominant conceptions of society and the development of new political strategies.[19] But how is one to account for the move from undecidability to the political *decision* to combat that domination? If deconstruction is the strictest possible determination of undecidability in the limitless context of, for want of a better word, experience, then this entails a suspension of the moment of decision. Yet, decisions have to be taken. But how? And in virtue of what? How does one make a decision in an undecidable terrain? I would claim, with Laclau, that an adequate account of the decision is essential to the possibility of politics, and that it is precisely this that deconstruction does not provide.[20] As an epigraph to his celebrated essay on Foucault, Derrida cites Kierkegaard: 'The instant of the decision is madness' (*ED* 51/*WD* 31). This is a good statement of the deconstructive dilemma: one has to make decisions, yet the moment of the decision is madness. I take a risk one way or another – I am for x or against x – but ultimately I do not know why I made this decision. I can no longer ground my political decisions on some ontological basis, or *eidos*, or on a set of *a priori* principles or procedures. Now, this may well be true. Perhaps the ground for one's political decisions is ultimately contingent. But is the madness of the decision itself an adequate account of political life? Is it even a valid description of how one arrives at one's political preferences and engages in political action? Might not Richard Rorty finally have a point in finding in Derrida's work a quest for ironical, private perfection which is politically useless and perhaps even pernicious?[21]

To summarize, is the account of politics given by Derrida either too formalistic and abstract at the level of undecidability or too contingent and empty at the level of the decision? More gravely, in the rigorous, quasi-transcendental delineation of undecidability as the dimension of political responsibility, is there not an implicit refusal of the ontic, the factical, and the empirical – that is to say, of the space of *doxa*, where politics takes place in a field of antagonism, decision, dissension, and struggle? In this sense, might one not ultimately speak of a refusal of politics in Derrida's work?

What I called above the impasse of the political in Derrida's work is now beginning to take shape. Before attempting to indicate a way out of this impasse with reference to Levinas's thematization of the passage from ethical responsibility to political questioning and critique, I would like to explore Lacoue-Labarthe's and Nancy's proposed re-tracing of the political.[22]

5.3 Lacoue-Labarthe and Nancy: Re-tracing the Political

I

The possible implications of Derrida's thinking for the question of politics are addressed with some urgency on the occasion of the 1980

Cérisy colloquium on 'The Ends of Man', which took Derrida's work as its starting point. In the initial description of the aims of the meeting, Lacoue-Labarthe and Nancy cited the opening sentence of the text from which the colloquium took its title: namely, 'Every philosophical colloquium necessarily has a political signification' (*M* 131/*MP* 111). They furthermore described the stakes of the colloquium as breaching the inscription of a wholly other politics (*d'entamer l'inscription d'une tout autre politique*) (*FH* 21). The possible content of this wholly other politics was provisionally discussed in the seminar on politics directed by Christopher Fynsk. Fynsk began his intervention by suggesting that there is a certain withdrawal (*retrait*), (*FH* 488) – I shall return to this word – with respect to politics in Derrida's work, a certain deliberate silence or hesitation with respect to the political. The latter theme was taken up by Lacoue-Labarthe in an improvised response to the intervention, in which he concurred with Fynsk that there is indeed a silence or withdrawal with respect to politics (*la politique*) in Derrida's work, although, he added, one can rethink the political (*le politique*) on the basis of deconstruction (FH 494).

Here one finds the introduction of the distinction that was to become determinant for Lacoue-Labarthe's and Nancy's discussion of the political: *le politique* refers to the essence (a word apparently employed with little deconstructive reticence) of the political – what, before Heidegger, one might have referred to as the philosophical interrogation of politics – whereas *la politique* refers to the facticity, or empirical event, of politics. (I shall have reason to question this distinction below.) For Lacoue-Labarthe, the essential political task arising out of Derrida's work is the need for a deconstruction of *la politique* and an interrogation of the essence of *le politique*. In particular, Lacoue-Labarthe declares the need for a deconstruction of Marxism and Marx's text. Clearly, for Lacoue-Labarthe, the most serious shortcoming of Derrida's withdrawal with respect to politics is his failure to engage deconstructively with Marxism. He goes on to argue that Marxism should not be sheltered from deconstruction (*à l'abri de la déconstruction*) (*FH* 496), and, as possible antecedents for such a deconstructive Marxism, he cites the work of the Situationist International and the *Socialisme ou Barbarie* group and their revolutionary critique of the bureaucratic counter-revolution implicit in Soviet-style socialism. Lacoue-Labarthe's point is confirmed by Derrida's response to a paper by Jacob Rogozinski, in which, contrary to the latter's thesis that deconstruction is essentially a deconstruction of the concept of revolution, Derrida claims that he has not argued against revolution as such (*FH* 526). More specifically, he did not attack the notion of revolution because his concern was not to weaken the revolutionary force of Marxism in France (*FH* 527). Very suggestively, he goes on to claim that his withdrawal with respect to Marxism should be read deconstructively as a blank (*un blanc*), that is, as a political gesture of solidarity with Marxism. Such is Derrida's cryptic rather than crypto-Marxism.

Some months after the Cérisy colloquium, Lacoue-Labarthe and Nancy were responsible for the establishment of the Centre for Philosophical Research on the Political at the École Normale Supérieure in Paris. The essence of Lacoue-Labarthe's and Nancy's position is spelt out in the paper given as the 'Ouverture' for the Centre in December 1980. The basic question of the Centre is 'How can one today interrogate the essence of the political?' (*RJ* 9). In question is a philosophical interrogation of the political, the difference being that the status of philosophy itself will be challenged in the process of interrogation. The posing of this question implies a deliberate and crucial choice: namely, that the direct, empirical approach to the political does not concern Lacoue-Labarthe and Nancy (*RJ* 13). They will only take into account the essential co-appartenance of the philosophical and the political. This very revealing (and question-begging) choice itself arises from the assumption that the move from the philosophical interrogation of the political to politics itself is henceforth no longer possible (*RJ* 13). Politics is impossible.

The reasoning behind this claim can be found in Lacoue-Labarthe's and Nancy's deeply Heideggerian analysis of the contemporary world. In brief, the present is marked by the installation of the philosophical as the political and the absolute domination of politics. The truth of the present is that 'everything is political'; that is, the political condition of contemporary societies is one in which all areas of social life are politicized. As I will show, this entails that the political form of contemporary societies is *totalitarian*. Furthermore, this understanding of the present political situation finds its condition of possibility in philosophy itself. To put this as simply as possible, within the metaphysical tradition, the political is not exterior to the philosophical, but rather – and this is how they understand the quotation from 'The Ends of Man' cited above – there is an essential co-appartenance of the philosophical and the political (*RJ* 14); the political is founded philosophically. This is also how Lacoue-Labarthe reads Heidegger's political adventure of 1933–4; Heidegger's Rectoral Address is one of the last grand philosophical gestures with regard to the political, one which attempts to ground politics on a philosophical foundation, namely science (*Wissenschaft*).[23] For the Heidegger of 1933, 'All science is philosophy, whether it knows and wills it or not.'[24] Philosophy is science – that is, science of Being (*Wissenschaft vom Sein*)[25] – and *Dasein* is that being who is capable of transcendence – that is, of going beyond itself, of projecting itself into the truth of its Being and Being itself. *Dasein* is the being capable of science. This gesture of foundation, or *instauratio*, of the political by the philosophical is not novel; it is *the* classical metaphysical gesture with respect to politics that one finds in Plato's *Republic*, where the *polis* must be founded on philosophy – that is, on the pursuit of *epistēmē* – and consequently the rulers must be philosophers. It is the metaphysico-political gesture *par excellence*, and it is one of the principal elements holding Heidegger's early thinking within the closure of metaphysics. However, if Heidegger's political commitment of 1933 is metaphysical and is a repetition (in Heidegger's sense of a *Wiederholung*, a recapitulation) of the metaphysico-political gesture of Plato's *Republic*,[26] then the first consequence of the much discussed failure of this engagement is the collapse of his transcendental project of fundamental ontology and the extension of that ontology to politics.

For Lacoue-Labarthe and Nancy, the present is marked by both a completion of philosophy (*la philosophie est finie*, both finished and finite) (*FP* 18/*HAP* 4) and a closure of the political (*la clôture du politique*) (*RJ* 15). These notions can be clarified by means of a telling allusion in the 'Ouverture' paper to Heidegger's collection of notes from the years 1936–46 published as 'Overcoming Metaphysics' (*Überwindung der Metaphysik*) (*RJ* 15).[27] I would claim that Lacoue-Labarthe's and Nancy's account of the closure of the political is consonant with Heidegger's analysis of the completion (*Vollendung*) of metaphysics as technology. This is to some extent confirmed by Lacoue-Labarthe's hypothesis in *La Fiction du politique* that Heidegger's politics is not to be found in 1933, but rather in the discourse following the war, the meditation on technology, in which

one finds an oblique, complex settling of accounts with National
Socialism (*FP* 82/*HAP* 53). In a manner which is not simply homolo-
gous – as they point out in the later paper 'Le retrait du politique',
their position is not *simply* Heideggerian (*RT* 187) – the thesis of the
absolute domination of politics is assimilable to Heidegger's analysis
of the contemporary world in terms of the total domination of technology, while the distinction between *le politique* and *la politique* is
assimilable to Heidegger's distinction between the essence of technology ('which is nothing technological') and technology itself.[28] If
politics is henceforth impossible, then there still remains the possibility of meditation upon the essence of *le politique*.

In Heidegger's terms, in those terrifying and profound paragraphs that conclude 'Overcoming Metaphysics', politics in the age
of technology means the total domination of rational calculability and
planning, the triumph of instrumental reason. The completion of
metaphysics unleashes what Heidegger calls 'the will-to-will' (*der
Wille zum Willen*), which manifests itself as an infinite desire to master
nature and dominate the earth, where the human being becomes
simply raw material in a never-ending circle of consumption (it is
worth noting that much of Heidegger's analysis presages the ecologi-
cal critique of capitalism[29]). In the bleak twenty-sixth paragraph of
'Overcoming Metaphysics' (*VA* 87–93/*EOP* 103–9), in passages
where Heidegger diagnoses the nascent political form of totalitarianism, the symptoms of technological domination are located in a
number of phenomena: in the effacing of the distinction between war
and peace that occurred, for Heidegger, at the end of the Second
World War; in the becoming unworld (*Unwelt*) of the world; in the
cult of leadership (*Führung*) and the leader (*der Führer*); in the development of artificial insemination, eugenics, and cybernetics; in the
division of human society into sectors and the development of what
Adorno would call the 'culture industry'; and in the need of business
to overcome national boundaries and become international, and the
consequent collapse of the distinction between the 'national' and the
'international'. In short, the domination of the political by technology
and the utter oblivion of Being implicit in this process entail a
homogenization of all areas of human life into complete uniformity
(*Gleichförmigkeit*). In this process, the human being, metaphysically
understood as an *animal rationale*, is transformed into the the figure
of the worker (Heidegger refers to Ernst Jünger's *Der Arbeiter* (*VA*

68/*EOP* 85)) in what Hannah Arendt would call the victory of the *animal laborans*.

How is this situation to be transformed? How is the completion of metaphysics in technology to be overcome? for Heidegger, the transformation cannot come from within the human being, but only from Being itself. 'No mere action can change the state of the world,' Heidegger writes; for action presupposes the activity of the will, which is the motor that drives the distress (*die Not*) of modernity. Heidegger's only offer of hope is a certain prospect of dwelling within the limits of the possible (*das Mögliche*), which the activity of the technological will is always attempting to exceed and push towards the impossible (*das Unmögliche*) (*VA* 94/*EOP* 109), and a receipt of the blessing of the earth (*der Segen der Erde*) (ibid.). Heidegger's famous remark in the Spiegel interview, that 'Only a god can save us', is no rhetorical flourish; it is completely consistent with the development of his later thinking, a development itself partly motivated by the failure of his own political activism.[30]

What is Lacoue-Labarthe's and Nancy's relation to the Heideggerian analysis? As I have already said, there is no simple homology here; but there is a structural equivalence, because the reduction of *la politique* to *le politique* echoes the Heideggerian move from technology to the thinking of its essence. The sole political recourse in a present dominated by *la politique* ('everything is political') is to reflect on the essence of *le politique*. In virtue of the fact that Lacoue-Labarthe and Nancy accept the description of the contemporary world in terms of the total domination of *la politique*, any move back into politics is necessarily prohibited as a collapse into metaphysics. It is revealing to note that they translate Sartre's famous formulation that 'Marxism is the horizon of our time that cannot be overcome' (*Le marxisme est l'horizon indépassable de notre temps*) by the sentence, 'Socialism (in the sense of "real socialism") is the completed and completing figure of philosophy's imposition' (*Le socialisme (au sens du 'socialisme réel') est la figure achevée, achevante, de l'imposition philosophique*) (*RJ* 16). By 'real socialism' – and this is crucial – they are not simply referring to Soviet, Chinese, or Eastern European 'socialist' regimes; they also include all radicalizations or continuations of the revolutionary socialist project in *Socialisme ou Barbarie* and other groupings. In short, what has attained closure or completion in the contemporary world is the entire discourse of revolution. For Lacoue-Labarthe and Nancy, 'actually existing socialism' (or, it would now be more correct to say, 'formerly existing socialism') represents the final figure in the philosophical determination of the political, and is equated with the phenomenon of totalitarianism. The Heideggerian analysis leads them to accept the inevitability and necessity of totalitarianism as the figure for the closure of *le politique* and the absolute domination of *la politique*.

The closure of the political and the completion of philosophy entail the political form of totalitarianism. Totalitarianism – and here they seem to be following Claude Lefort's analysis (*RJ* 20) – is that political form of society governed by a logic of identification whereby all areas of social life represent incarnate power: the proletariat is identified with the people, the party with the proletariat, the politburo with the party, the leader with the politburo, and so on. It is the representation – or rather, fantasy – of a homogeneous and transparent society, a unified people among whom social division or difference is denied (as is difference of opinion, of faith, and so forth). Totalitarianism is a modern despotism in which the social is represented as something without anything beyond it – that is to say, without any transcendence. In totalitarianism, power has no outside; it is the total immanence of the social in the political. It is politics without transcendence, without remainder or interruption; what Nancy calls 'immanentism' (*CD* 16).

The closure of the political is both the total domination of politics in all areas of social life – the complete atrophy of transcendence in an immanent society – and the absence of any reflection on the political as such. The alleged complicity of traditional philosophy in the political project that results in totalitarianism shows that philosophy has failed to think the political essentially. Thus Lacoue-Labarthe and Nancy diagnose what they see as a withdrawal, or retreat, of the political, exploiting both senses carried by the word *retrait* in French. It is necessary first to engage in a withdrawal with respect to *la politique* (that is, totalitarianism) in order to think the essence of *le politique* as such; second, there is a need for a re-trait, or re-tracing, of the political in its essence. One withdraws before politics in order to re-trace the political more essentially. The approach to the political is governed by this double movement of withdrawal: a re-treat and a re-trait. Thinking back to Lacoue-Labarthe's intervention at the Cérisy colloquium, it is now clear that Derrida has completed the first part of this movement, but has failed to go on to the second.

II

But is this analysis of the present condition of politics accurate? Is totalitarianism indeed the horizon of our time that cannot be overcome? What about the societies that pride themselves on being called 'the democracies'? Lacoue-Labarthe and Nancy respond to certain objections made against their position in the 'Ouverture' paper in 'Le "re-trait" du politique', a text which, in an empirical sense, functions as the *clôture* of the Centre, since it closes the second and final volume of papers published under its name (*RT* 183–200). In this paper, Lacoue-Labarthe and Nancy reaffirm their position on the co-appartenance of the philosophical and the political and the common closure of the political and the philosophical that manifests itself in the form of totalitarianism (*RT* 187). Totalitarianism, as the attempted re-in-*corpor*-ation or re-*organ*-ization of the body politic into a transparent, homogeneous unity without any remainder or transcendence is a process that emerged historically as a response to the crisis of liberal democracy (for example, in Weimar Germany and in post-First World War Italy). Now it is precisely on the question of the distinction between totalitarianism and democracy that a very revealing dimension of Lacoue-Labarthe's and Nancy's work can be discerned. As Nancy Fraser correctly points out, the most provocative intervention into the Centre's work was Claude Lefort's paper 'The Question of Democracy', given in January 1982. Lacoue-Labarthe and Nancy respond to this intervention by taking a critical distance from Lefort's analysis of democracy and questioning whether Western societies can indeed be described as democratic.

Lefort's paper adopts an extremely provocative tone, and is addressed to an audience that has, he believes, refused the task of political philosophy and failed to see the link that ties philosophical reflection to democratic experience. For Lefort, the extreme theoretical sophistication of philosophers attending the Centre – for example, both Derrida and Lyotard were in the audience for Lefort's paper – becomes the most presumptuous realism when applied to politics. Lefort remarks:

> Is it possible to handle with subtlety the ontological difference, and to
> rival the wonders of the combined development of Heidegger, Lacan,
> Jakobson and Lévi-Strauss, and yet to return to the most presump-
> tuous realism when it is a question of politics? (*RT* 72)

For Lefort, politics is the constitution of social space, of the *form* of
society; and the task of contemporary political philosophy is to return
to the ancient philosophical question: namely, what are the different
forms of society? In Lefort's view, to rethink the political in our times
is to analyse the form of totalitarianism, and Lefort's work has been
devoted to this task ever since his early critique of the Trotskyite
belief that the bureaucratic socialism of the Soviet Union was only a
temporary phenomenon. For Lefort (and Castoriadis, when both were
members of *Socialisme ou Barbarie*), the failure of the French Left to
criticize the Soviet Union was symptomatic of a failure to recognize
the nascent political form of totalitarianism. Totalitarianism is neither
a passing phenomenon nor a description of a particular political
regime; it is rather a distinct and novel societal form.[31]

In his paper to the Centre and in a move that mirrors the development of his own work, Lefort goes on to re-examine democracy
and to distinguish the latter from totalitarianism. Following de
Tocqueville's *De la démocratie en Amérique* – although, ultimately, he is
critical of de Tocqueville's resistance to what he calls 'the unknown
(*l'inconnu*) of democracy' (*RT* 79–80) – Lefort understands democratic
society to be committed to an equality of conditions for all citizens.
However, democracy is founded on a contradiction: namely, that it is
a societal form in which the foundation of the social has disappeared.
Democracy is founded on the absence of foundation; what Lefort
means by this can best be seen by following his analysis of the absolute monarchy of the *ancien régime*. In absolute monarchy, the monarch
has two bodies: he is the incarnation of both secular power and divine
power; he is both mortal and immortal, a mediator between God and
man and between men and an ideal of justice. His body is two bodies,
and its division is paradoxically a symbol for the unity of the king-
dom. In the language of traditional metaphysics, the king is the
unconditional substance, or subject, that founds the social order;
monarchy is a politicized metaphysics of substance. With the advent
of democracy in the French Revolution, the place of power became an
empty space (*un lieu vide*). In democracy, those who govern cannot

incarnate power; rather, the holding of power is submitted to periodic changes as a result of elections. The important point here is that in democracy the source of power is contested; it is open to competition, struggle, and antagonism. In democracy, power is not occupied by a king, a party leader, an egocrat, or a *Führer*; rather, it is ultimately empty; no one holds the place of power. Democracy entails a disincorporation of the body politic, which begins with a literal or metaphorical act of decapitation. In Bataille's terms, democracy is the headless community of *Acéphale*.

At a more practical level, this disincorporation of the body politic entails a division of what Lefort calls the spheres of law, power, and knowledge (RT 83), which echoes Montesquieu's separation of legislative, executive, and juridical power. Democracy enacts 'a dialectic of exteriorization' (ibid.) in all spheres of social life, a dialectic that is not, as Marx thought, reducible to alienation. In democracy, power is an empty place that is sustained by a tension or contradiction: on the one hand, democracy is people power; it is power sustained by the principle of universal suffrage; yet, on the other hand, at the very moment when popular sovereignty manifests itself in an election, the electorate is reduced to an abstract number. The individual in a democracy is no longer dependent on or in bondage to a leader or monarch: he or she is free to choose and judge; yet that same individual is alienated in a society in which the exercise of that freedom is perhaps felt to be worthless. Democracy is an indeterminate political form founded on the contradictions of individual freedom versus anonymous alienation, affirmation of difference versus complete uniformity, recognition of human rights versus the formalization and abstraction of those rights in practice. The formation of totalitarianism out of democracy is explicable, in Lefort's view, on the basis of the latter's very fragility, its open, uncertain, non-foundational character. Democracy installs a metaphysical agnosticism, or perhaps even a metaphysics of absence, at the heart of political life. If this is taken into account, it is not difficult to understand why a philosopher like the early Heidegger (and he is far from being alone in this) should be suspicious of democracy in the name of a National Socialist *totale Staat*, a suspicion which, as the *Spiegel* interview makes clear, persisted until the end of his life.[32]

In the transcript of the discussion that followed Lefort's paper, the response is univocal, immediate, and perhaps unsurprising. Derrida and others ask: Does not present-day democracy conceal a totalitarian threat? Is not democracy another, perhaps more subtle, form of totalitarianism? (*RT* 86–7). This point is echoed and reinforced in 'Le "re-trait" du politique'. After stating that they accept Lefort's analysis and definition of totalitarianism in the societies of Eastern Europe and the Soviet Union, Lacoue-Labarthe and Nancy go on to ask: Is not a more insidious, 'softer' (*plus 'douce'*) (*RT* 190) form of totalitarianism experienced by Western societies in the guise of a techno-scientific ideology? Interestingly, they then claim that this soft totalitarianism is what is described by Lyotard under the title, *The Postmodern Condition*. In terms derived from Lefort's own analysis of ideology, it could be asked: Is there not an *invisible* ideology at work in Western societies, which aims at the same social homogenization as totalitarianism, but does so more surreptitiously, through mass consumption and the mass media, whereby one is encouraged to become at home in society, to enter its *entre-nous*?[33] To this powerful (although far from original) objection, Lacoue-Labarthe and Nancy add a further question. I quote in full:

> A certain ready made and widespread opposition between totalitarianism and democracy, even if it is true and the differences are glaring, is not in reality so simple. We do not have camps, and our police, whatever their 'technological advances', are not an omnipresent political police. But that does not mean that the democracy that we have is that described by Tocqueville. And if Tocqueville's democracy contained the germ of classical totalitarianism, nothing proves that our democracy is not in the process of secreting something else, an unheard of form of totalitarianism. This is at the very least a question that poses itself and as a consequence it does not seem aberrant for us to generalize (once again, at a certain depth) the concept of totalitarianism. (*RT* 191)

Thus, Lacoue-Labarthe and Nancy generalize Lefort's description of totalitarianism, and extend it to an analysis that includes Western liberal democratic societies. In this way they blur the distinction between totalitarianism and democracy. The strength of their objection is that while it is true to say that citizens of Western liberal democracies do not experience totalitarianism in the same way as certain societies experienced it until recently or continue to experience it (as violation of human rights, the existence of a secret police and a system of informants, internment of dissidents, single party dictator-ship, denial of freedoms of speech, of movement, of belief, of political and artistic expression), it is also true to say that those citizens certainly do not inhabit the sort of democracy described by de Tocqueville. It is doubtful, to say the very least, that Western liberal democratic societies are committed to the full equality and develop-ment of all their citizens or to genuine possession of power by the people. Thus, one might conclude that the distinction between totalit-arianism and democracy is too simple and too rigid to describe the complexities of contemporary political reality.

Moreover, the weakness of Lefort's analysis of democracy can be expressed in other terms. Thus I would claim that Lefort runs the continual risk of conflating democracy with liberal democracy.[34] It is perhaps too easy and too tempting to read Lefort's analysis as a descriptive apologetics for Western liberal democracy. Following C. B. Macpherson's classic analysis, it is evident that the historical basis for the development of liberal democracy was a liberal state commit-ted to a competitive party system and a competitive market economy, onto which was eventually grafted, after much struggle and blood-shed, a universal democratic franchise.[35] The important point to grasp here is that there is nothing *necessarily* democratic about the liberal state. To interpret de Tocqueville's analysis of democracy and then transpose it to contemporary, often post-totalitarian, liberal democracies is an extremely questionable procedure, both historically and hermeneutically. Furthermore, one might question the extent to which Lefort's analyses are generalizable or whether they are culturally and historically specific. For example, his view of the tran-sition from absolute monarchy to revolutionary democracy makes sense in the context of French political history; but what of the evol-ution of other forms of liberal democracy, such as constitutional monarchy on the British model, not to mention the historical experi-ence of many other European and non-European peoples?

But even if one accepts these criticisms of Lefort's account of democracy, is one then forced to conclude that the political form of Western societies is an 'unheard of' or 'soft' totalitarianism? Lefort's response to this charge – and the democratic revolutions of 1989 provide an empirical confirmation of this hypothesis – would be that, far from undergoing homogenization and increasing totalization, present-day democracy is experiencing increasing division and fragmentation. Contrary to the Heideggerian and Heidegger-inspired analysis that would see the present as undergoing depoliticization and a move towards uniformity, one might employ Laclau's notion (already present in de Tocqueville) of 'democratic revolution'[36] and claim that the present is marked by an increasing fragmentation of society, a proliferation of new antagonisms, and a consequent increase in political possibilities. I shall return to these themes in conclusion, but let me note provisionally that as a response to the claim that actually existing liberal democracy conceals a totalitarian threat, a claim that has much to recommend it in many respects, one must not restrict oneself to conceiving of democracy as the description of an existent political form – and certainly not as a descriptive apologetics for Western liberal democracy – but must begin to think of democracy as a task or project to be attempted. *Democracy does not exist*; rather, it is something to be achieved because it is the incomplete (*l'inachevé*) *par excellence*. In Derridian terms, democracy has a futural, or *différantial*, structure; it is always democracy to come (*la démocratie à venir*). This is the future of deconstruction.

III

What is of interest in Lacoue-Labarthe's and Nancy's critique of democracy is that it is entirely consistent with the premises of their position, as described above. The thesis of the withdrawal of the political cannot be a partial withdrawal, it *must* be total. The analysis of the dual closure of the philosophical and the political *must* see totalitarianism as the final figure in the development of political forms: complete withdrawal of *le politique* in the face of the absolute domination of *la politique*. Lacoue-Labarthe and Nancy *must* therefore diagnose Western liberal democracies as being subject to an unheard-of totalitarianism. Before concluding with a sketch of this re-tracing of the political, a project with which I substantially agree, I would like to raise some critical questions as to hardness of this *must*.

In an excellent discussion of Lacoue-Labarthe's *La fiction du politique*, Dominique Janicaud notes that the former's analysis strives to be 'more Heideggerian than Heidegger' (*plus heideggerien que Heidegger*).[37] What this slogan implies is that there is seemingly a complete accord between Lacoue-Labarthe and Heidegger on the ontologico-historical schema of interpretation that is to be employed; that is, the history of Being. Apart from a disclaimer, in one of the Postscripts to *La fiction*, to the effect that 'One should not attribute to me the positions I am analysing', in which he claims that he does not subscribe to the thesis of the 'unicity-singularity of the History of Being', a history within which he is prepared to include 'scansions' other than those indicated by Heidegger (*FP* 144–45/*HAP* 101), Lacoue-Labarthe does not appear to doubt the validity of Heidegger's account of the history of the West. Indeed, I would go further and claim that it is the integrity of this account that gives force to the thesis of the inevitability of totalitarianism as the political form of society during the completion of metaphysics. Perversely, the fact that Lacoue-Labarthe does not question Heidegger's ontologico-historical schema is what gives a book like *La fiction* its strength and its persuasive force. It is a book that comes across as a brave, bold, honest settling of accounts with Heidegger (even if the prose is sometimes marred by an irritating, sub-Heideggerian grandeur of tone). What happened in 1933 was neither an accident nor an error, the real failure in Heidegger's thought being failure at the level of thinking itself, a failure in the duty of thought. For Lacoue-Labarthe, as for Levinas – I shall come back to this below – it is a question of Heidegger's failure to speak out on the Holocaust, exemplified in his failure to address Paul Celan, a failure obliquely reflected in the latter's poem 'Todtnauberg'.[38] *La fiction du politique* writes the supplement to this failure. Lacoue-Labarthe says what Heidegger should have said, what the logic of his thinking obliged him to say, but what his work failed to say: namely that 'In the Auschwitz apocalypse, it was nothing less than the West, in its essence, that revealed itself' (*FP* 59/*HAP* 35), or again, that 'God in fact died at Auschwitz' (*FP* 62/*HAP* 37). Lacoue-Labarthe borrows the concept of the caesura from Hölderlin's remarks on Sophocles' *Oedipus Rex* and *Antigone*, and interprets Auschwitz as the caesura within Western history (*FP* 64–72/*HAP* 41–6). The caesura is that pure or null event that interrupts history and opens up or closes another possibility of history.

A first, seemingly tangential, critical question can be raised here as to whether it is adequate to transfer a concept gleaned from Hölderlin's remarks on Greek tragedy to the event of the Holocaust. What is involved in such a transfer? Although Lacoue-Labarthe qualifies his position by saying that Auschwitz belongs to a sphere

'beyond tragedy' (*FP* 72/*HAP* 46), does not this insertion of the
Holocaust into an ontologico-historical schema produce an interpretation that is too formal and too transcendental to contribute to any
concrete understanding of the Holocaust? By including the Holocaust
within the destinal unfolding of the West, is it thereby claimed that
the Holocaust is somehow necessary? A necessary sacrifice? Surely
not. Employing the terms of Heidegger's thinking, Lacoue-Labarthe
claims that he cannot see that any logic other than 'spiritual' or
'historial' (*FP* 75/*HAP* 48) governed the Holocaust, and he goes on
to speak of it as a 'pure metaphysical decision' (ibid.). But, to turn
Lacoue-Labarthe's words back upon his own analysis, is not this
position on the Holocaust 'scandalously inadequate' (*FP* 58/*HAP*
34)? Following Janicaud's critique, I would claim that in wanting
to be more Heideggerian than Heidegger, Lacoue-Labarthe risks
presenting and ennobling the criminal absurdity of the Holocaust as a
destinal historical necessity. Is it not rather the sheer facticity of the
Holocaust that is most terrifying?

It is precisely this question of facticity that allows one to pass from
the analysis of the Holocaust to the question of politics, and specifically the interpretation of the political in terms of the inevitability
of totalitarianism. In both analyses there is constant reduction of the
factical, the empirical, the contingent, the ontic – that is to say, *la
politique*. But why is this significant? My claim is that the reduction of
la politique to *le politique*, upon which Lacoue-Labarthe's and Nancy's
analysis rests and which serves as the starting point for their reflection on the political, is an exclusion of politics itself, if by the latter
one understands an empirical, contingent field of antagonism, conflict,
and struggle, the space of *doxa*. For Lacoue-Labarthe and Nancy, the
legitimacy of the reduction of *la politique* to *le politique* rests on the
Heideggerian determination of the contemporary world as the epoch
of completed metaphysics and of the completion of metaphysics
taking place as a planetary technological domination, with totalitarianism as the political form of societies undergoing this domination.
Although, for separate reasons, I would want to take issue with this
Heideggerian determination of the contemporary world as being too
exclusive and too unconditional an account of modernity, for the
purposes of the present argument one can see how this account
informs Lacoue-Labarthe's and Nancy's position, thereby prohibiting
any move back into *la politique*. The only possibility of non-totalitarian

political thinking is a certain dwelling on the essence of *le politique*. Lacoue-Labarthe and Nancy's reduction of *la politique* to *le politique* leads to a synoptic and transcendental vision of the political in which any trace of *la politique* must be excluded. But it is precisely this gesture that I want to question, because rejection of *la politique* means rejection of the very genre of political debate, of dispute and dissension, persuasion and the battle over *doxa*.

Further, if the reduction of *la politique* to *le politique* leads to an exclusion of politics, certain other questions must be asked. First, and naïvely, is the reduction of *la politique* to *le politique* possible? Is this reduction not simply a quasi-transcendental reduction of the natural attitude, and might one not ask, with Merleau-Ponty, whether the most important lesson to be learnt from the reduction is the impossibility of a complete reduction?[39] Moreover, following Derrida's reading of Husserl's attempted reduction of meaning to expression and the exclusion of indication outlined above, should it not be asked whether there remains a trace, or *grapheme*, of empiricity and facticity in the reduction of *la politique* to *le politique* that disrupts or deconstructs the possibility of such a reduction? Is there not an inextricable contamination of *le politique* by *la politique*, and vice versa? Second, and here I take up a hint from Nancy Fraser,[40] is not this reduction of *la politique* itself a refusal of the 'dirty hands' that must accompany any intervention in political struggle? I would argue that there is no politics without dirty hands, in that politics is concerned with struggle, dissension, contestation, and negotiation. Is not the desire for an interrogation of *le politique* a desire for clean hands? And is this not a classical philosophical desire in the Platonic sense: namely, to determine the essence of the *polis* without having to act (or, at best, act reluctantly) within that *polis*? Only a philosopher could declare the impossibility of politics.

Third, is the return to *la politique* necessarily prohibited as being a collapse back into metaphysics? Janicaud calls the politics of the later Heidegger 'a politics of awaiting' (*une politique de l'attente*)[41] – that is, a politics based upon the realization that human action cannot transform the world and that we must wait for the transformation to come from within Being itself: we are too late for the gods and too early for the god who is to come (*der kommende Gott*). Lacoue-Labarthe and Nancy repeat the logic (if not the pathos) of this Heideggerian position; but this begs the vast question of the adequacy of the

Heideggerian analysis. Perhaps political action is metaphysical; but how exactly is this charge to be avoided without lapsing into political quietism and despairing resignation? Should the charge that any return to *la politique* is a collapse back into metaphysics necessarily halt that return? In a note to an annex in *Le retrait du politique*, Derrida revealingly relates his unease when faced with the political demands of the philosophers associated with Charter 77 in Czechoslovakia. How can one reconcile their demand for human rights, individual freedom and autonomy, with the claim that these philosophemes must be deconstructed because they are implicated within a metaphysical or logocentric tradition? (*RT* 203–4). Is the fear of metaphysics also a fear of dirty hands? Coming at the same problem from the opposite perspective, this also relates to the question of whether there is a co-appartenance of the metaphysical and the political in the manner described by Lacoue-Labarthe and Nancy. It is true to say that, in Plato's *Republic* and Heidegger's Rectoral Address, for example, the metaphysical serves to found the political. The possible metaphysical presuppositions of the political forms of totalitarianism and monarchy have also been mentioned. But is this necessarily true in the same way for other political forms? Might not democracy, as it is described by Lefort, possess a different metaphysical structure? Might one not speak of democracy as a metaphysical agnosticism or, more provocatively, as the political form that is founded on the absence of any metaphysical foundation? The substantive question here concerns the unilateralism of the Heideggerian account of metaphysics as a basis for the interpretation of political forms. Is there not a need for a more subtle and variegated account of the relation between metaphysics and politics and perhaps, more speculatively, the possibility of a democratic politics that would be non-metaphysical?

To sum up, I have claimed that Lacoue-Labarthe's and Nancy's diagnosis of the withdrawal of the political and the reduction of *la politique* to *le politique* leads to an exclusion of politics, understood as a field of antagonism, struggle, dissension, contestation, critique, and questioning. Politics takes place on a social terrain that is irreducibly factical, empirical, and contingent. Thus Lacoue-Labarthe's and Nancy's account of the inevitability of totalitarianism and their critique of democracy effectively prohibit any return to *la politique*, a prohibition which I shall challenge below, by tracing Levinas's passage from ethics to politics. By continuing and deepening what I have called the impasse of the political in Derrida's work, Lacoue-Labarthe and Nancy reveal the limitations of deconstruction when faced with the question of politics and awaken the need for a supplement to deconstruction.

IV

However, beyond this critique, I would like to conclude by insisting that Lacoue-Labarthe and Nancy's project of a re-tracing of the political can still contribute to a rethinking of politics. This re-tracing emerges most clearly at the end of 'Le "re-trait" du politique' and again in Nancy's *La communauté désœuvrée*.[42] The problem negotiated in these texts can be summarized in the following way: given the analysis of totalitarianism outlined above, an 'unheard-of' total-itarianism that applies to both 'actually existing socialism' and West-ern liberal democracy, and given that totalitarianism is defined as a form of society that aims at the complete immanence and trans-parency of all areas of social life, what Nancy calls 'immanentism', in which all alterity or transcendence is reduced, the problem of politics becomes, to recall my leitmotif, the problem of whether a politics that does not reduce transcendence is still possible. The *retrait* of the political is the complete withdrawal of the transcendence or alterity of the political in an immanentist society, and the re-tracing of the politi-cal is therefore an attempt at a re-inscription of the transcendence of the political. However, this re-inscription does not aim at restoring transcendence by founding the political on the transcendental sig-nified of God, man, history, or destiny; rather, it is necessary to rethink the political without nostalgia for a lost plenitude of presence. Thus, the task of re-tracing the transcendence of the political is not a matter of bringing the political out of its withdrawal or of founding the political in a new act of *instauratio*; it is rather a matter of focusing the question of the political precisely around this withdrawal, where the transcendence of the political is, it could be said, the alterity of an absence.

Lacoue-Labarthe and Nancy indicate that this re-tracing of the political is broadly consonant with both Lefort's analysis of democ-racy, in which the place of power is 'un lieu vide' (*RT* 194), and Bataille's analysis of sovereignty, in which 'La souveraineté n'est

RIEN" ('Sovereignty is NOTHING') (*CD* 49), since it 'is' the excessive or ecstatic character of human finitude irreducible to immanence. Nancy explores this reading of Bataille in more depth in *La communauté désœuvrée*, where he attempts to think a notion of community irreducible to immanentism – that is to say, irreducible to community as a fusion of beings, a unifying organic whole, the dream of transparent social organization based on the specular recognition of the self in the other. An immanentist community is one that seeks to produce its own essence as a work (*une œuvre*), as is the case in what Lacoue-Labarthe calls Heidegger's 'national aestheticism' (*FP* 91/*HAP* 58). National aestheticism is the desire to produce or create the community as a living artwork, a project that is sketched in the closing pages of Heidegger's 'Origin of the Work of Art'.[43] It is the desire that a people, in this case the German people, create itself anew as a *Gesamtkunstwerk*, that the community produce itself as a vast collective entity represented by a leader or head, who incarnates the entire community. It is this dream of a community as an architectural edifice that Bataille's work never ceased to undermine through the act of writing itself – writing against architecture.[44] Immanentism is another name for that aesthetic ideology that begins with Schiller and that one finds in Schelling, the early Nietzsche, and Heidegger.[45]

In opposition to this aestheticization of politics and its dream of the *polis* as a living artwork, Nancy seeks to think a community rooted in the refusal of immanence, a community based on a certain transcendence, alterity, or incompletion – that is to say, a community of *désœuvrement*, of worklessness; an idling, unoccupied, out-of-work community that refuses to create itself as a work. A community *désœuvrée* is a community found wanting, a community of lack, and this is what transcendence or, to use Bataille's word, the sacred (*le sacré*), consists in (*CD* 86, 88). The community in which transcendence is not reduced is, for Nancy, a community of *partage* – that is, of both sharing and division. Community as *partage* is expressed in the polysemic formula 'Toi (e(s)t) (tout autre que) moi' (*CD* 74), which expresses the sharing and commonality of the community, in the relation between you and me (*toi et moi*), where you are me (*toi est moi*); but where this sharing is itself sustained by the recognition of division, where you are wholly other than me (*toi est tout autre que moi*). Nancy is seeking to rethink the social bond as a relation that is at the same time unbound and founded on what Levinas would call the 'relation without relation' (*TeI* 295/*TI* 271), a recognition of division, or difference. For Nancy, the political can be re-traced only on the basis of such a conception of community.

The second leitmotif to this chapter is the question: what meaning can community take on in difference without reducing difference? That is, the question of politics, as I see it, becomes a question of how the community can remain a place for commonality while at the same time being an open, interrupted community that is respectful of difference and resists the closure implicit within totalitarianism and immanentism. What conception of politics would be necessary in order to maintain this thought of community? This is the question. In Nancy's critique of immanentism and his rethinking of community in terms of transcendence and alterity, one finds, I would argue, the beginnings of a response to the impasse of the political in deconstruction. In the next section, I will offer a different response to this impasse, one which takes its inspiration from Levinas rather than Bataille. In a nutshell, the way in which transcendence is to be reintroduced into politics is through Levinas's complex thematization of ethical transcendence. Transcendence enters into politics in the relation to the singular other, the being who interrupts any synoptic vision of the totality of social life and places me radically in question. The community remains an open community in so far as it is based on the recognition of difference, of the difference of the Other to the Same: community as *différance* affirmed through Yes-saying to the stranger. I shall argue that access to a just conception of politics can only be mediated ethically.[46]

5.4   A Levinasian Politics of Ethical Difference

> All I have is a voice
> To undo the folded lie,
> The romantic lie in the brain
> Of the sensual man-in-the-street
> And the lie of Authority
> Whose buildings grope the sky:
> There is no such thing as the State
> And no one exists alone;
> Hunger allows no choice

To the citizen or the police;
We must love one another or die.

Defenceless under the night
Our world in stupor lies;
Yet, dotted everywhere,
Ironic points of light
Flash out wherever the Just
Exchange their messages:
May I, composed like them
Of Eros and of dust,
Beleaguered by the same
Negation and despair,
Show an affirming flame.[47]

I

I have claimed that there is an impasse of the political in Derrida's work, which, in a complex manner, is continued and deepened in Lacoue-Labarthe's and Nancy's deconstruction of the political. I now want to indicate a way (*nota bene*: *a* way and not necessarily *the* way) out of this impasse by returning to Levinas, and in particular to the passage from ethics to politics that is traversed all too briefly in *Totality and Infinity* (*TeI* 187–90/*TI* 212–14) and taken up again in greater detail in the fifth chapter of *Otherwise than Being* (*AE* 199–207/*OB* 156–62). In these passages, Levinas attempts to build a bridge from ethics, understood as a responsible, non-totalizing relation with the Other, to politics, conceived of as a relation to the third party (*le tiers*), to all the others, to the plurality of beings that make up the community. The passage from ethics to politics – and here I return to the theme of the discussion of *Of Spirit* – is approached by Levinas in terms of 'the latent birth of the *question* in responsibility' (*la naissance latente de la* question *dans la responsabilité*) (*AE* 200/*OB* 157). The passage from ethics to politics is synonymous with the move from responsibility to questioning, from the proximity of the one-for-the-other to a relation with all the others whereby I feel myself to be an other like the others and where the question of justice can be raised (*TeI* 56/*TI* 84). At stake therefore is the *question* of politics, or politics conceived of as a space of questioning. However, it should be noted that this return

to the order of the question from the ethical dimension of responsibility (the question of the question) does not indicate a return to the
primacy of questioning as seen in the early Heidegger; rather, questioning is rooted in the priority of ethical responsibility.

The Levinasian account of the passage from ethics to politics leads
to a different vision of political space from that seen in Derrida,
Lacoue-Labarthe, and Nancy: what I shall call 'a politics of ethical
difference', where politics must be mediated ethically. (It is significant – and much could perhaps be made of this – that Derrida barely
mentions this move to the third party, politics and justice, in his
essays on Levinas (cf. *ED* 156n./*WD* 314, n.37).) For Levinas, I
would claim, ethics is the disruption of totalizing politics: anti-
semitism, anti-humanism, National Socialism. As the French and
Hebrew epigraphs to *Otherwise than Being* make clear, National Socialist anti-semitism is not restricted to a hatred of the Jewish people, but
is expanded by Levinas to mean a hatred of the other person as such.
Anti-semitism is an anti-humanism, if by 'humanism' one understands
a humanism of the other human being. National Socialism is an
exemplar of all forms of totalizing politics or forms of immanentism
that are premised on a refusal, or reduction, of transcendence. The
crematoria at Auschwitz are testimony to the attempted destruction of
transcendence and otherness. The philosophy of Levinas, like that of
Adorno, is commanded by the new categorical imperative imposed by
Hitler: namely, 'that Auschwitz not repeat itself' (*daß Auschwitz nicht
sich wiederhole*).[48]

In both his major works, *Totality and Infinity* and *Otherwise than
Being*, the exposition begins with the statement of the domination of
totalizing politics, which for Levinas is always associated with the fact
of war. This means both the empirical fact of war, which, Levinas
claims, 'suspends morality' (*TeI* ix/*TI* 21), and the Hobbesian claim
that the peaceful order of society is founded on the war of all against
all. Levinas writes: 'It is then not without importance to know if the
egalitarian and just State in which man is fulfilled...proceeds from a
war of all against all, or from the irreducible responsibility of the one
for all, and if it can do without friendship and faces' (*AE* 203/*OB*
159–60). Levinasian ethics is a reduction of war (which, as will be
shown, is not a complete reduction). For Levinas – and here his
analysis rejoins the description of totalitarianism given above – the

domination of totality is also the total domination of politics, where 'everything is political'. Left to itself, politics engages in the reduction of all areas of social life, and more particularly that of ethics to politics. The primacy of politics is the primacy of the synoptic, panoramic vision of society, wherein a disinterested political agent views society as a whole. For Levinas, such a panoramic vision, not only that of the philosopher but also that of the political theorist, is the greatest danger, because it loses sight of ethical difference – that is, of my particular relation to and obligations towards the Other. As Levinas notes, 'Politics left to itself bears a tyranny within itself' (*TeI* 276/*TI* 300), and it is necessary to oppose the particular ethical relation with the Other to the panoramic vision of political life that views society only as a whole. Of course, to the totalizing political philosopher, this ethical relation will appear ridiculously naïve; Levinas remarks: 'Politics is opposed to morality as philosophy to naïveté' (*TeI* ix/*TI* 21). Thus Levinas's thinking is, in a genuine sense, a critique of politics, in so far as he is opposing the domination of politics enacted in totalizing or immanentist conceptions of society. However, if one were tempted to claim that his critique of politics is directed only against narrowly defined totalitarian regimes, then it should be noted that he also criticizes liberal politics, in so far as it has been dominated by the concepts of spontaneity, freedom, and autonomy. In the 1990 Preface to a republished essay, he wrily notes, 'We must ask ourselves if liberalism is all we need to achieve an authentic dignity for the human subject.'[49] The Levinasian critique of politics is a critique of the belief that only political rationality can answer political questions. To take a concrete and far from neutral example, Sadat's visit to Jerusalem in 1977 and the peace agreement reached between Israel and Egypt were, for Levinas, phenomena irreducible to the operation of political rationality. Levinas claims that what took place on both sides was a recognition of the Other in their otherness; ethical peace overriding and guiding political reason.[50]

Levinas's disruption of totalizing politics permits the deduction of an ethical structure irreducible to totality: the face-to-face, proximity, substitution, and responsibility prior to questioning. However, Levinas's critique of politics and his insistence on the primacy of ethical difference does not result in an a-politicism, in a quietism or a 'spirituality of angels' – that is the source of his critique of Buber's I–Thou relation (*TeI* 187–8, 40–1/*TI* 213, 68–9).[51] Rather, ethics

leads back to politics, responsibility to questioning, to the interroga-
tive demand for a just polity. I would go further and claim that, for
Levinas, *ethics is ethical for the sake of politics* – that is, for the sake of a
new conception of the organization of political space. The leitmotif
for the latter is a verse from Isaiah 57, cited in *Otherwise than Being*:
'Peace, peace, to the neighbour (*le prochain*) and to the one far off (*le
lointain*)' (*AE* 200/*OB* 157). Peace, or responsibility, to the near one,
the neighbour, *is* peace to the one far off, the third party, or human
plurality. All humanity looks at me in the eyes of the Other. My claim
is that politics provides the continual horizon of Levinasian ethics,
and that the problem of politics is that of delineating a form of political life that will repeatedly interrupt all attempts at totalization.

Of course, in these discussions, we have not really left the orbit
of *l'affaire Heidegger*, which provided my access to the question of
deconstruction and politics. Heidegger's politics – whether National
Socialist, national aestheticist, or what Janicaud identified as *une
politique de l'attente* – provides the prime modern philosophical
example of a totalizing politics that is reductive of ethical difference.
Despite Levinas's early, almost juvenile, enthusiasm for Heidegger,
revealed in his dissertation and essays from the years 1930–32,[52] and
despite his ongoing belief that *Being and Time*, in its critique of traditional notions of rationality, objectivity, and scientificity, remains
one of the 'eternal books in the history of philosophy',[53] his opposition to Heidegger's politics took a written form as early as 1934,[54]
and has been continuous ever since. Unlike Hannah Arendt, Levinas
was unable to see Heidegger's political engagement as an 'episode';[55]
for him, the relations between Heidegger and National Socialism 'are
forever' (*sont à jamais*).[56] However, Levinas is willing to forgive much
that Heidegger did; for example, he appears to be willing to overlook
the mistakes and excesses of the rectorate and his subsequent, more
tacit support for Nazism as the *immoralités inévitables* (both inevitable
and unavoidable immoralities) of politics.[57] Nonetheless, Levinas
cannot forgive Heidegger's silence after the war and his refusal to
speak out on the Holocaust. He writes:

> But doesn't this silence, in time of peace, on the gas chambers and
> death camps lie beyond the realm of feeble excuses and reveal a soul
> completely cut off from any sensitivity, in which can be perceived a
> kind of consent to the horror (*comme un consentement à l'horrible*).[58]

However, there is a crime *worse* than silence, and Heidegger committed it in his by now infamous remark, cited by Lacoue-Labarthe, 'Agriculture is now a mechanized food industry. As for its essence, it is the same thing as the manufacture of corpses in the gas chambers and the death camps, the same thing as the blockades and the reduction of countries to famine, the same thing as the manufacture of hydrogen bombs' (*FP* 58/*HAP* 34). In response to this passage, Levinas comments: 'This stylistic turn of phrase, this analogy, this progression are beyond commentary *(se passent de commentaires)*.'[59] For Levinas, by speaking on the Holocaust in this way, Heidegger shows complete insensitivity to the specificity and extremity of its evil.

Towards the end of 'Mourir pour...', a paper given at the same conference as Derrida's *Of Spirit* in 1987, Levinas comments on paragraph 47 of *Being and Time*, from the death analysis, where Heidegger is seeking the authentic signification of Being-towards-death (*SuZ* 237–41). Here Heidegger makes a short digression into the significance of experiencing the death of others and the consequence of such experience for trying to get a complete grasp on the totality of *Dasein*. After discussing the idea of going to one's death for another *(für einen Anderen in den Tod gehen)* (*SuZ* 240), he immediately withdraws from this possibility, writing that to die for the other, 'always means to sacrifice oneself for the other' *(für den Anderen sich opfern)* – (ibid.). For Heidegger, in order to get a complete grasp of the totality of *Dasein*, death must be in every case my own, and in facing up to the finitude of my Being, I experience authentic individuation. To die for the Other is always secondary within the logic of fundamental ontology; it would always be but a sacrifice. Now, for Levinas, it is precisely the ethical relation, understood as the priority that the Other has over me that is primary; the fact that I would be prepared to sacrifice myself for the Other, to substitute myself and die in the Other's place. One might further claim that this refusal of sacrifice by Heidegger is a refusal to conceive of my *Dasein* as a sacrifice for the other – that is, as *ein Opfer, to holocauston*, an offering. The intriguing and complex question here is whether and to what extent Levinas is correct in his judgement or whether the Heideggerian text can be read in terms of a thematics of sacrifice or holocaust as an offering to the Other. To choose a far from politically neutral example, what does Heidegger mean in 'The Origin of the Work of Art' when he claims that one of the ways in which truth grounds itself is 'the essential sacrifice' *(das wesentliche Opfer)*?[60]

For Levinas, politics begins as ethics, that is, as the possibility of sacrifice; and this leads him to articulate a form of political life that would interrupt all attempts at totalization, totalitarianism, or immanentism. The interruption of the political order of totality occurs with the infinity of the ethical, the moment of transcendence that maintains the community as an open community, an interrupted community. On the basis of Levinas's work, I would argue, one can begin to envisage a politics that does not reduce transcendence, because of the irreducible ethical difference between myself and the Other. The slogan 'Politics begins as ethics'[61] means that political space is based on the irreducibility of ethical transcendence, where the community takes on meaning in difference without reducing difference. Political space is an open, plural, opaque network of ethical relations which are non-totalizable and where 'the contemporaneity of the multiple is tied around the dia-chrony of the two' (*AE* 203/*OB* 159). Levinasian politics is the enactment of plurality, of multiplicity.

II

I should now like to follow this movement from ethics to politics in some textual detail. Although Levinas discusses it from as early as the 1954 essay, 'The Ego and the Totality' (*CPP* 25–45), I will begin by focusing on a couple of pages from *Totality and Infinity* entitled 'The Other and the Others' (*Autrui et les Autres*). Levinas begins by stipulating that what takes place between the Same and the Other concerns everyone; that the ethical relation with the face 'places itself in the full light of the public order' (*TeI* 187/*TI* 212). The discourse between myself and the Other does not result in complicity; the ethical relation is not a clandestine, private relation between lovers, in which the seriousness and frankness of ethics 'turns into laughter or cooing (*roucoulement*)'. The ethical relation is not, Levinas claims, like Buber's I–Thou relation, 'self-sufficient' and 'forgetful of the universe'; rather, 'The third party looks at me in the eyes of the Other – language is justice' (*Le tiers me regarde dans les yeux d'autrui – le langage est justice*) (*TeI* 188/*TI* 213). It is here that Levinas introduces the crucial theme of *le tiers*, the third party who ensures that the ethical relation always takes place within a political context, within the public realm.

Levinas's claim here is that the third party looks at me in the eyes of the Other, and therefore that my ethical obligations to the Other open onto wider questions of justice for others and for humanity as a whole.

Levinas insists that the passage from ethics to politics, or from the Other to the third, is not chronological: 'It is not that there first would be the face and then (*ensuite*) the being it manifests or expresses would concern itself with justice; the epiphany of the face as face opens humanity.' The ethical relation does not take place in an a-political space outside the public realm; rather, ethics is always already political, the relation to the face is always already a relation to humanity as a whole. One quickly realizes the stakes involved in this claim; for the move to *le tiers* allows Levinas to introduce the concept of equality. The ethical relation is a relation of obligation to 'the poor one and the stranger'; that is, it is a relation with a being who is not my equal, but who is destitute (*le démuni*) and speaks to me from a position of height. There is therefore a radical inequality or asymmetry between the terms of the ethical relation, which, as it were, provokes my obligation. However, Levinas continues, the Other also presents him or herself as an equal in so far as the relation to the Other is a relation with *le tiers*. The relation to the third is the communal bond, a relation among equals, a *we*.

> The *thou* is posited in front of a *we*. To be *we* is not to 'jostle' one another or to get together around a common task. The presence of the face – the infinity of the other (*l'Autre*) – is destitution, presence of the third party (that is, of the whole of humanity that looks at us). (*TeI* 213/*TI* 188)

Thus my ethical relation to the Other is an unequal, asymmetrical relation to a height that cannot be comprehended, but which, *at the same time*, opens onto a relation to the third and to humanity as a whole – that is, to a symmetrical community of equals. This simultaneity of ethics and politics gives a doubling quality to all discourse, whereby the relation to the Other, my Saying, is at the same time the setting forth of a common world, what in this context Levinas calls 'prophecy'.[62] Levinas would appear to be thinking of prophecy here in the sense that the prophet is the person who puts the community under the word of God, who binds the community and makes it a commonality. He continues:

By essence the prophetic word responds to the epiphany of the face, doubles all discourse (*double tout discours*), not as a discourse about moral themes, but as an irreducible movement of a discourse which is essentially aroused by the epiphany of the face inasmuch as it attests the presence of the third party, of humanity as a whole, in the eyes that look at me. (Ibid.)

The passage from the ethical to the political is not a passage of time, but rather a doubling of discourse, whereby the response to the singularity of the Other's face is, at the same time, a response to the prophetic word, to the word that makes the community a commonality. Thus – and this is a decisive insight – *the community has a double structure;* it is a commonality among equals which is at the same time based on the inegalitarian moment of the ethical relation. 'The essence of society', as Levinas puts it, does not derive from a war of all against all or from a 'struggle of egoisms', but from the ethical relation. The coincidence of beings in a community is, for Levinas, based on the non-coincidence of the Same and the Other in the ethical relation. To express this dialectically, *community is the coincidence of coincidence and non-coincidence*, what Levinas calls, in a rather uncomplicated manner, 'human fraternity' (*la fraternité humaine*).

Fraternitas: a community of brothers bound around a double bind.

Human fraternity has then a double aspect: it involves individualities whose logical status is not reducible to the status of ultimate differences in a genus, for their singularity consists in each referring to itself...On the other hand, it involves the commonness of a father, as though the commonness of race would not bring together enough. (*TeI* 214/*TI* 189)

Levinas names this double community – both equal and unequal, symmetrical and asymmetrical, political and ethical – with the name *monotheism*. 'Monotheism signifies this human kinship, this idea of a human race that refers back to the approach of the Other in the face, in a dimension of height, in responsibility for oneself and for the Other' (ibid.). The patriarchal and seemingly onto-theo-logical implications of these lines should be neither reduced nor elided. There is a powerful logic that links together the question of God and the question of community in Levinas's text. The passage to *le tiers*, to justice and humanity as a whole, is also a passage to the prophetic word, the

commonness of the divine father in a community of brothers. One
might say that there is a divine horizon to politics in Levinas's work.
Continuing the line of argument outlined in chapter 3, one plausible
way of reading Levinas would be to emphasize critically the way in
which transcendence enters into politics by anchoring the community
in God – a divinity, moreover, whose alleged neutrality (the 'Il' of
Illeity) once again reveals Levinas's constant subordination of sexual
difference to ethical difference and the feminine to the masculine.
However, complicating such a reading, the singular character of this
transcendence would have to be noted, because the transcendence of
the divine in Levinas is the alterity of the trace, an order irreducible
to presence and the possibility of incarnation. Levinas's God is not
the God of onto-theo-logy, but rather, like Lefort's *lieu vide*, God
'is' an empty place, the anarchy of an absence at the heart of the
community. One finds a similar logic at work in *Otherwise than Being*,
where, in the discussion of *le tiers*, Levinas writes that it is ' "Thanks
to God" that I am an Other for the others' (*AE* 201/*OB* 158). That
is to say, my relation to all the others takes place only in so far as
it binds me to the other person whose alterity stands in the trace of
Illeity. What prevents the community from becoming wholly immanent to itself is the transcendence of the relation with the Other, a
transcendence that comes from the order of the trace, the trace as the
opening of the divine as an absence.

III

Turning from the brief discussion of the relation of ethics to politics
given in *Totality and Infinity*, one finds a fuller and more nuanced
discussion of the same topic in *Otherwise than Being*. However, between
the two books, both a continuity and a discontinuity should be noted.
First the continuity: the move from ethics to politics or, more precisely, to *le tiers* occurs at the same point in the argument of both
books. The move back to politics occurs after the ethical moment has
been delineated, whether in the 'Ethics and the Face' chapter of *Totality and Infinity* or in the central 'Substitution' chapter of *Otherwise than
Being*. Moreover, the discussion of *le tiers* in *Otherwise than Being* refers
back to 'The Other and the Others' passage in *Totality and Infinity* in a
number of ways: the terminology of *Totality and Infinity*, especially the
notion of *le visage*, is more present in these pages than elsewhere in

Otherwise than Being; the metaphor of Deucalion's creation of the human race by casting stones over his shoulder occurs in both discussions (*TeI* 189/*TI* 214; *AE* 202/*OB* 159); and a footnote, in a way that is rare in *Otherwise than Being* – I know of only one other instance (*AE* 201/*OB* 199) – refers back explicitly to the prior discussion of *le tiers* (*AE* 201/*OB* 199).

But there is also a marked discontinuity between the two discussions. First, the entire argument for the move to *le tiers* is given in much greater depth and detail in *Otherwise than Being*, and occupies a much more important place in the argumentative development of the book. Second, and more significantly, if the innovation of *Otherwise than Being* is the introduction of the model of the Saying and the Said as a way of explaining how ethics signifies within ontological language, then the move to *le tiers* is, for Levinas, clearly also a move from the Saying to the Said. As I will show, the passage to politics is a return to the Said; which is, at the same time, a return to questioning, ontology, and philosophy.

With this in mind, the argument of *Otherwise than Being* can perhaps be divided into three moments. The exposition begins at the level of the Said, of entities exposed in their essence in the facticity of war and the domination of totality. The second moment is the move from the Said to the Saying, by peeling off the layers of ethical subjectivity until the structure of substitution is delineated in chapter 4. However, in a third moment, chapter 5 moves from the Saying back to the Said (*du Dire au Dit*), in order to reopen the questions of justice, politics, community, ontology, and philosophy, as well as the question of the question itself. But here we must ask: Is the Said of the first moment perhaps different from that of the third moment? Are there two 'Saids' in Levinas's work, and are they in contradiction? I would argue that there is only one Said for Levinas, but that the difference between the Said of the first and third moments is the difference between an *unjustified* and a *justified* Said.[63] The return from the Saying to the Said in chapter 5 is an attempt to thematize a justified Said, or a Said that is informed and interrupted by the trace of the Saying. The originality of *Otherwise than Being* perhaps consists in its recognition of the need for an account of the justified Said – that is, of a political language of philosophical questioning that does not reduce ethical transcendence. This is not so much 'ethics as first philosophy', as 'philosophy as ethics first'.

In chapter 5 of *Otherwise than Being* then, Levinas is once again intent on showing the passage from the ethical relation to the Other to the political relation to all the others, the difference being that this passage is described as a movement back to ontology, philosophy, and questioning. Levinas writes: 'It is not by chance, through foolishness or through usurpation that the order of truth and essence...is at the first rank in Western philosophy' (*AE* 199/*OB* 156–7). The domination of ontology in the philosophical tradition is not accidental; and Levinas is intent on showing the *necessity* of the betrayal of the Saying in the Said. The question becomes 'Why knowledge? Why problems? Why philosophy?' (*Pourquoi savoir? Pourquoi problème? Pourquoi philosophie*) (*AE* 199/*OB* 157). To this list, one might add: 'Why is there a question here?' or 'Why why?'

Once more, it is a question of the question itself, of the latent birth of the question in ethical responsibility. Levinas responds:

> If proximity ordered me to the Other alone, 'there would not have been any problem' – in any and even the most general sense of the term. A question would not have been born, nor consciousness, nor self-consciousness. The responsibility for the other is an immediacy anterior to the question: precisely proximity. It is troubled and becomes a problem with the entry of the third party. (*AE* 200/*OB* 157)

This is a compact, elliptical sentence; but it would seem that Levinas is arguing that *if* I inhabited an angelic I–Thou relation without a relation to others – ethics without politics – then there would be no problem and no question of raising a question. The responsible relation with the Other would be one of pure immediacy, a moment of sense-certainty where I would not even be conscious of the relation or capable of self-consciously reflecting on its status. However, despite the fact that this is what many of Levinas's less sympathetic readers understand to be the argument of *Otherwise than Being*, the above passage suggests that there is no pure immediacy of responsibility prior to questioning, a Saying without a Said, or ethics without ontology. As I argued above, to say that the ethical relation is troubled and becomes a problem with the entry of *le tiers* is to say that the ethical relation is *always already* troubled and problematized. The passage from the Other to the others is not chronological; rather, 'the others concern me *from the first*' (*les autres* d'emblée *me concernent*) (*AE*

202/*OB* 159). From the first, my ethical discourse with the Other is troubled and doubled into a political discourse with all the others: a double discourse. The immediacy of the ethical is always already mediated politically. This is the reason why there is a question, or knowledge, or problems, or philosophy. However, what question is being addressed here exactly?

Le tiers has always already entered into the ethical relation, troubling and doubling it into a political discourse. This is also to say that *le tiers* always already 'introduces a contradiction into the Saying whose signification before the other until then went in one direction (*un sens unique*)' (*AE* 200/*OB* 157). The *sens unique*, or ethical 'one-way street', that always directs me from myself to the Other must now bear the weight of two-way traffic. That is to say, the ethical response given to the Other is given back to me in the form of a question, engaging me in a movement of reflection that takes place at the level of self-consciousness. The third party introduces a limit to responsibility and allows the 'birth of the question'. The question that is born at the limit of responsibility is, for Levinas, the question of *justice*: 'what do I have to do with justice?' (*AE* 200/*OB* 157) or again, Cain's question: 'Am I my brother's keeper?' (*AE* 150/*OB* 117). However, recalling Socrates' question – and I shall return to this theme in my conclusion – it should be asked: What is justice?

'*Il faut la justice*', Levinas writes:

> Justice is necessary, that is, comparison, coexistence, contemporaneousness, assembling, order, the *visibility* of faces, and thus intentionality and the intellect, and in intentionality and the intellect, the intelligibility of a system, and thence also a co-presence on an equal footing as before a court of justice. (*AE* 200/*OB* 157)

Justice is, paradoxically, the limit of responsibility. It is the moment when I am no longer infinitely responsible for the Other, and consequently no longer in an asymmetrical, unequal relation. Rather, justice is 'an incessant correction of the asymmetry of proximity' (*AE* 201/*OB* 158), where I become the Other's equal. In justice, I am no longer myself in relation to an Other for whom I am infinitely responsible, but I can feel myself to be an other like the others (*TeI* 56/*TI* 84) – that is, one of a community that can demand its rights regardless of its duties. If ethical responsibility is 'the surplus of my duties over my rights' (*AE* 203/*OB* 159), then the order of justice is one in which rights override duties. In the order of justice, I and the Other can be compared as contemporaries, or peers, occupying the same synchronic order – what Levinas calls the order of co-presence. At the level of justice, I and the Other are co-citizens of a common *polis*.

In these pages, then, one sees Levinas negotiating the passage from ethics to politics, in which the evanescence of the Saying becomes fixed into a Said, 'is written, becomes a book, law and science' (*AE* 202/*OB* 159). In this way, Levinas responds to a common objection raised against his thinking: namely, that if I am infinitely responsible to the Other, how can I ever judge or question the Other's actions? One can respond by claiming that, ethically, I have no right to judge the Other; I am simply called to be responsible to him or her, and whether the Other responds or reciprocates the gesture is his or her business, not mine (*EeI* 94–5). Ethically, I cannot demand that the Other be good. However, the extremity of this position must be tempered by the thought that, at the level of politics and justice, at which I am a citizen of a community, I *am* entitled to judge, to call the Other to account, to raise Cain's question. For Levinas, judgement is political judgement; and, as I shall show presently, the Socratic function of philosophy in the *polis* is persistently to raise the question of justice.

However, is this return to the order of the Said, ontology, and philosophy simply a betrayal of ethical Saying? The response to this question turns on the meaning of what was called above 'the justified Said'. The return to the Said is not a return to the pure Said of ontology, but rather to a Said which maintains within itself the trace of ethical Saying. Levinas writes:

> The one for the other is not a deforming abstraction. In it justice is shown from the first (*d'emblée*); it is thus born from the signifyingness of signification, the one-for-the-other of signification. This means concretely or empirically that justice is not a legality regulating human masses, from which a technique of 'social equilibrium' is derived, harmonizing antagonistic forces – that would be a justification of the State delivered over to its proper necessities. Justice is impossible without the one that renders it finding himself in proximity. (*AE* 202/*OB* 159)

For Levinas, justice cannot be conceived as some abstract or formal legality regulating society, reducing antagonism and producing social harmony. Such would be a description of an immanentist or totalizing community, a transparent society without friendship and faces. Justice must be informed by proximity; that is to say, the equality and symmetry of the relations between citizens must be interrupted by the inequality and asymmetry of the ethical relation. There must be a certain creative antagonism between ethics and politics which ensures that justice is done in the sight of the Other's face. The just, egalitarian society is one that is based on the inequality of the ethical relation, a society that permits the proliferation of antagonism and transcendence – what I called above a doubled community and what I shall go on to describe as a democratic polity. Injustice – not to mention racism, nationalism, and imperialism – begins when one loses sight of the transcendence of the Other and forgets that the State, with its institutions, is informed by the proximity of my relation to the Other.

Levinas continues:

> Justice only remains justice in a society where there is no distinction between those close and those far off (*entre proches et lointains*), but in which there also remains the impossibility of passing by the closest (*du plus proche*); where the equality of all is borne by my inequality, by the surplus of my duties over my rights. (*AE* 203/*OB* 159)

The justified Said is a political discourse of reflection and interrogation, a language of decision, judgement, and critique that is informed and interrupted by the responsibility of ethical Saying. A relation to all the others is justifiable only in so far as it is based on the recognition of the impossibility of passing by the Other. Thus the move to *le tiers* in Levinas, and the consequent turn to politics, the Said, ontology, and philosophy, is not a betrayal of ethical Saying, but rather represents the attempt to traverse the passage from ethics to politics without reducing the dimension of transcendence. In this way, rather than claiming to be done with ontological language, Levinas recognizes the necessity for privileging it in questions of politics and justice. As I mentioned at the end of the last section, the thrust of Levinas's argument is to show how the universality of political rationality cannot ignore the pre-rational singularity of my ethical respect for the Other, what Levinas calls a 'rationality of peace' (*AE* 203/*OB* 160). The anarchic, pre-original relation to the Other needs to be supplemented by the measure of the *archē*: of principles, beginnings, and origins. Ethical subjectivity needs to be shown in its political role of '*citizen*' (*AE* 204/*OB* 160), speaking 'in the autonomy of its voice of consciousness' (*AE* 206/*OB* 161).

Towards the end of his discussion of the passage from ethics to politics, Levinas completes his argument by offering a reinterpretation of the function of philosophy. He writes:

> From responsibility to the problem – such is the way. The problem is posed by proximity itself, which, as the immediate itself, is without problems. The extraordinary commitment of the Other with regard to the third party calls for control, to the search for justice, to society and the State, to comparison and possession, and to commerce and phil-osophy, and, outside of anarchy, to the search for a principle. Philos-ophy is this measure brought to the infinity of the being-for-the-other of proximity, and it is like the wisdom of love (*la philosophie est cette mesure apportée a l'infini de l'être-pour-l'autre de la proximité et comme la sagesse de l'amour*). (*AE* 205/*OB* 161)

The passage from the Other to *le tiers* is the move from ethical responsibility to the problem of politics. The anarchy of ethical responsibility to the Other needs to be measured by the search for principles of justice and the establishment of the just society. The name for this measure brought to the excessiveness (*démesure*) of my responsibility for the Other is *philosophy*. Why philosophy? Most obvi-ously, in virtue of the claim that the immediate ethical relation to the Other is always already politically mediated, a necessary domain of questioning is opened, one that might be called philosophy. How-ever, a singular inversion in the definition of philosophy should be noted; Levinas does not define philosophy in the usual manner as the love of wisdom (*l'amour de la sagesse*), but rather as the wisdom of love (*la sagesse de l'amour*).[64] Why this inversion? In chapters 1 and 4, I discussed how, for Levinas, philosophy is not simply reducible to ontology and how the philosopher's effort should consist in the reduction of the Said to the Saying, causing a disturbance within language that allows the ethical to signify within ontology. For the later Levinas, philosophy occupies a liminal position, being both the language of the Said and the language whereby the reduction of the Said to the Saying is shown. Levinas writes: 'Philosophy is called upon to think ambivalence, and to think it in several times' (*AE* 206/*OB* 162). Even though the discourse of philosophy takes place at the level of synchrony and the Said, it remains, Levinas claims, 'the handmaiden of the Saying' (*la servante du Dire*) (ibid.), signifying the diachronic relation between myself and the Other. Levinas repeats: 'Philosophy: wisdom of love at the service of love' (*La philosophie: sagesse de l'amour au service de l'amour*) (ibid.). Love is therefore ethical Saying, whereas philosophy is that language of the Said and justice that is called on to serve love.

I spoke above of the double discourse of the community in Levinas, a discourse that expresses the commonality of the community while simultaneously expressing the ethical difference upon which that community is based. It is clear now that *philosophy* is this double discourse of the community, the language of wisdom at the service of love. Levinas writes:

> Philosophy serves justice, by thematizing difference and by reducing the thematized to difference. It brings equity into the abnegation of the one for the other, justice into responsibility. Philosophy – in its very diachrony – is the consciousness of the rupture of consciousness. In an alternating movement, like that which leads from scepticism to the refutation that reduces it to ashes, and from its ashes to its rebirth, philosophy justifies and criticizes the laws of Being and the City, and finds again the signification that consists in detaching the absolute one-for-the-other both the one and the other. (*AE* 210/*OB* 165)

That is, philosophy serves justice by both thematizing difference and reducing the thematized to difference. The ambivalent, oscillating movement of philosophy both brings the measure of wisdom, reason, and universality to the ethical relation and shows how the rational order of justice is itself derived from the proximity of love. Philosophy both betrays (*trahit*) the ethical Saying and conveys (*traduit*) the Saying within the treasonable Said. Philosophy is the enactment of this alternating movement between the Saying and the Said, between ethical love and political wisdom, a double movement that both justifies and criticizes the laws of the *polis*. Thus the rational order of the *polis* is justified by a philosophical language which criticizes the *polis* in the name of what it excludes or marginalizes, the pre-rational one-for-the-other of ethics. Philosophy is this activity of justification and critique; the political order is justified only in so far as it is simultaneously capable of being criticized subversively. Political discourse must be both a language of justice and a language of critique, legitimizing the *polis* while simultaneously letting the *polis* be interrupted by that which transcends it: a politics of ethical difference.

5.5   Conclusion: Philosophy, Politics, and Democracy

Within the *clôtural* logic that has been thematized in this book and has governed its development, any attempt at a conclusion would entail a moment of interruption, an opening to the Other, whose siginificance would be ethical. The gesture of conclusion and the closure that it imposes upon a text calls for the type of *clôtural* reading outlined above. In closing this book, therefore, I will broach a series of issues that will hopefully open a subsequent text. A risk, then, a 'fine risk', as Levinas would say, which is always to be run in philosophy (*AE* 24/*OB* 20).

My general thesis in this chapter has been that there is an impasse of the political in Derrida's work, which is extended and deepened by Lacoue-Labarthe and Nancy. I have shown a way out of this impasse by following the movement from ethics to politics in Levinas's work. The general argument of this book is that Derridian deconstruction has a horizon of responsibility or ethical significance, provided that ethics is understood in the Levinasian sense. Deconstruction, as 'the most rigorous determination of undecidability in a limitless context' or as a 'philosophy of hesitation', opens an ethical space of alterity or transcendence. However, the move that deconstruction is unable to make – what I have called its impasse – concerns the passage from undecidability to the decision, from responsibility to questioning, from deconstruction to critique, from ethics to politics. Political space is understood here as a factical, ontic, or empirical terrain, on which politics is conceived as an activity of questioning, critique, judgement, and decision; in short, as the creation of antagonism, contestation, and struggle – what one might call the battle over *doxa*. In Lacoue-Labarthe and Nancy, for reasons that are essential to their analysis, this dimension of politics – *la politique* – was excluded in favour of a meditation upon *le politique*. I have argued that there is a need for a political *supplement* to deconstruction, in the full sense of that word, as something which both makes up for a lack and adds to what is already complete. I believe that this supplement is necessary in order to prevent deconstruction from becoming a fail-safe strategy for reading – an empty formalism – which, as Rorty would have it, is a means to private autonomy that is publicly useless and politically pernicious. Thus, in order for there to be a future for deconstruction, it has been necessary to engage in the writing of this supplement.

This chapter traces a way out of this impasse of the political in deconstruction by following the Levinasian move from the Other to *le tiers,* from responsibility to the question, from the anarchy of ethical responsibility to the question of the *archē* of the political order. This move resulted in a re-articulation of the political function of philosophy. Philosophical discourse is a language of questioning that asks after the legitimacy of the political order; it is a universal demand to justify and criticize the *polis.* The properly philosophical moment is not that of founding the *polis* upon science, knowledge, or wisdom, but, rather, consists in raising the *question* of legitimacy by calling the political order into question: What is justice? Following Hannah Arendt's interpretation,[65] I see this as the properly Socratic moment of philosophy, which sees the latter as a way of criticizing or interrupting the *polis,* of calling the *polis* to judgement, of judging the duty of citizenship to be the wisdom of love at the service of love. Arendt distinguishes the Socratic moment of the interruption or critique of the *polis* from the Platonic moment of founding the *polis* on the absolute foundations of philosophical knowledge – what Arendt calls Plato's 'tyranny of truth' (p. 78). It is this Platonic moment of grounding the *polis* on a philosophical foundation that is so disastrously repeated in Heidegger's Rectoral Address. Arendt writes:

> The role of the philosopher is not to rule the city but to be its 'gadfly', not to tell philosophical truths but to make citizens more truthful. The difference with Plato is decisive: Socrates did not want to educate the citizens so much as he wanted to improve their *doxai,* which constituted the political life in which he took part.[66]

The philosopher is not one who wants to subordinate *doxa* to *epistēmē,* thereby establishing politics on an absolute foundation; rather, the philosopher is one who dwells in the *polis,* which is the space of *doxa,* and who questions, criticizes, and judges *doxai.* The political function of the philosopher is to be a gadfly, not a king. Let us suppose that the Delphic oracle was sincere, that Socrates was the wisest man in Greece because he did not know, and that the philosopher's wisdom consists in a self-conscious agnosticism that is at the service of love. Philosophy should not envision the abandonment of *doxa* – or, indeed, the cave – as the place where politics takes place; rather, philosophy is a constant activity of criticizing and legitimizing *doxai*. Socratic midwifery is simply the process of critical dialogue upon the *doxai* of a particular community which enables citizens to come to the truth of *doxa*. There is, I believe, an urgent need to re-establish the political link between philosophy, as critical reflection on *doxai*, and citizenship, as a reflective stance with regard to one's political duties and rights: philosophy as citzenship and citizenship as philosophical activity.

Such a conception of the political function of philosophy (which is, of course, far from novel; indeed, perhaps it is the very furthest from novelty) needs to be integrated with a different understanding of political space. The space of the *polis* is not an enclosed or immanent structure, but rather a multiplication of spaces, a structure of repeated interruptions, in which the social totality is breached by the force of ethical transcendence. I have shown how the community has a double structure in Levinas, as a relation both to the Other and to all the others, were 'toi (e(s)t) (tout autre que) moi'. Any attempt to bring closure to the social is continually denied by the non-totalizable relation to the Other. Social space is an infinite splintering, or fragmentation, of space into spaces in which there is consequently a multiplication of political possibilities. Philosophy, as the wisdom of love at the service of love, is the discourse which, through its activity of open, agnostic critique, ensures that the community remains an open community, at the service of ethical difference. Philosophical critique, like Antigone herself, is the eternal irony of the community, the fact that the community is legitimized only by calling the legitimacy of the community into question.[67] The just polity is one that can actively maintain its own interruption or ironization as that which sustains it. If Levinasian politics is a politics of the multiple, of the second and the third persons, then philosophy is the language that is respectful of this multiplicity, that 'thematizes difference and reduces the thematized to difference'. To quote Arendt once again:

> If philosophers, despite their necessary estrangement from the every-
> day life of human affairs, were ever to arrive at a true political philos-
> ophy they would have to make the plurality of man, out of which
> arises the whole realm of human affairs – in its grandeur and misery –
> the object of their *thaumadzein*.[68]

If philosophy begins in wonder, then political philosophy – the reflective activity of *polis*-dwelling beings – begins in wonder at the fact
of human plurality.

Furthermore, such a conception of political space is, I would claim,
democratic. I understand democracy to be an ethically grounded form
of political life which is continually being called into question by
asking of its legitimacy and the legitimacy of its practices and
institutions: what is justice?[69] In this sense, legitimate communities
are those which have themselves in question; and, to that extent,
legitimate communities are philosophical. The political wisdom of
democratic societies consists in their service to love, to the irreducibility of ethical difference. The political responsibility of the citizen
of a democracy consists in the questioning of the axioms and
foundations of democratic society, a questioning which has its horizon in responsibility for the Other. Democracy is the form of society
committed to the political equality of all its citizens and the ethical
inequality of myself faced with the Other. However, returning to the
above discussion of Lefort, the central feature of democratic politics
is that the source of power is contested, through elections or through
parliamentary or extra-parliamentary activism and debate. In democracy, power does not disappear; rather, it is the site of antagonism,
competition, and struggle. Such is the risk of democracy, the fact that
democratic life is always exposed to the danger of collapsing into
tyranny and totalitarianism. The trial and death of Socrates provide a
first and permanent reminder of the risk of democracy, and offer an
explanation of why Plato and an entire tradition of political philosophy extending to Heidegger should be so suspicious of democracy.
Democracy is a fragile, agnostic, doxic form of political life, where
fragility is the price to be paid for the refusal of all forms of
immanentism. Democracy is the politics of difficulty, opacity, and
dirty hands, of the fact that the social is not a complete, transparent
œuvre, that political action is always taken on an open, undecidable

terrain. Democracy is a permanent risk, a risk that is well worth running – 'a fine risk' – because it is only when political space is organized democratically – that is, dis-*organ*-ized as an open, interrupted community – that one can envisage a politics that does not reduce transcendence, a community that thinks difference without reducing difference. Democracy is the politics of ethical difference, political wisdom at the service of ethical love.

In this way, one can re-open negotiation on the best route between Jerusalem and Athens. That is to say, the hierarchy and totality of the Athenian democratic political order and the philosophical question that Socrates raises about the legitimacy, or *archē*, of that order need to be supplemented by the anarchic ethical particularity of Jerusalem. In the discussion that followed his paper 'Transcendence and Height', Levinas argued that 'both the hierarchy taught by Athens and the *abstract* and slightly *anarchical* ethical individualism taught by Jerusalem are *simultaneously necessary* in order to suppress violence' (*TH* 103). I emphasize 'simultaneously necessary'; for democratic political life is not to be built on a philosophical, theoretical, or even aesthetic foundation. Rather, democracy practices the on-going interruption of politics by ethics, of totality by infinity, of the Said by the Saying. For this, both the question and the question of the question are needed.

However, *democracy does not exist*. As I mentioned above, one must not restrict oneself to conceiving of democracy as an existent political form (and, once again, certainly not as an apologetics for Western liberal democracy). Rather, one must begin to think of democracy as a task, or project, to be attempted. *Democracy does not exist*; that is to say, starting from today, and every day, there is a responsibility to invent democracy, to extend the democratic franchise to all areas of public and private life. 'Once more an effort', *encore un effort*, as Derrida has recently noted; this is the germ of democracy.[70] To say that democracy does not exist is to say that democracy is always democracy to come (*à venir*). Democracy is an infinite task and an infinite responsibility directed towards the future (*l'avenir*); its temporality is that of *advent*. To think of democracy as futural is to take up the ethico-political obligation to invent democracy, more and better, today and every day. Democracy is a political form characterized by incompletion and deferral, which is to say that democracy has a *différantial* structure. Of course, to say this is no longer to criticize

Derrida; on the contrary, it is to imagine the future of deconstruction and perhaps the future of Derrida's own work. *Democracy as the future of deconstruction?* In this closing chapter, I have tried to open this future by raising a question of politics.

NOTES

1 I refer to John Sallis, 'Flight of Spirit', in *Diacritics*, 19, nos 3–4 (1989), pp. 25–37; and Geoffrey Bennington, 'Spirit's spirit spirits spirit', in *Of Derrida, Heidegger and Spirit*, ed. David Wood, Northwestern University Press, Evanston, Forthcoming.

2 The proceedings of this colloquium appeared in *Research in Phenomenology*, 17 (1987), pp. 1–188.

3 'Die Sprache im Gedicht', in *Unterwegs zur Sprache* (Neske, Pfullingen, 1959), hereafter *US*, pp. 35–82, Peter D. Hertz in *On the Way to Language* (Harper and Row, New York, 1971), hereafter *OL*. pp. 159–98.

4 Paul de Man, *Allegories of Reading* (Yale University Press, New Haven and London, 1979), p. 277.

5 Heidegger, *Vorträge und Aufsätze* (Neske, Pfullingen, 1952), p. 40; tr. W. Lovitt in *Martin Heidegger. Basic Writings* (Routledge and Kegan Paul, London and Henley, 1978), p. 317.

6 See e.g. Victor Farias, *Heidegger and Nazism* (Temple University Press, Philadelphia, 1989).

7 See e.g. Luc Ferry and Alain Renaut, *La pensée 68. Essai sur l'anti-humanisme contemporain* (Gallimard, Paris, 1985), ch. 4. Ferry and Renaut continue their critique of the anti-humanism of French Heideggerianism with particular reference to Derrida in *Heidegger et les Modernes* (Grasset et Fasquelle, Paris, 1988).

8 This remark by Adorno is cited in *FP* 150–1/*HAP* 105 and 117–18.

9 'Kleiner (Tübinger) Programmentwurf. Philosophie heute und jetzt – Ein paar Überlegungen', *Frankfurter Rundschau*, 5 March 1988; partially quoted by Habermas in 'Work and Weltanschauung: The Heidegger Controversy from a German Perspective', *Critical Inquiry*, 15 (Winter 1989), pp. 431–56.

10 Derrida, 'Comment donner raison', *Diacritics*, 19, nos 3–4 (1989), p. 8.

11 In this regard, see the first two sections of the 'Exposition' in *OB*: 'Questioning and Allegiance to the Other' and 'Questioning and Being: Time and Reminiscence' (*AE* 29–39/*OB* 23–31). Blanchot responds to Levinas's remarks on questioning in *Otherwise than Being*, and relates them to his own theme of disaster in *L'Écriture du désastre* (Gallimard, Paris, 1980), pp. 21, 27, 43–4, 53.

12 Derrida employs a very similar formulation in *LSS*: 'Responsibility, if there is any, requires the experience of the undecidable as well as that irreducibility of the other' (*MPM* 210/*LSS* 639).

13 Derrida, 'L'autre cap', *Liber, Revue européenne des livres*, no. 5 (October 1990), pp. 11–13; reprinted in book form as *L'autre cap* (Minuit, Paris, 1991), pp. 11–101. I refer to the earlier version.

14 Reprinted with all other articles from the period in Paul de Man, *Wartime Journalism, 1939–1943*, ed. W. Hamacher *et al.* (University of Nebraska Press, Lincoln and London, 1988), p. 45.

15 Derrida, 'L'autre cap', p. 13.

16 See Derrida's remarks on the Gulf War and international law in an interview with *Magazine Littéraire*, in a special issue devoted to his work, no. 286 (March 1991), pp. 27–8.

17 'Il y a une limite où l'exercice d'un art, quel qu'il soit, devient une insulte au malheur. Ne l'oublions pas' (Blanchot, *L'Écriture du désastre*), p. 132.

18 See the exchange between Aletta Norval and Ernesto Laclau on the topic of apartheid in Laclau, *New Reflections on the Revolution of Our Time* (Verso, London and New York, 1990), pp. 133–74.

19 See the important opening essay in Laclau, *New Reflections on the Revolution of Our Time*, pp. 3–84.

20 See Laclau, 'Totalitarianism and Moral Indignation', *Diacritics*, 21 (Spring 1991).

21 See Rorty, 'From Ironist Theory to Private Allusions: Derrida', in *Contingency, Irony, and Solidarity* (Cambridge University Press, Cambridge, 1989), pp. 122–37. Rorty forcefully restates his interpretation of Derrida in 'Habermas, Derrida and the Functions of Philosophy', to appear in *Revue International de Philosophie* (I quote from an unpublished typescript). Crudely stated, the core of Rorty's argument lies in the distinction between the private and the public, the former being concerned with 'idiosyncratic projects of self-overcoming', the latter with those activities 'having to do with the suffering of other human beings' (p. 1). Rorty sees Derrida's work as confined to the private realm, to the ironist's personal quest for perfection and autonomy, which has no public or political significance. Roughly, my disagreement with Rorty's interpretation is that, in so far as deconstruction is ethical – that is, in so far as it is a certain opening on to the Other – Derrida's work has an irreducibly public function by Rorty's own definition; that is, it is concerned with the suffering of the Other. On my reading, the crucial distinction to be drawn in relation to deconstruction is between the relation to the Other, or ethics, and the relation to others as a whole, or politics.

22 For helpful, related discussions of Lacoue-Labarthe and Nancy's work, see Nancy Fraser, 'The French Derrideans: Politicizing Deconstruction or Deconstructing the Political?', *New German Critique*, 33 (1984), pp. 127–54; and David Ingram, 'The Retreat of the Political in the Modern Age: Jean-Luc Nancy on Totalitarianism and Community', *Research in Phenomenology*, 18 (1988), pp. 93–124. Bill Readings takes issue with Fraser's article in 'The Deconstruction of Politics', in *Reading de Man Reading*, ed. L. Waters and W. Godzich (University of Minnesota Press, Minneapolis, 1989), pp. 242–3, n. 31.

23 See Lacoue-Labarthe, 'La transcendance finit dans la politique' (*RJ* 189–92), tr. P. Caws in Lacoue-Labarthe, *Typography* (Harvard University Press, Cambridge, Mass., 1989), pp. 280–2.

24 Heidegger, *Die Selbstbehauptung der deutschen Universität*, bilingual edn (T.E.R., France, 1982), p. 8; tr. K. Harries, 'The Self-Assertion of the German University', *Review of Metaphysics*, 38 (March 1985), p. 472.

25 Heidegger, *Die Grundprobleme der Phänomenologie* (Vittorio Klostermann, Frankfurt am Main, 1975), p. 15; tr. A. Hofstadter, *The Basic Problems of Phenomenology* (Indiana University Press, Bloomington, 1982), p. 11.

26 A point made by Gadamer in ' "Back from Syracuse?" ', *Critical Inquiry*, 15 (Winter 1989), pp. 427–30.

27 Lacoue-Labarthe and Nancy refer particularly to paras 19–28 of this text, in Heidegger, *Vorträge und Aufsätze* (Nesde, Pfullingen, 1952), pp. 83–95; tr. Joan Stambaugh in *The End of Philosophy* (Harper and Row, New York, 1973), pp. 99–110.

28 Heidegger, *Vorträge und Aufsätze*, p. 9; *Basic Writings* (Routledge and Kegan Paul, London and Henley, 1978), p. 287.

29 Cf. Dominique Janicaud, 'Face à la domination. Heidegger, le marxisme et l'écologic', *Cahier de l'Herne. Heidegger* (Editions de l'Herne, Paris, 1983), pp. 477–95.

30 Heidegger, ' "Only a God Can Save Us": The *Spiegel* Interview', tr. W. J. Richardson, in *Heidegger, the Man and the Thinker* (Precedent Publishing Inc., Chicago, 1981), pp. 45–67.

31 See the Editor's Introduction and the essays collected in Lefort, *The Political Forms of Society*, ed. J. B. Thompson (Polity Press, Cambridge, 1986).

32 Heidegger, ' "Only a God Can Save Us" ', p. 55.

33 See Lefort, *The Political Forms of Modern Society*, pp. 224–36.

34 I owe this insight to conversations with Jay Bernstein.

35 C. B. Macpherson, *The Real World of Democracy* (Oxford University Press, New York and Oxford, 1966), esp. pp. 1–11.

36 Laclau, *New Reflections on the Revolution of our Time*, p. 81. For the concept of democratic revolution in de Tocqueville, see his *De la*

démocratie en Amérique, ed. H. G. Nicholas (Macmillan, London, 1961), pp. 8–9.

37 Janicaud, *L'Ombre de cette pensée* (Jérôme Millon, Grénoble, 1990), p. 133.

38 Celan, *Selected Poems*, tr. M. Hamburger (Penguin, Harmondsworth, 1990), pp. 292–4.

39 Merleau-Ponty, *Phenomenology of Perception*, tr. Colin Smith (Routledge and Kegan Paul, London and Henley, 1962), p. xiv.

40 Fraser, 'The French Derrideans', p. 150.

41 Janicaud, *L'Ombre de cette pensée*, p. 158.

42 See also Nancy's important book *L'Expérience de la liberté* (Galilée, Paris, 1988), a text which would require a separate, extensive commentary. See esp. ch. 7, 'Partage de la liberté. Egalité, fraternité, justice', where Nancy's thoughts on community are extended to the notion of a revolutionary politics of inaugural liberty taking place at the level of *la politique*.

43 Heidegger, 'Der Ursprung des Kunstwerkes', in *Holzwege*, 6th edn (Vittorio Klostermann, Frankfurt am Main, 1980), pp. 61–4, and 'Nachwort', pp. 65–7; tr. A. Hofstadter in *Poetry, Language, Thought* (Harper and Row, New York, 1971), pp. 75–81.

44 See Denis Hollier, *Against Architecture: The Writings of Georges Bataille* (MIT Press, Cambridge, Mass., and London, 1989).

45 I refer to the notion of aesthetic ideology developed in Paul de Man's later work and to an unpublished typescript of the 1983 lecture 'Kant and Schiller'. This and other essays will appear in *Aesthetic Ideology*, ed. A. Warminski (University of Minnesota Press, Minneapolis).

46 Of course, for Lacoue-Labarthe, ethics (and he specifically refers to Levinas (*FP* 51/*HAP* 31)) is no longer possible for the reasons set out in the discussion of Heidegger's 'Letter on Humanism' in chapter 1. He asks rhetorically: 'How and from where could one *philosophically* get back beyond Heidegger's delimitation of ethics and humanism?' Thus the category of the ethical has to to be suspended because it suffers from a 'general exhaustion of philosophical possibilities' (ibid.). I have already tried to address this question in chapter 1 by following Derrida's response to this Heideggerian objection; but for a compelling critique of Lacoue-Labarthe on the question of the possibility of ethics, see once again Janicaud, *L'Ombre de cette pensée*, pp. 123–8, where he argues that there is an inconsistency, or *glissement* (p. 127) on Lacoue-Labarthe's part, in that, on the one hand, he wants to condemn Heidegger in the name of a wrongdoing, but on the other hand, refuses to see that wrongdoing in ethical terms. The question here is how one can condemn Heidegger's political activism as wrongdoing while at the

same time maintaining that ethics and ethical judgement are exhausted. Is not ethical judgement silently and continually introduced after the statement of its impossibility? Lacoue-Labarthe argues that 'what has occurred this century...has subjected the very idea of ethics to an unprecedented shock and perhaps definitively destroyed its foundations'. Thus, in the ethical realm, we are 'entirely without resources' (*FP* 51/*HAP* 31). While agreeing with this as historical description, I would want to draw the opposite conclusion: namely, that the events of this century, particularly the event of the Holocaust, have indeed stripped us of traditional ethical resources, but that this state of affairs need not lead to a suspension of the ethical; on the contrary, the very lack of ethicality shown by the events of this century impose on us an imperative to maintain the imperative mode in order that those events not repeat themselves.

47   W. H. Auden, 'September 1st 1939', in *Selected Poems*, ed. E. Mendelson (Faber and Faber, London and Boston, 1979), pp. 88–9.

48   Adorno, *Negative Dialektik* (Suhrkamp, Frankfurt am Main, 1966), p. 356; tr. E. B. Ashton, *Negative Dialectics* (Continuum, New York, 1973), p. 365.

49   Levinas, Prefatory Note to 'Reflections on the Philosophy of Hitlerism', *Critical Inquiry* 17 (Autumn 1990), pp. 62–3.

50   Levinas, 'Politique Après!', in *L'Au-delà du verset* (Editions de Minuit, Paris, 1982), pp. 221–8.

51   It is, at the very least, an open question as to whether this is an accurate reading of Buber. For an authoritative account of the dialogue between Buber and Levinas, see Robert Bernasconi, ' "Failure of Communication" as a Surplus: Dialogue and Lack of Dialogue between Buber and Levinas', in *The Provocation of Levinas*, ed. R. Bernasconi and D. Wood (Routledge, London and New York, 1988), pp. 100–35.

52   See Levinas, *La Théorie de l'intuition dans la phénoménologie de Husserl* (Alcan, Paris, 1930); tr. A. Orianne as *The Theory of Intuition in Husserl's Phenomenology* (Northwestern University Press, Evanston, 1973); *idem*, 'Martin Heidegger et l'ontologie', *Revue Philosophique de la France et de l'Etranger* 113, nos 5–6 (May–June 1932), pp. 395–431; reprinted in modified and abridged form in *EDE* 53–76.

53   See Levinas, ' "Mourir pour..." ', in *Heidegger. Questions Ouvertes* (Osiris, Paris, 1988), pp. 255–64, esp. p. 256.

54   See Levinas, 'Reflections on the Philosophy of Hitlerism'.

55   Hannah Arendt, 'Martin Heidegger at Eighty', in *Heidegger and Modern Philosophy*, ed. Michael Murray (Yale University Press, New Haven and London, 1978), pp. 293–303.

56   See Levinas, 'Comme un consentement à l'horrible', *Le nouvel observateur*, 22–8 January 1988; tr. Paula Wissing, *Critical Inquiry*, 15 (Winter 1990), pp. 485–8.
57   Ibid. p. 487.
58   Ibid.
59   Ibid.
60   Heidegger, 'Der Ursprung des Kunstwerkes', p. 48; *Poetry, Language, Thought*, p. 62. In a commentary on *Glas*, I tried to show how Derrida gives a Heideggerian reading of Absolute Knowing in Hegel, a reading that focuses on the theme of sacrifice or holocaust; Critchley, 'A Commentary on Derrida's Reading of Hegel in *Glas*', *Bulletin of the Hegel Society of Great Britain*, no. 18 (Autumn/Winter 1988), pp. 21–7.
61   'Begins' must here be understood phenomenologically. I cannot give a full account of Levinas's complex and ambivalent relation to Husserlian phenomenology, except to say that his allegiance to phenomenology, like that of the early Heidegger, is *methodological*. That is to say, Levinas's allegiance is to the spirit rather than the letter of the Husserlian text; thus, 'Our analyses claim to be in the *spirit* of Husserlian philosophy, whose letter has been the reminder to our epoch of permanent phenomenology restored to its rank as a method for all philosophy' (*AE* 230/*OB* 183). Levinas does not, of course, deny the sociohistorical, genealogical, psychoanalytic, or structuralist accounts of the construction and conditioning of ethical subjectivity; he even acknowledges them, claiming that the critique of the primacy of the autonomous humanist subject clears a place for a rethinking of ethical selfhood (*AE* 164/*OB* 128). 'Politics begins as ethics' means that the latter has phenomenological priority, reducing the natural attitude and investigating the profound structures of intentionality, structures such that it eventually proves necessary to move beyond intentionality and beyond phenomenology (cf. Levinas, 'Beyond Intentionality', in *Philosophy in France Today*, ed. A. Montefiore (Cambridge University Press, Cambridge, 1982), pp. 100–15.
62   On the meaning and modulation of sense that this word undergoes in Levinas's work, see Fabio Ciaramelli, 'Levinas's Ethical Discourse between Individuation and Universality', in *RRL* 83–105, esp. 98–101.
63   I owe this insight to conversations with Fabio Ciaramelli.
64   Of course, a singular inversion in Levinas's use of the word 'love' should be noted here. In TI there is virtually an opposition between the terms 'love' and 'ethics', which echoes the distinctions between need and desire, symmetry and asymmetry; 'The metaphysical event of transcendence – the welcome of the Other, hospitality, desire and language – is not accomplished as love' (*TeI* 232/*TI* 254). This inversion was noted by Jean-Luc Marion during a debate with Levinas in

which he said: 'It is remarkable that today you are more willing to accept the use of the word love. Some years ago you refused it, saying that it was the most prostituted word' (*Autrement que savoir* (Osiris, Paris, 1987), p. 74). On the relation between Marion and Levinas, see chapter 2, note 44.

65 Hannah Arendt, 'Philosophy and Politics', *Social Research*, 57, no. 1 (Spring 1990), pp. 73–103. Of course, there is a vast question as to the historical and hermeneutical accuracy of Arendt's interpretation of Socrates and Plato. Arendt's wish to distinguish the Socratic from the Platonic could be said to result in a monological reading of Plato that ignores †he irony and endless ambiguity of Platonic dialogue. For a completely opposed, but none the less erudite and compelling interpretation of the historical Socrates, see I. F. Stone, *The Trial of Socrates* (Picador, London, 1989), which denounces Socrates as a 'snobbish', anti-democratic aristocrat, who wanted to become a martyr in order to leave an eternal stain on Greek democracy. It should be noted that I am using Arendt's interpretation of Socrates merely as a heuristic device to illuminate the relation between politics, philosophy, and democracy, not to confirm any substantive claims about the truth of the historical Socrates. Also, in my allusions to the Greek *polis*, I am not making any politically utopian or nostalgic assumptions about the *sittlich* world inhabited by the Greeks, which is no longer ours.

66 Ibid., p. 81.

67 Cf. Hegel, *Phenomenology of Spirit*, tr. A.V. Miller (Oxford University Press, Oxford, 1977), p. 288. See too Luce Irigaray, 'The Eternal Irony of the Community', in *Speculum of the Other Woman* (Cornell University Press, Ithaca, 1985), pp. 214–26.

68 Arendt, 'Philosophy and Politics', p. 103.

69 Cf. Robert Bernasconi, 'Rousseau and the Supplement to the Social Contract: Deconstruction and the Possibility of Democracy', *Cardozo Law Review*, 2, nos 5–6 (July/August 1990), p. 1563.

70 Cf. Derrida, 'La démocratie ajournée', in *L'autre cap*, p. 123. On democracy in Derrida, see 'the idea of democracy' as referring to something which is 'never given' (*n'est jamais donnée*) but 'which remains to be thought and to come' (*qui reste à penser et à venir*) (*Liber*, p. 13). This sentence is given an expanded formulation in the longer version of this text, where Derrida speaks of a democracy *à venir*: 'Not that it will certainly arrive tomorrow, not the *future* democracy (national and international, at the state and trans-state level), but a democracy that should have the structure of the promise' (*L'autre cap*, p. 76). See also the discussion of *La démocratie à venir* in Derrida, *Du Droit à la philosophie* (Galilée, Paris, 1990), pp. 41–54.

Index